D0853611

HATRED & CIVILITY

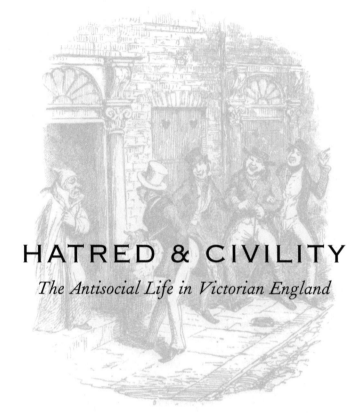

HATRED & CIVILITY

The Antisocial Life in Victorian England

CHRISTOPHER LANE

COLUMBIA UNIVERSITY PRESS   New York

COLUMBIA UNIVERSITY PRESS
Publishers Since 1893
New York   Chichester, West Sussex

The Northwestern University Research Grants Committee has provided partial support
for the publication of this book. We gratefully acknowledge this assistance.

Library of Congress Cataloging-in-Publication Data
Lane, Christopher, 1966–
Hatred and civility : the antisocial live in Victorian England / Christopher Lane.
p.   cm.
Includes bibliographical references and index.
ISBN 0–231–13064–3 (acid-free paper)
1. English literature—19th century—History and criticism.   2. Misanthropy in
literature.   3. Literature and society—England—History—19th century.
4. England—Social life and customs—19th century.   5. Great Britian—
History—Victoria, 1837–1901.   6. Alienation (Social psychology) in literature.
7. Interpersonal relations in literature.   8. Manners and customs in literature.
9. Courtesy in literature.   10. Hate in literature.   I. Title.

PR468.M56L36 2004
823'.809353—dc21

2003055146

Columbia University Press books are printed on permanent and
durable acid-free paper.
Printed in the United States of America
Designed by Linda Secondari

c 10 9 8 7 6 5 4 3 2 1
p 10 9 8 7 6 5 4 3 2 1

These days we know less about the feeling of hatred than in times when man was more open to his destiny. . . . These days subjects do not have to shoulder the burden of the experience of hatred in its most consuming forms. And why? Because our civilisation is itself sufficiently one of hatred. Isn't the path for the race to destruction really rather well marked out for us? Hatred is clothed in our everyday discourse under many guises, it meets with such extraordinarily easy rationalisations.

—Jacques Lacan, *The Seminar of Jacques Lacan*, BOOK I

CONTENTS

ILLUSTRATIONS

ACKNOWLEDGMENTS

IN HIS BIOGRAPHY OF W. C. FIELDS, Robert Lewis Taylor repeats the saying that "most persons . . . harbor a secret affection for anybody with a low opinion of humanity."[1] I trust the power of this maxim in thanking the following (few of them actually misanthropes) for their generous help: Mark Bauerlein, Leo Bersani, A. S. Byatt, Dane Claussen, Tim Dean, Michael A. Elliott, Jonathan Freedman, Christine Froula, Peter Gay, Judith Feher Gurewich, Barbara Hardy, Christopher Herbert, Daniel Karlin, Laura Kipnis, Jules Law, Deborah Luepnitz, Russell Maylone, Walt Reed, Michael Riley, and Oliver Sacks.

I am grateful to Jason K. Friedman and Jan McInroy for their copyediting expertise, and to the University Research Council at Emory for a generous yearlong fellowship that aided my research. Thanks are also due my graduate students at Northwestern and Emory—especially Jason Jones, who tracked down several sources—and the many helpful librarians in the rare books collections at the British Library, the University of Chicago, Columbia, Emory, the University of Georgia, Harvard, the National Library of Scotland, the New York Public Library, Northwestern, and Yale. I am also grateful to the staffs at the Ashmolean Museum, Oxford; Glasgow University Library's Special Collections; the Metropolitan Museum of Art, New York; Musées de Strasbourg; Northwestern Library's Special Collections; the Pace/MacGill Gallery,

New York; the Science and Society Picture Library and Victoria and Albert Museum Archives, London; and the University of Wisconsin–Madison's Special Collections for giving me permission to reprint several images.

The English departments at the University of Utah and Northwestern heard earlier versions of the Eliot and Brontë chapters, respectively, and attendees at Harvard's Humanities Center responded valuably to an earlier version of the Browning chapter, helping me sharpen several claims. Ronald Paulson and two readers at *English Literary History* guided publication of the Brontë chapter, and Andrew Miller and three readers at *Victorian Studies* gave invaluable feedback on a slightly different version of the Bulwer chapter, also reprinted with permission. Generous funding from Northwestern's Graduate School and University Research Grants Committee defrayed the cost of reproducing the illustrations.

Two readers at Columbia Press offered excellent advice during the final stages of revision. Sincere thanks to them, to Juree Sondker and Anne McCoy at the press, and above all to Jennifer Crewe, my editor, who secured the reports, kept everything on time, and provided throughout unstinting encouragement and practical help.

John David Smith and my family in England offered the best kind of support—as well as reprieve from the material in this book—sharing generous love and laughter in their own inimitable ways.

PROLOGUE

WHEN I BEGAN WRITING THIS BOOK, actors appeared nightly on U.S. television, warning viewers that hateful thoughts could lead to hate crimes, "so watch what you say. Hate destroys."[1] Advertisements flooded network television, offering Paxil (paroxetine hydrochloride) to an estimated ten million Americans experiencing "social anxiety disorder" (SAD).[2] And a team of psychiatrists in California announced that Samson, the biblical figure, may have suffered from "antisocial personality disorder" (ASPD).[3] This seemed fitting, if scarcely plausible, when they added that generalized anxiety disorder "afflicts more than one-half the general [U.S.] population." The psychiatrists doubtless boosted that figure by including as examples of social phobia fears about eating alone in restaurants, writing in public, and using public rest rooms.[4]

A staple of American life before the terrorist attacks on September 11, 2001, these claims flourished while Americans enjoyed the longest period of peace and prosperity in more than two generations. Polled in December 1997, however, 57 percent of them believed that "the people running the country don't really care what happens to you."[5] If we can trust that figure, then collective happiness is neither a simple nor a logical effect of social harmony and increased wealth. Indeed, that greater prosperity can magnify incivility is a problem for politicians, cultural theorists, and writers tackling the social scene.

Journalists and scholars have made similar claims on the other side of the Atlantic, the principal focus of this book. In the British political magazine *Prospect*, expatriate Michael Elliott recently accused "Rude Britannia" of becoming "rougher as it gets richer" and of turning "incivility" into "a real social problem."[6] Although Elliott blamed both outcomes on the collapse of Britain's empire and the country's "modernisation and liberalisation," he conceded that "it's easier to dislike anti-social behaviour than to measure its impact; and it's easier to do either of those than to figure out how to persuade people to behave better."[7] Elliott didn't view the demand for "satisfactory adjustment to society" as a problem in its own right, yet one dictionary now defines this adjustment as a condition of *mental health*. The same dictionary glosses *normal*, tendentiously, as "free from any mental disorder."[8] Given the above percentages about generalized anxiety, presumably this last definition is rather optimistic.

Let me stress at the outset: This book doesn't try to persuade people to behave better. It admits the difficulty of measuring, much less diminishing, antisocial behavior. And it shows that incivility predates the collapse of Britain's empire, filling the very works of Victorian fiction and nonfiction that many still view as morally exemplary. Dickens's *Our Mutual Friend*, Eliot's *Daniel Deronda*, and Trollope's *The Way We Live Now*—just three of many exceptions to popular characterizations of the Victorians today—don't merely caution readers to settle for less while urging them to treat their spouses, neighbors, and relatives better. All three works advance bleaker explanations for rancor. Often deriving more pleasure from discord than from harmony, their characters view neighbors as severe obstacles to happiness and fulfillment. Allegedly schooling readers in good manners, these novels actually portray hatred in nearly insoluble forms. In this book I examine the resulting tension, calling it systemic, because it stems from impulses, emotions, and forms of rebellion that society can't integrate. I also challenge the myth that nineteenth-century England was simply a breeding ground for today's precarious civility. Indeed, if understanding antisocial behavior in contemporary Britain and the United States is truly our goal, then rereading Victorian fiction would be a good place to start.

Received wisdom about Victorian culture has, I think, blinded us to the range and intensity of its antisocial dynamics, including the cultural prevalence of acute misanthropy and schadenfreude (joy in another's sorrow). *Hatred and Civility* unmasks these dynamics, eliciting their disruptive energy in readings of Victorian novels, plays, poetry, and journalism, as well as sermons, philosophical essays, and medical tracts. Granted, some scholars before me (Peter Gay, Daniel Karlin, and Victor Brombert among them) have complicated others' widespread assumptions that the Victorians were essentially charitable and genial, but I approach these and related issues from a different perspective, asking why the Victorians blamed misanthropes in particular for betraying a set of values that many ordinary citizens found unsustainable. Given the severity of this blame, it is all the more ironic that narrow assumptions about Victorian morality recur in contemporary Britain and North America as an ideal by which both societies are measured and found deficient. Victorian scholars may dismiss these assumptions, calling their suggestion of "manners and morals" inaccurate and prim, but that doesn't alter popular judgments about the nineteenth century, which stoke powerful arguments today about the family and "traditional values."

Consider a recent example of this evaluative struggle—the art exhibition "Exposed: The Victorian Nude," which showed at the Tate Gallery, London, in 2001 and, for several months in 2002, at the Haus der Kunst, Munich, and the Brooklyn Museum of Art. What was striking about the exhibition's mixed reviews was not the critics' polar assessments of the art's aesthetic merits, which in today's climate are quite predictable, but the service to which those assessments were put. Writing in London's *New Statesman*, Eliot biographer Kathryn Hughes applauded the exhibition's "cogent" arrangement but criticized it for appealing to outmoded stereotypes about the Victorians. "When it comes to titling anything to do with the Victorians," she observed, "there is a tiresome tendency to lean on the image of dark secrets being brought to the surface," a tendency that the word *exposed* seems to confirm.[9] Instead, the *New Statesman* subtitled the review "Kathryn Hughes Finds That the Victorians Differed Little from Us in Their Response to Nudity," a tack that Matthew Sweet also adopted in his recent study, *Inventing the Victorians*.[10] In "Undressing the Victorians," by contrast, art historian and conservative critic Roger Kimball tries to keep the Victorians mysterious and foreign, and thus balks at material hinting at their and our shared interest in nudity. He begins his review for the *New Criterion* with an epigraph from Burke's "Letters on a Regicide Peace": "Manners are of more importance than law," then complains that the exhibition's very rationale means "yet another chapter in the so-called culture wars," a chapter he views as "a battle about everything the Victorians are famous for: . . . cleanliness, hard work, strict self-discipline, etc."[11] "The assembled works of art," Kimball intones, "provide the excuse to fight some contemporary ideological battles: battles about the place of sexuality in public life, the ideals of modesty and seemliness, the concept of sexual normality."[12]

The empirical evidence that Kimball saw clearly did nothing to dislodge this assessment, and the military rhetoric shaping his judgment allegedly does nothing, in turn, to up the ante. Still, Hughes and Kimball agree, from very different perspectives, that at stake in such evaluations is nothing less than our entire conception of the Victorians. Scholars no longer can afford to ignore this yawning gulf in Victorian studies or the canards that shape it. If I begin by tackling such resilient assessments of Victorian culture and society, it's to expose the half-truths that they veil. Kimball might in fact recall Walter Houghton's chastening, if rather broad, indictment of Victorian hypocrisy, in his now classic study *The Victorian Frame of Mind*: "The Victorians . . . pretended to be better than they were. They passed themselves off as being incredibly pious and moral; they talked noble sentiments and lived—quite otherwise."[13]

Arguments about civility or sociability did not, we'll see, emerge in the nineteenth century independent of a wide body of literature highlighting the lively hostile impulses an individual should aspire to control. Yet hatred and repression also did not coexist in anything like a simple cause-effect relation—an idea leading many to champion repression as a way to eliminate these tensions or to put them to fresh use. Arguments like these not only imply that literature and art sublimate such emotions, promoting only sociability, but also downplay the kinds of struggle that precede narrative or poetic closure, including the upheaval awaiting readers disturbed by their excited response to dramatized hostility. Claiming that culture teaches us to thwart unruly passions, moreover, ignores that collective judgments—especially in late-Victorian fiction—often are injurious to individuals and foster outrage at social hypocrisy, double standards, and punitive rectitude. Above all, these works often entertain readers with outlandish scenarios giving antisocial behavior a thrilling, if vicarious, emancipatory appeal. That such excitement may occur at the expense of other parties may be unpleasant, even unethical, but that these scenarios are fictional shouldn't blind us to their exhilarating effects. What's striking about Victorian fiction, as will emerge, is less its moral didacticism than its willingness to let hatred and civility collide in Jekyll-and-Hyde fashion—often at the expense of sociability and similar ideals.

In Robert Louis Stevenson's enormously popular novel, for example, Henry Jekyll describes his asocial counterpart, Edward Hyde, as "a being inherently malign and villainous," whose "soul boil[ed] with causeless hatreds."[14] Hyde's demonic rage and blithe capacity for murder clearly push us beyond the realm of misanthropy, yet it's a mistake to attribute unwavering civility to Dr. Jekyll. As he acknowledges, the being that "shook the very fortress of [his] identity" isn't separate but something emanating from him that generates "perennial war" in his consciousness (57, 55). "I was radically both," he admits of a creature reveling in "ape-like spite" (56, 70). "This, too, was myself" (58).

Dr Jekyll and Mr Hyde is doubtless the best-known account of acute hatred and doubtful civility in Victorian literature, but its willingness to ascribe these extremes to a transforming powder, and to eliminate them with Jekyll's suicide, skews a fascinating conflict in less extravagant works. The novel's ending lets Victorian and contemporary readers imagine that the "perennial war" it stages is soluble and normally invisible, rather than one that, to a much lesser degree, afflicts us all. No society can tolerate the full expression of every impulse, hostile or murderous, crossing the minds of its diverse citizenry. What, though, of works that voice this hostility in less egregious forms?

"Other people are quite dreadful," sniffs Lord Goring in Wilde's *An Ideal Husband*. "The only possible society is oneself."[15] First performed in January 1895, three months before Wilde's first trial over accusations of "gross indecency," his play is a deft commentary on sanctimony. Doubtless, Goring's claim provoked as many Victorians to laughter as to anger, but in doing so it tested the bounds of credible sociability. How would a modern Goring or his author view today's sociopolitical climate, a time of anthrax, enemy combatants, and terrorists in our midst? Strange to say, the question presses our faith in Victorian values and sociability. As Felice Charmond cries in Hardy's *Woodlanders*, "The terrible insistencies of society—how severe they are, and cold, and inexorable. . . . Oh! why were we given hungry hearts and wild desires if we have to live in a world like this?"[16] Her question accents a tension between social control and individual satisfaction, indicating that Victorian society is to her more a cause of misery than a means of alleviating it. Tired of society's "terrible insistencies"—its corruption, inequality, and relentless pressures—many today would voice harsher indictments of this entity.[17]

What, then, do we owe our friends and neighbors, to say nothing of complete strangers? What is required of us, as distinct from what we choose to give?[18] These earnest questions may first engage duty, morality, and altruism, but accompanying and undercutting them is the equivalent of Don Juan's infamous suggestion, in Byron's poem, that "hatred is by far [our] longest pleasure; / Men love in haste, but they detest at leisure."[19] Given the Victorians' hope of finding societal explanations for good and evil, we must raise these questions when reading their works, and it's useful to imagine their most gifted thinkers asking us the same thing.

In *A Dream of John Ball*, William Morris says "fellowship is heaven, and lack of fellowship is hell: fellowship is life, and lack of fellowship is death."[20] Shunning the "vapour-bath of hurried and discontented humanity," his metaphor for urban life, Morris summed up his predicament in 1894, two years before he died: "Apart from the desire to produce beautiful things, the leading passion of my life has been and is hatred of modern civilization."[21] Believing himself "born out of his due time," Morris found happiness evoking life five centuries earlier, in medieval England.[22] But while he and other Victorians earnestly practiced the biblical injunction "Love thy neighbor as thyself," an injunction that Morris could reconcile with his socialist beliefs, many other nineteenth-century works voice a different message: Fear—sometimes hate—thy neighbor.

One reason this aspect of Victorian culture remains underexplored is because misanthropes—once prized for their integrity and disdain for humanity's worst excesses—came to appear immoral, degenerate, and even quasi-criminal. As my introduction explains in some detail, the evolution of this judgment in the nineteenth century highlights the changing role of communities in deciding who belongs, who doesn't, and why. Exposed at such moments is the barely veiled underside of better-known claims about positivism and communitarianism—the assumptions that humanity is inching toward perfectibility and that society is the best means of ensuring this outcome. Because the resulting thematic collision stems from a structural difficulty, moreover, it can't be remedied by murdering villains, dissolving a character's egoism, or creating conditions that demand greater altruism—stock remedies in Victorian fiction that the major writers examined here quickly left behind. That is why this book examines complex issues like "surplus" enmity, failures of sociability, ties between narration and hostility, and the kinds of antisocial impulses that, for Dickens, Browning, and Conrad, push their characters from conventional psychology to eschatology. These writers helped fashion a move from self-responsibility to interest in the limits and extinction of personality, the threat of asocial drives, and the duplicity that illusions of civility can mask.

"Victorian misanthropy" is thus a protean term, and leading literary and philosophical works conclude differently about how to define it. This makes it difficult to give one account of hatred in the nineteenth century; we must consult more sources and juggle varied, sometimes contradictory perspectives. Neither the Victorians nor scholars today can say with certainty that misanthropes are petty but not wise, mean rather than charitable. As an unnamed character declares in Dostoyevsky's *Brothers Karamazov*: "The more I love mankind in general, the less I love human beings in particular."[23] In "compensating" for the apparent imbalance, he clings to an ideal love of humanity but finds it impossible to love individuals a fraction more: "The more I . . . hated human beings in particular, the more ardent has become my love for mankind in general" (62). Posing difficulties for social theorists and visionaries, such paradoxes are difficult to interpret without importing preexisting assumptions from psychology, sociology, and philosophy (especially communitarianism, old and new). Still, theorists in these disciplines often skirt those paradoxes, hoping less to tolerate misanthropy and antisocial behavior than to explain them away. To understand misanthropy in all its complexity, we must therefore turn to literature, which recasts social issues in imaginative ways and lets responsibility take a backseat to representation.

The word *misanthropy* stems from the Greek *misánthropos* (*misein*, to hate + *anthropos*, man). Although the *Oxford English Dictionary* defines this noun as simply "hatred of mankind," it lists five different uses of the word, ranging from "bad opinions of mankind" (James Harris's 1781 *Philological Inquiries*) to the "revenge" we take on humanity "for fancied wrongs it has inflicted on us" (William Alger's 1867 meditations *The Solitudes of Nature and of Man*).[24] Since the Middle Ages, moreover, the verb *to hate* has supported both "strong" and "weak" definitions: "to hold in very strong dislike; to detest; to bear malice to," and a second, milder response: "to dislike greatly, be extremely averse (to do something)" (*OED* 7:6). While the Victorians generally coupled misanthropes with the first definition of *hate*, thereby associating their hatred with "very strong dislike" and "malice," subtle variations in how and why they hated make interpretation pressing but difficult. As the *OED*'s examples show, the Victorians and their forebears could employ *hate* imprecisely, and they sometimes turned *misanthropy* into a synonym for *enmity*, *rancor*, and *antipathy*—emotions whose object ordinarily wouldn't encompass all humanity.

When using these terms interchangeably, however, most Victorians took for granted hatred's pathological status, which therefore exacerbated the condition of misanthropes. Compelled to socialize, pressured into thinking more than their forebears were that companionship is healthy, misanthropes at the time faced a bitter irony: the expectation that a social answer would dispel their problems. As Carlyle insisted in "Characteristics," "Society is the genial element wherein [man's] nature first lives and grows; the solitary man were but a small portion of himself and must continue for ever folded in, stunted, and only half alive."[25] A few pages later, in a voice for which he's better known, he nonetheless praises solitude by lamenting the height to which "the dyspepsia of Society [has] reached; as indeed the constant grinding internal pain, or from time to time the mad spasmodic throes, of all Society . . . too mournfully indicate."[26]

As such ambiguous statements imply, my title *Hatred and Civility* is not contradictory. Nor does it blame nineteenth-century intellectuals—Carlyle among them—for believing citizens should strive for collective fulfillment. Instead it highlights the partial collapse of this ideal in literature, as well as the persistence of so-called irrational hatred in Victorian fiction and society, which generates antisocial perspectives and, occasionally, full-blown misanthropy. The result corrects our misshapen idea of the Victorians, describing a significant historical, cultural, and ethical shift in what sociability at the time meant and entailed. *Hatred and Civility* shows what happened when the Victorians' faith in community buckled under the pressure of sustaining fellow feeling, letting more intemperate emotions emerge.

The nineteenth century offers so many examples of hatred that the first question any critic faces is what to leave out. Although discussion of these subjects in French, German, Russian, and North American cultures would generate several books, I interpret this material only when it has a clear relation to hatred and misanthropy in nineteenth-century Britain. For example, my chapter on Dickens includes a brief section on Dostoyevsky's *Notes from Underground*, because the latter is central to accounts of hatred burgeoning at the time, and Dickens almost certainly influenced Dostoyevsky's work. Additionally, many late-Victorian writers (including Stevenson, Gissing, and Wilde) considered Dostoyevsky an important antecedent, and for good reason.

Although my interest is British hatred in general and misanthropy in particular, I acknowledge that these phenomena are distinct in scope and style. Characters hate humanity in the works I examine; societies display acute forms of cruelty and violence. Of course, the wealth of available material means that no one could give an exhaustive account of British writers interested in these interrelated topics. Still, readers may be surprised that Hardy, despite his prominent disdain for "madding crowds" and "shoddy humanity," isn't a player here.[27] Though he took a dim view of humanity, Hardy wrote parables about social bigotry rather than justified misanthropy.

Consider the poem "In a Wood," composed as he was reading articles on Arthur Schopenhauer and Eduard von Hartmann, and discovering French impressionist painting. In the poem's opening stanza, the speaker asks broadly, rhetorically,

> When the rains skim and skip,
> Why mar sweet comradeship,
> Blighting with poison-drip
> Neighbourly spray?

"Heart-halt and spirit-lame," he looks for peace in a remote wood, only to unearth a Darwinian nightmare in which anthropomorphized trees are "combatants all!," destroying one another as they compete for light and space. Rank and embattled vegetation certainly were recurring motifs in midcentury art and photography, roughly two decades before Hardy wrote his poem, and in Albert Moore's watercolor *Trunk of an Ash Tree with Ivy* (1857) and John Dillwyn Llewelyn's photograph *Lastrea Filix Mas* (c. 1854), the artists' fascination with decay hovers between delight and hints of menace (FIGURES 0.1 and 0.2). But while his Romantic spirit is similarly crushed, Hardy's speaker describes additional alienation from humanity and language—a common lament in Victorian poetry. Longing for solace, he turns "back to my kind," grudgingly conceding that there "now and then, are found / Life-loyalties."[28] The passive voice in this clause makes clear that from the speaker's perspective, loyalty arrives by chance, not design. Many other passages in Hardy's work display similar concerns, often with gloomier conclusions: "*Done because we are too menny* [*sic*]" is the plaintive explanation young Father Time gives for hanging his sister, baby brother, and himself near the end of Hardy's last novel, *Jude the Obscure*.[29]

Other, obvious candidates for inclusion in this book include Thackeray, Arnold, and Carlyle. The first (despite his middle name, Makepeace) was notorious for ridiculing his rivals while condemning the misanthropy of others, like Swift; the second was renowned for his fear of mobs and fascination with solitude;[30] the third, infamous for railing against greed and stupidity. The number of other texts worth discussing is vast, including Disraeli's early fiction; Morris's and James Thomson's horror of urban humanity in, respectively, *The Pilgrims of Hope* and *The City of*

FIGURE O.1 *Trunk of an Ash Tree with Ivy* (1857). Albert Moore. Watercolor. *Courtesy the Ashmolean Museum, Oxford.*

Dreadful Night; and Meredith's and H. G. Wells's late work, especially Wells's *Mind at the End of Its Tether*. While researching this book, I also read a large number of articles on hermits, eremites, misers, and crowds—most dating from the 1850s and 1860s. Such topics merely touch on hatred and misanthropy but raise a host of related questions about political reform and religious debate to which an encyclopedic approach could only begin to do full justice.[31] Clearly, the list of possible works to engage could go on and on, but as brevity and space require a focused approach, these topics and figures generally appear in my notes only.

This book, then, is neither a sociological nor an exclusively historical account of hatred in Victorian Britain, and its emphasis isn't reducible to

FIGURE O.2 *Lastrea Filix Mas* (c. 1854). John Dillwyn Llewelyn. Collodion. *Richard Morris, private collection.*

psychological and biographical concerns. My primary goal is not to unearth links between fictional accounts of hatred and authorial sadism, or to view fiction as a means of restraining readers' malice by venting before curbing our schadenfreude. Instead, I take a different tack, asking why readers gloat when characters we're encouraged to revile suffer and even die. What "providential" design secures in Victorian fiction a form of justice that life at the time so often denied? Dickens and Browning pursued these questions with keen intelligence, Browning in particular forging a style that's faithful to poetic, not political, justice. In comparison with other Victorian works, book 11 of his *Ring and the Book* arguably is unsurpassed in highlighting the pleasure of vengeance blind to its own self-defeating consequences. The result isn't quite cathartic, as I explain more fully in chapter 5. Judging pleasure a zero-sum element, Browning provokes, rather than diminishes, the full poetic power of schadenfreude.

These revenge scenarios may be deeply satisfying (Carker's grisly death in Dickens's *Dombey and Son* and Baldassarre's long-awaited retribution in Eliot's *Romola* are other examples that I consider), but they blur the line between misanthropy and villainy. Although villains conventionally harm specific targets and misanthropes' ubiquitous hatred often helps them abstain from violence, hatred itself can corrupt or dissolve these comforting distinctions. Is Baldassarre untainted by misanthropy when soliloquizing, "I am not alone in the world; I shall never be alone, for my revenge is with me"?[32] The question becomes muddier if, as Eliot's narrator permits, we consider his revenge warranted—owing to Tito's betrayal—and thus unlike his son's villainy.

Hatred and Civility also interprets works by writers (including Eliot and Charlotte Brontë) who, despite their frequent avoidance of admirers and occasional statements about others' disloyalty, are rarely called misanthropes.[33] They appear in this book because misanthropy is a factor they represented and struggled to diminish in their work. Moreover, the following chapters combine historical arguments with philosophical claims about hatred, including the limits of fellowship and humanity's near limitless capacity for malice—topics close to Eliot's heart, since many of her siblings and friends rejected her for living unmarried with George Henry Lewes. As an accompaniment to my allusion to *Romola* and a foretaste of later inquiry, Eliot's readers might ponder why her fictional teachers and intellectuals invariably are curmudgeonly (for example, Bartle Massey in *Adam Bede*, Bardo de' Bardi in *Romola*, and the scabrous Edward Casaubon in *Middlemarch*) or confirmed misanthropes (Latimer in *The Lifted Veil*, and Touchwood, Proteus Merman, and the narrator in *Impressions of Theophrastus Such*). In this last, eccentric book, completed just before Eliot died, the long-suffering Merman is "lacerated," "pilloried[,] and as good as mutilated" by the community of scholars he hopes to join. His fate is written as an allegory and given the richly sardonic title "How We Encourage Research."[34]

Biographical details in the following chapters may help readers gauge whether a character's opinions replicate an author's ideas, but fiction overall should not be confused with psychobiographical and social concerns. I stress this, because the esteem in which critics hold Eliot and Brontë risks eclipsing the way antipathy in their novels corrupts fellow feeling. Eliot is a good litmus test for this problem. Invoking her countless statements on fellow feeling, some critics recoil at the thought that enmity imbues her later fiction. Justly observing that much has been written on vindictiveness in *Romola*, *Felix Holt*, *Middlemarch*, and *Daniel Deronda*, others contend that arguments about hatred's persistence in her work are now so obvious as to be almost banal. Both reactions are a problem for those working on Eliot and hatred. While offering proof of this emotion risks eclipsing Eliot's well-known thoughts on fellow feeling, resulting in merely a fatuous preoccupation with evidence, a stronger account of what hatred does in her work won't satisfy those who believe Eliot resolved her fictions' moral ambiguities in the first place.

The problem deepens when one implicates several truisms in Eliot studies: Her critical and narrative perspectives often clash; her later works differ considerably from her earlier fiction; perspectives on fellow feeling shift imperceptibly within novels; and what Eliot achieves in her fiction frequently produces effects she denounces in her letters and essays. With other writers—say, Edward Lytton Bulwer—these tensions are easier to explain and somehow matter less. With Eliot, even sophisticated critics view her fiction and philosophy as mutually reinforcing. As with perhaps no other Victorian writer, scholars search her essays and letters for the exact cause of her literary arguments. Given these factors, can one plausibly examine her works' multiple concerns without appearing mildly contradictory?

I suspect not. If after detailing Eliot's preoccupation with ill will one provides her thoughts on fellow feeling, he or she risks accusing her improbably of idealism or naïveté. Yet given Eliot's remarkable talent as a writer, even the smallest allusion to ethical failure can seem patronizing, translating easily into presumptions about artistic deficiency. As this dilemma raises wider questions about interpretive method and the status of literature in this book, let me add that even the most stolidly realist narrative or didactic tract may convey fantasies contradicting its stated design. To that end, it is paradoxical but not naïve to assert that fiction

alternately buttresses and challenges hypotheses about society. Moreover, for good or ill, young Victorians arguably derived more instruc-
tion from reading novels than by reading philosophy, sermons, tracts,
biographies, and even conduct books. Admittedly, these contentions
about fiction's effects may vex historians, just as too many speculative
claims could lead us to echo Thomas Gradgrind, Dickens's ardent utilitarian in *Hard Times*: "Now, what I want is, Facts. . . . Facts alone are
wanted in life."[35] Certainly, *Hatred and Civility* reproduces a fair number of them. But a purely empirical approach to hatred—like a literalist
approach to fiction—can't account for hatred's and fiction's counterintuitive effects. As Browning's speaker declares suggestively in *Ferishtah's Fancies*: "Soul—too weak, forsooth / To cope with fact—wants
fiction everywhere!"; the latter alone blends "things visible and invisible."[36] "Whoever enlists fiction to assist in the hunt for knowledge,"
adds Peter Gay in his recent study, *Savage Reprisals*, "must always be
alert to authorial partisanship, limiting cultural perspectives, fragmen-
tary details offered as authoritative, to say nothing of neurotic obses-
sions."[37] To assess the ensuing literary effects, one must surely combine
Gay's approach to intellectual and cultural history with a form of close
reading that poets such as Browning practiced.

While parsing these concerns in my Eliot chapter, I question more
broadly in this book whether aesthetic harmony requires an ethical resolution of narrative conflict, and whether hatred in novels is gratifying
because it voices a set of tensions that Victorian society symbolized
more reluctantly. This is where I depart from Gay's fascinating claim
that novelists such as Dickens, Flaubert, and Thomas Mann composed
several works in revenge against personal slights.[38] Focusing less on the
relation between biography and creativity, I explore the philosophical
repercussions of extreme hatred in Victorian culture, before weighing
their effect on, say, Eliot's fictional communities and her statements
about compassion. Eliot arguably could picture the latter only in abstract, impersonal forms; solicitude fails when her fiction makes altruism
bridge deeply embittered conflicts among neighbors. More broadly, that
her largely intellectual interest in hatred could tarnish her reputation
sadly confirms what misanthropy has come to mean for us. To those insisting on a clear correspondence between her fiction and her life, I can

only add that despite cultivating a persona exuding warmth, Eliot chafed at being put on a pedestal. Like Jane Austen, she also wrote in her letters comments on other people that might surprise a few of her readers.

As this book draws on some material unknown to Victorianists and general readers (the pages of many sole surviving editions at the British Library being previously uncut), I supplement analysis of rare works with salient quotations. Despite the mediocrity of these works, they signal what was published on hatred in eighteenth- and nineteenth-century Britain.

Readers interested in the history of misanthropy should consult *Not in Timon's Manner*, Thomas Preston's lively account of "feeling, misanthropy, and satire in eighteenth-century England."[39] Among the growing number of studies on Victorian misanthropy, four stand out as particular influences: Gay's *The Cultivation of Hatred*, volume 3 of *The Bourgeois Experience, from Victoria to Freud*, and *Savage Reprisals*; Daniel Karlin's *Browning's Hatreds*; and Victor Brombert's *In Praise of Antiheroes*.[40] With these key texts, Adam Gillon's *The Eternal Solitary: A Study of Joseph Conrad* proved indispensable, as did John Portmann's philosophically rich account of schadenfreude in *When Bad Things Happen to Other People*.[41] I also found compelling Barbara Ehrenreich's observations in *The Snarling Citizen* and Nobel Prize winner Wisława Szymborska's poem "Hatred," which asserts that this emotion "knows how to make beauty," even though it creates a face "twisted in a grimace / of erotic ecstasy."[42] Among the many philosophical works influencing this project were Giorgio Agamben's oblique but fascinating *Language and Death: The Place of Negativity*; Alain Badiou's provocative study *Ethics: An Essay on the Understanding of Evil*; Joan Copjec's collection *Radical Evil*; Renata Salecl's *(Per)Versions of Love and Hate*; and Slavoj Žižek's *Tarrying with the Negative: Kant, Hegel, and the Critique of Ideology*.[43] Finally, for a wryly intelligent overview of misanthropy, focusing especially on contemporary people-hating in North America, one should read Florence King's *With Charity Toward None: A Fond Look at Misanthropy*.[44]

HATRED & CIVILITY

Victorian Hatred, a Social Evil and a Social Good

So, What Are Victorian Values?

DR. ROBERT DUNCAN is blessed with all the right virtues: He's earnest, loyal, and good. But after his father is swindled and left penniless, the doctor's love of humanity sours. His Victorian values take a nosedive. "From henceforth he hated the world, and swore there should be war to the knife between him and the world."[1]

Duncan is the hero of *A Philanthropic Misanthrope*, an oddly named novel by "Joseph Somebody." Hackneyed and predictable, the work is a moral fable for the 1850s, long before the corporate scandals rocking us today. The moment Somebody tests his protagonist, Duncan's family dies with alarming rapidity, his sister Ada collapsing first, followed swiftly by both parents. This is but the start of Duncan's decline and embitterment, yet three hundred pages later justice prevails: the villain, John Stubbs, dies in gratifying pain (someone else's horse and carriage run him over repeatedly), and the well-heeled doctor marries Louise, his sweetheart, whose "gentle, humanising influence" restores his goodwill. "In time Louise convinced her beloved husband that his misanthropy was only theoretical, that it was merely the hatred of all that was bad, and mean, and dishonourable in mankind, but not a hatred of mankind itself" (346–47).

Now languishing in the rare books section of the British Library, *A Philanthropic Misanthrope* seems an unlikely representative for Victorian culture. In truth, it's closer to a caricature of the period's piety, and thus a point of departure for this book. Still, the novel sums up ideas that many Victorians inherited and transformed: Love cancels misanthropy, and extreme hatred is a pathology marking a character for death. Later examples will confound this picture, compromising writers and challenging intellectuals by putting their characters in more complex light. But the sentiment flourishing at the end of Somebody's novel recurs in popular nineteenth-century fiction, and it clouds many assessments of the Victorians today.

Take Lord Macaulay, the nineteenth-century liberal historian, who proudly declared, "The public mind of England has softened while it has ripened, and . . . we have, in the course of ages, become, not only a wiser, but also a kinder people." "The more we study the annals of the past," he added, in a Whiggish claim for progress favoring Victorian society over its 1685 counterpart, "the more shall we rejoice that we live in a merciful age, in an age in which cruelty is abhorred, and in which pain, even when deserved, is inflicted reluctantly and from a sense of duty."[2]

True to Macaulay's hope, we rarely label the Victorians people-haters. We know them better for creating charities and philanthropic organizations, for writing some of our best novels about society, and for upholding what Samuel Smiles, in his midcentury best-seller *Self-Help*, enshrined as Victorian values—duty, thrift, and self-sacrifice. These values allegedly kindled devotion to family, neighborly regard, and love of nation, building on Burke's now-famous statement that loving "the little platoon we belong to in society, is the first principle (the germ as it were) of public affections. It is the first link in the series by which we proceed towards a love to our country and to mankind."[3] In sermons and conduct manuals, in journalism and fiction, the Victorians praised these sentiments so highly that our first instinct might be to dismiss the term *Victorian hatred* as contradictory.

Hatred and Civility shows that doing so would be inaccurate and unwise. Examining rare and well-known works that cast the nineteenth century in a darker light, this study asks whether the Victorians actually were ardently sociable, much less consistently moral and philanthropic, and what happened to individuals who defied or even mocked their ideals. As we'll see, Macaulay's fructifying metaphors ("the public mind . . . has softened while it has ripened") could anticipate a fine national harvest only if the fruit did not go bad or include too many rotten apples.

Numerous Victorians believed "public affections" and "love [of] mankind" could trounce moral evil. But like those whose obsession with cleanliness compels them to unearth more and more dirt, they were pre-occupied by hatred and anxious to eliminate it. Some bewailed "the great mystery" of turpitude, fretting, "We cannot be in the enjoyment of good without the knowledge of evil."[4] Others realized that "hatred of the old murderous kind" is not, as "so many of our instructors would have us believe[,] . . . entirely obsolete—killed by education, and intel-ligence, and what is known as 'deeper sympathy.'"[5] Sly and unsettling, this last idea jeopardizes many contrary expectations. Indeed, the author of this 1890 article added, "There is nothing in intelligence of itself to extinguish hate . . . , and to understand [it] accurately may only make you understand more clearly the hatefulness of the person hated."[6] Bod-ing poorly for society, these remarks let gifted writers rethink existing values and assumptions. Novelists like George Moore gauged the bene-fit—and the price—of belonging to a community, and Moore conclud-ed the price was too high. "Oh, vile, filthy, and hypocritical century," he announced in *Confessions of a Young Man*, "I at least scorn you."[7]

These examples not only point to recurring social concerns in the nineteenth century but also indicate how difficult it is to generalize about this era; a subtler, even piecemeal approach is necessary. Making matters more complex, the adjective *Victorian* has different connotations for conservatives and liberals today, who use their associations to buttress arguments they favor and to dismiss those they don't. Whereas a con-servative historian like Gertrude Himmelfarb praises the Victorians for their dignity and self-control, wishing Britons and North Americans today would emulate them,[8] liberal scholars cite Michel Foucault's influ-ential claim that nineteenth-century society was adept at punishing mis-creants, enforcing norms, and regulating desire.[9] How, then, could mis-anthropes and others voice their dissent and vent their spleen? Taking issue with both sets of critics, this book shows that hatred escapes regu-lation in many literary and cultural texts, forging visions of individual freedom more imaginative than Foucauldians and conservatives generally admit.

Examining the Victorians' varied, often contradictory responses to hatred and misanthropy, this introduction explains how many of them challenged orthodox medical, psychiatric, theological, and philosophical judgments, especially about vexed but fascinating links between satisfaction and sociability. Those links in fact recur throughout this book. My introduction also revisits key debates from previous centuries, when secular alternatives to theological discussion of evil took hold and philosophers wrangled over the difference between abstract and practical hatred of humanity.

The Victorians interpreted these arguments in ways as dynamic as the culture they inhabited and produced. Casting society as the best judge of moral evil and communities as a fine way of fulfilling individual needs, many of them nevertheless pathologized misanthropy so dramatically that a journalist could argue in 1901, with some justification, that the time when one could "be a 'good hater' ha[d] ceased."[10] "Hatred of certain causes and principles we have everywhere treated," the author conceded, "but individual, personified enmity, intense enough to last a lifetime, and bending all the events of existence to its malignant will, is employed very charily nowadays in literary or dramatic work[s]."[11] Apparently, misanthropy died with Queen Victoria, leaving the Edwardians queasy about hatred, an emotion whose appearance in literature could "shock [them] as bad art."[12] Though one need only glance at my epilogue to find holes in this argument, the status of misanthropy changed dramatically in the Victorian era, and the following pages explain why.

Misanthropes in all ages deserve our respect, but heroism is not their goal. As persons "who distrust . . . men and avoid . . . their society,"[13] they share several traits. For starters, they are more often antisocial than asocial, so differing from hermits, prophets, and those practicing autarky—complete self-sufficiency. But although misanthropes aspire to be independent, their ornery behavior and pride in judging humanity often defeat this end, bringing them into volatile contact with the failings they abhor. Moore and others didn't hide their contempt when calling humanity "despicable vermin" (186); they published it.

The ensuing strain touches on psychology and philosophy. As truculent idealists, misanthropes are society's conscience and scold. Like revolutionaries, they question what we expect from other people; unlike revolutionaries, they can't stand other people.[14] Dismissing the idea of harmonious coexistence, misanthropes scorn fellow feeling, to say nothing of loyalty, conformity, and altruism. Ignoring Enlightenment philosophers who claimed that humans rationally would pursue pleasurable activities, many nineteenth-century misanthropes realized they would experience more happiness spoiling other people's. "Who believes in philanthropy nowadays?" asks Moore. "We are weary of being good. . . . Humanity be hanged!" (136, 126, 185).

"The misanthrope is not merely different from other men," writes David Konstan. "He perceives himself as the representative of a social ideal which others have betrayed, and condemns his fellows for their perversity and hypocrisy. And yet society abides, and it is the misanthrope who cannot fit. He is rigid and surly, a natural target for comic deflation."[15] Unlike Konstan's essay, this book doesn't treat misanthropes as "a reflex of the history of social forms themselves"; nor does it presume that all such persons are male (98).[16] Instead, it shows that individuals have a complex, unpredictable relationship to society and themselves, and that the Victorians often stigmatized the ensuing diffidence and self-strangeness because both jeopardize fellowship and citizenship (*civitas*), probing the foundations on which they rest. This is just one reason I modify the claim, in "The Decline of Hatred," that misanthropy died with Queen Victoria.

Potent in Renaissance drama and refined by such eighteenth-century satirists as Swift, Gay, and Dr. Johnson, hatred of humanity acquired fresh significance in the age of Bentham, Mill, and Darwin. Rocked by a series of religious crises in the 1830s, the Victorians tried to develop increasingly secular and societal remedies for what were once considered theological and metaphysical concerns. As Auguste Comte explained, theology's "treatment of . . . moral problems [is] exceedingly imperfect," given its "inability . . . to deal with practical life."[17] As such claims took hold, they allowed citizens to spurn those who disagreed with society's determining role. Indeed, a host of philosophical, scientific, and psychiatric assumptions began circulating at midcentury, arguing that misanthropes default on human relations and abdicate group responsibility—beliefs that left the culprits vulnerable to charges of moral and social delinquency. Hostility toward misanthropes gathered momentum as Romanticism waned, and, as we'll see, disdain for misanthropy properly dates to the final decades of the eighteenth century. But unique in the 1850s and 1860s was a set of psychological and psychiatric judgments casting misanthropy as not merely eccentric or irritating, but also a condition bordering on insanity.

William Alger argued accordingly in *The Solitudes of Nature and of Man* that "the man who separates himself from mankind to nourish dislike or contempt for them, has in him a morbid element which must make woe."[18] We could ignore that making woe for others differs greatly from baring unhappiness, but Alger put his claim in the imperative. "However natural it may be to do so," he added, "there is no justification for those who, when wronged, turn against mankind with retaliating animosity" (107). Perspectives like his oriented many hotly debated topics at the time, including capital punishment, irrational conduct, and rapacious imperialism. Indeed, Alger partly summed these up when asserting, "Misanthropy, as a dominant characteristic, if thoroughly tracked and analyzed, will be found almost always to be the revenge we take on mankind for fancied wrongs it has inflicted on us" (123). By the time the Hungarian writer and physician Max Nordau revisited this subject in the 1890s, his assessment was unambiguously negative: "Anti-social instincts . . . [make] life in common with the race difficult or impossible, worsening consequently its vital conditions, and preparing its ruin indirectly."[19]

Misanthropes Ancient . . .

In accepting these judgments, many Victorians overturned earlier accounts of people-hating, in which "retaliating animosity" did not epitomize misanthropy, and redress—when it existed—could appear justified, even natural. Britain's golden age of misanthropy in fact occurred almost three centuries before Victoria's reign. The *OED*'s first entry for *misanthrope* is Barnabe Googe's *Eglogs, Epytaphes, and Sonettes* (1563), and the noun *misanthropy* appeared almost one hundred years later, in 1656, just a few decades after the first published use of *philanthropy* in 1606.[20] One of the period's best accounts of misanthropy—*Timon of*

Athens, published in 1623 and attributed to Shakespeare—adapts Plutarch's *Lives of the Noble Grecians and Romans* as well as Lucian's dialogue *Timon the Misanthrope* (second century A.D.).[21]

In Plato's *Phædo*, another vital antecedent, Socrates calls misanthropy "discreditable," because it stems from "ignorance of the world." Allegedly, misanthropes hate rashly, unearthing falsehood when they expect to find integrity.[22] Socrates reproaches such individuals for prejudging the whole from faults in the part: "Misanthropy arises out of the too great confidence of inexperience." After trusting men who "turn . . . out to be false and knavish," the irascible "at last hates all men, and believes that no one has any good in him at all" (1:474).

People-hating was also well known to many other Greek, Roman, and Indo-Greek writers, including Euripides, the cynic Diogenes, Horace, and Menander, who authored *Dyskolos*, often translated as *The Bad-Tempered Man; or, The Misanthrope*.[23] Menander was a pupil of Theophrastus, whose philosophy informs George Eliot's last book, *Impressions of Theophrastus Such*. Moreover, it was Horace's speaker who declared, "I hate the profane mob and keep them at a distance," insisting, "Our generation is prolific in evil."[24]

. . . Augustan and Romantic . . .

For much of the eighteenth century, by contrast, writers and philosophers drew sharper distinctions between cerebral and heartfelt hatred, as well as between hatred of specific individuals and loathing of the entire species. Those who hated a few generally fared better than those who indulged in heartfelt contempt for all, but the latter could still defend themselves without being called mad, iniquitous, or perverse. Eighteenth-century intellectuals also upheld this distinction, because it helped them separate love of individuals from disgust for human weaknesses, so redeeming the benevolent misanthrope as one waging a personal crusade against vice. As Percival Stockdale declared, quite confusingly, in his 1783 *Essay on Misanthropy*, "There is a Misanthrope, who is as acute, and severe in his observations, as he is gentle, and placid in his conduct."[25] In this miraculous interpretive shift, "speculative" misanthropy becomes morally edifying, defending individuals against worldly corruption by establishing the foundations necessary for fellow and religious feeling:

> This latter Misanthropy will keep us calm and serene amid the tumults of life. It will arm us completely against the selfishness, malignity, and barbarity of mankind: We shall not be discomposed; for we shall not be disappointed. It will secure us esteem, respect, content, and satisfaction; and, however paradoxical the assertion may seem, it will tend to make us good Christians: It will even warm and dilate our hearts with the tenderest and most expanded humanity; and it will adorn our conduct with universal and active benevolence. (9)

Of course, Stockdale's vague thesis wrests "speculative" misanthropy from any suggestion of hatred, thereby rendering the term *misanthropy* almost meaningless. His concession about "the selfishness, malignity, and barbarity of mankind" also sits uneasily beside his claims for "universal . . . benevolence," making any thought of turning the other cheek rather unwise. But that's why his argument is interesting. In advancing such shaky distinctions, he and other eighteenth-century writers sought to defend "speculative" misanthropy from its invidious counterpart. Disappointment at other people's weaknesses could seem honorable, but generalized vengeance against humanity was beyond the pale.

In light of such arguments, one can appreciate why William Hazlitt's 1823 essay "On the Pleasure of Hating" was so scandalous. Hatred, claims Hazlitt, is inspiring and unexceptional. By tarnishing everyone's thoughts, it creates "a moral basis . . . radically *opposed* to the standard of utility."[26] "The spirit of malevolence survives the practical exertion of it," he insists. "We learn to curb our will and keep our overt actions within the bounds of humanity, long before we can subdue our sentiments and imaginations to the same mild tone. We give up the external demonstration, the *brute* violence, but cannot part with the essence or principle of hostility."[27]

Why not? Focusing on intractable forms of malice, Hazlitt established a rationale for hatred that wreaked havoc on rationalist arguments about behavior, including Robert Owen's early belief that individuals are determined entirely by their environment and Jeremy Bentham's desire to promote "the greatest happiness of the greatest number" by vanquishing our "malevolent or dissocial affections."[28] Poking fun at such noble utilitarian aims, Hazlitt destroyed the myth that the pathological alone plumb the depths of enduring hatred. "There is a secret affinity, a *hankering* after evil in the human mind," he says, and "it takes a perverse, but a fortunate delight in mischief, since it is *a never-failing source of satisfaction*" (12:128; second emphasis mine). Though such satisfaction turns out to be a mixed blessing, first to go in this account is any idea of fellow feeling. "The greatest possible good of each individual," he insists, in obvious mockery of Bentham's maxim, "consists in doing all the mischief he can to his neighbour: that is charming, and finds a sure and sympathetic chord in every breast!" (12:129). Many Regency and Victorian sketches portray this glee, including Cruikshank's amusing studies "Sheer Tyranny" and "Sheer Tenderness" (FIGURES 01.1 and 01.2).

. . . and "Modern"

Although they were fascinated by these antecedents, the Victorians generally drained their satirical and antisocial associations. They did so, as William Alger shows, by refining another, predominantly eighteenth-century assumption—that people-hating is a psychological affliction

SHEER TYRANNY.
Cropping a poor wanderer, who has slept one night in the Croydon workhouse, before he is liberated in the morning.

SHEER TENDERNESS.
Cropping a long-haired bacchanal, convicted at the Mansion-house of drunkenness, instead of fining him.

FIGURES 01.1 AND 01.2 *Sheer Tyranny* and *Sheer Tenderness* (n.d.).
George Cruikshank. Woodcut illustrations. *George Cruikshank's Omnibus* (London, 1842). *Courtesy the University of Wisconsin–Madison Special Collections.*

caused largely by unrequited love.[29] Still, other judgments circulated in the nineteenth century, especially among those who asserted that a little misanthropy would help keep society honest and self-critical.

In "The Modern Misanthrope," published in April 1863, Edward Lytton Bulwer hewed this line, accusing his fellow Victorians of "masked misanthropy" when they tried thwarting aggression.[30] Gone was the previous century's "ruder age," he lamented, when contempt was heartfelt and individuals fled society in admirable disgust (477). Indeed, Bulwer inherited from German Romanticism the idea of weltschmerz (literally, "world-pain"), one of whose meanings is still "mental depression or apathy caused by comparison of the actual state of the world with an ideal state."[31] Claiming his peers were engaged merely in fashionable sniping, Bulwer implied that a sounder morality would generate stronger attacks on the "actual state of the world." Doubtless, he was partly recalling the vicious denunciation of his own work in *Fraser's Magazine* and *The Age*, as well as the enmity he experienced in the early 1830s from rivals like Thackeray—material that I explore in chapter 1 alongside Bulwer's complex thoughts on sympathy and social progress.

The myths that we inherit about Victorian fellowship and repression aren't the whole story, then, but they contain a grain of truth. "The movement from Romantic to Victorian years," writes John Reed, was "a movement also from aggressive heroism, or what might be called the imperial will, to controlled heroism, or the reflective will." The "need to renounce selfishness in favor of a larger purpose was," he adds, "characteristic of much Victorian writing."[32] As Joseph Somebody's novel helps indicate, many Victorian novels encourage self-renunciation so fervently they punish hatred while teaching individuals to balance self-regard with judicious attention to other people. So it isn't surprising that we feel confident, turning the last page of such works, that love and goodwill prevail over a range of social evils, including treachery and adultery. As the author of "The Natural History of Hatred" declared in 1871, with some justification, "Our modern novel-writers never attempt to offer us a study of revenge, or, if they do attempt it, break down hideously. . . . Hatred, real downright hatred, is far less common than is supposed, and is far more potent. We may admit without difficulty that it is unchristian."[33] Such attempts at dissolving "unchristian" hatred were for centuries inseparable from assumptions about Providence. Like their cultural antecedents, in other words, nineteenth-century novels harm villains and confer happiness on those practicing benevolence.

But as Bulwer's essay and a host of other works show, it would be wrong to view this as a complete account of the period or to suggest that novels taught the Victorians only to repress their hatred. The *Spectator* was right to caution that "what we see around us, in fact, is not the extinction of hate, but an increase of self-restraint in its manifestation. . . . It is intelligence as to consequences which we fear the modern method is diffusing, and not a better heart at all."[34] Arguably, the Victorians gave hatred new life when trying to curb antipathy, for, besides their literature on moral evil, they also produced a vast number of works on mobs, demonstrations, and class hatred at home. And a brief glance at the international stage shows that, for many of them, these issues were a global concern. In 1863 and 1866, respectively, *Littell's Living Age* reprinted short pieces titled "Japanese Hatred of Christianity" and "Irish Hatred of England." By the mid-1880s and throughout the 1890s, this and other journals were running articles or editorials on every conceivable form of hostility, including "Race-Hatred in India," "The Hatred of England," "The Growth of National Hatred," "The Hatred of Authority," "American Hatred of England," "The Hatred of the Poor for the Rich," "Hatred of Jews," 'Hatred of Foreigners," "Holy Hatred," "International Hatred," and "Racial Hatred."[35]

Informing—sometimes guiding—such disparate hostilities was a set of amorphous claims about racial enmity, voiced by adherents to such relatively new "sciences" as phrenology and eugenics. Allegedly, biological predispositions could account for factors as varied as wealth, intelligence, sympathy, and benevolence.[36] In 1824–25, for example, the *Phrenological Journal* included an essay "On the Coincidence between the Natural Talents and Dispositions of Nations, and the Development of Their Brains," which argued that a "common type" defines the "brains of different EUROPEAN NATIONS": "They are decidedly larger than the Hindoo, American Indian, and Negro heads; and this indicates superior force of mental character."[37] These assertions implicitly endorsed British imperialism by justifying its support for racial hierarchies: They made the scramble for Africa and other continents not only proof of the fittest nation but also, for many, an act of massive philanthropy.[38] While guiltlessly appropriating land, the jingoistic could believe that biological patterns had rendered non-Europeans somehow less godly or human than they. As the Scottish anatomist and surgeon Robert Knox put it, "Can the black races become civilized? I should say not; their future history, then, must resemble the past. The Saxon race will never tolerate them—never amalgamate—never be at peace."[39] An otherwise freethinking socialist and profeminist Karl Pearson, professor of applied mathematics at University College, London, could still advance similar claims half a century later, in 1900, attributing internecine strife in "large districts in Africa" not to European rapacity but rather to "bad stock" marring the cultures of "the Kaffir and the Negro." "If you want to know whether the lower races of man can evolve a higher type," he declared, "I fear the only course is to leave them to fight it out among themselves."[40] Not content with advocating such detachment, Pearson, in the midst of the Boer War, became a proponent of apartheid and, when necessary, of racial extermination in the name of national welfare: "The only healthy alternative" to the "evil" of racial coexistence was, he said, that the white man "should . . . completely drive out the inferior race" (21).

Despite their being published to bolster Victorian theories about the "family of man," these arguments rendered Victorian notions of fellowship so specious that Euro-American sociability could appear inseparable from bigotry. As Knox enthused, "What an innate hatred the Saxon has for [the Negro]. . . . There is, there can be, nothing more wonderful in human history than this dislike of race to race: always known and admitted to exist, it has only of late assumed a threatening shape" (161, 223). Unlike Pearson, who wanted above all to bolster "the case of the civilized white man" (*National Life* 34), Knox conceded that Britain's and Europe's political strength derived from their capacity for, and willingness to commit, genocide: "Empires, monarchies, nations, are human contrivances often held together by fraud and violence." "Man's gift is to destroy," he added, "not to create" (*Races* 11–12; 312). In short, as I've argued elsewhere,[41] the empire became for such thinkers a vehicle for the expression of group hatred, of misanthropy on a grand scale.

In his excellent study of European hatred, Peter Gay sums up this deplorable chapter of Victorian society:

The nineteenth-century bourgeoisie engaged in continuous, often acidulous debates over the moral nature and adaptive properties of aggression. These altercations were bound to be most ferocious when nation clashed with nation, class with class, interest group with interest group, but they proved only marginally less spirited when fought out over subtler issues. These controversies suggest that many Victorians were alert to the varieties of aggressiveness and stood ready to attack or defend one or another of its manifestations.[42]

"But," he cautions, "conscious and contentious attitudes toward aggression coexisted with aggressive ideas and acts that were not recognized as such."[43] As we've seen, the *Spectator* anticipated this point in 1890. Yet because writers and politicians were sometimes poor evaluators (or good rationalizers) of their motives, we can't take their statements simply on trust. Consequently, this book examines a range of Victorian fantasies, including the specious idea that love and fellowship annul hatred; it focuses on irreconcilable tensions between individuals and society, particularly when the former failed or refused to conform to the demands of the latter.

Victorian Misanthropes: Take Two

To simplify their moral and social concerns, many Victorians tried putting misanthropes in separate camps, depending on whether the bitterness was temporary, and thus basically harmless, or lasting, and thus morally reprehensible. That villains are innately venal and misanthropes merely appear so is an idea that flourished in simpler fiction of the time, settling the outcome of, say, Somebody's *Philanthropic Misanthrope*, M. J. M'intosh's equally facile story, "The Young Misanthrope," and Romantic antecedents such as *Hatred, or the Vindictive Father* and Catharina Smith's *The Misanthrope Father; or, The Guarded Secret*.[44] But as the best writers realized, these schemas are neither credible nor aesthetically interesting. The subject of chapters in this book, these gifted authors either couldn't sustain this distinction or chose not to for artistic and philosophical reasons. In probing how individuals' impulses and satisfactions clash violently with the sanctioned expression of such feelings in

society, these authors encourage a book-length analysis of related philosophical claims about pleasure and sociability, including the pleasure of
shunning—or retaliating against—other people.

Consider Dickens's last complete novel, *Our Mutual Friend*. In it, the
aptly named Mr. Venus exemplifies the belief that misanthropes hate for
want of love. When Pleasant Riderhood returns Venus's passion at the
novel's end, his mild antipathy softens and he returns to society a mar-
ried, productive citizen. But as I show in chapter 2, part of Dickens's
achievement in this novel is to tarnish with misanthropy almost every
character *except* this "harmless misanthrope."[45] Revoking pat solutions,
such shifts in perspective turn society into a source of hatred, inviting us
to ask, with protagonist Eugene Wrayburn, What if society were so corrupt, prejudicial, and even despicable that our sole happiness consists in
obstructing it?

Granted, this modifies the sentimentalism flourishing in some of
Dickens's earlier works, including *Sketches by Boz*, in which misanthropes—also shorn of hatred—are eccentric and endearing. But Dickens was almost unique in oscillating deftly between radical and maudlin
haters, and he appealed to popular tastes in milking misanthropes for all
their comic potential. In "The Bloomsbury Christening," Nicodemus
Dumps ("long Dumps") is a hilarious curmudgeon whose idea of toast-
ing his godson's life is telling the baby it will soon experience "trials,
considerable suffering, severe affliction, and heavy losses!"[46]

A few other writers also used misanthropy as rich material for laughter. In the mid-1870s, *Vanity Fair* ran a series of witty articles, later reprinted as *Our Own Misanthrope*, poking fun at subjects like salesmen, the
Swiss, Philistines, fake aristocrats, children, and the badly dressed. The
articles drew on such popular antecedents as James Beresford's *Miseries
of Human Life*—already in its eleventh edition by 1826, and reissued in
1856—in which the character Mr. Testy insists, "*Timon* or *Diogenes*, if
you will—*these* are the Recluses for me."[47] But "Ishmael," the author of
these *Vanity Fair* articles, is more bitter than either Mr. Sensitive or Mr.
and Mrs. Testy, and has little time for those practicing "charity":

> Every great philanthropist, and every great misanthrope, must in
> his turn damn the nature of things. . . . In truth, love and hate are

so very much alike that it takes something more even than angelic powers to analyze the difference; just as dust is mud in high spirits, as dirt is matter out of place, so philanthropy and misanthropy combine in a common dislike to humanity as it is; only one wishes to alter by leniency, the other by punishment.[48]

"Ishmael" clearly had read Dickens's *Bleak House*, in which Mrs. Jelly-by practices "telescopic philanthropy" and Mrs. Pardiggle hectors the poor and the sick, while bullying her own children.

As Bulwer found most lighthearted views of people-hating disingen-uous, his perspective in the 1863 essay resembles that in *Our Mutual Friend*, which Dickens began serializing the following year. According to Bulwer, the rage fueling Elizabethan and Jacobean malcontents sadly had begun to wane. Bulwer's lament is worth heeding, his argument dif-ficult to refute. For reasons we must examine, readers of Victorian liter-ature encountered less often the bile flourishing in plays by, say, Chap-man, Jonson, Marston, Shakespeare, Tourneur, and Webster. Gone too was much of the idealism motivating "benevolent misanthropy" in the eighteenth century, a term describing people who were disillusioned with humanity but not hostile toward all of it. If they abhorred their neighbors' greed, apparently it was less from spite than out of serious concern for their souls.[49] Such changes don't mean, however, that the Victorians always kept their word or fulfilled their lofty ideals. Nor, as Gay reminds us, did such concern make their culture and society intrin-sically less hostile than before. Even the liberal journalist and essayist Walter Bagehot, one of the most influential journalists midcentury, was prepared to write: "You may talk of the tyranny of Nero and Tiberius; but the real tyranny is the tyranny of your next-door neighbor."[50] Bage-hot was being sardonic, but readers surely got his point.

Churlish Victorians

When Victorian rhetoric and reality failed to correspond, misan-thropes—struggling to justify their hatred in the first place—became easy scapegoats for zealots. In a society bent on proclaiming fellowship, they stood out as symptoms of failed civility. More important, they drew attention to aspects of behavior that society couldn't contain, including impulses, passions, and forms of enjoyment arising at the *expense* of those needing charity and neighborly concern. As the author of "Confession of a Misanthrope" opined in April 1893, "That horrible word 'altruism' cuts a large figure in the discussions of the day. . . . I sometimes wonder if, in this modern world of general benevolence, there are any misanthropes extant beside myself. Certainly, if any such exist, they keep themselves extremely dark."[51] Betraying many reigning concerns, this material helps us see where Victorian ideals showed signs of collapse, spotlighting surplus enmity the culture couldn't integrate.

Adept at promoting "alibis for aggression," the Victorians imbued with violence such disparate topics as commerce, mass demonstrations, and colonialism, to say nothing of public executions and war.[52] So even statements hailing Victorian progress should be read with a pinch of salt, as Cruikshank's parody *The Grand "March of Intellect"* makes clear (FIGURE 01.3; see also FIGURE 01.4). When Macaulay proudly insisted he lived in "an age in which cruelty is abhorred, and in which pain, even when deserved, is inflicted reluctantly and from a sense of duty," he was invoking earlier penal reforms and echoing Kant's and Claude-Joseph Tissot's concern that punishment for crimes be compassionate, not vengeful.[53] As Gay puts it, Macaulay wanted society to show a "mounting willingness to forgo the emotional dividends of revenge."[54] Pandering to humanity's baser instincts—especially when punishing criminals—struck such commentators as unseemly, replacing justice with retaliation. Macaulay insisted relatedly, in his 1828 essay on Henry Hallam, that "misanthropy is not the temper which qualifies a man to act in great affairs, or to judge of them."[55]

But some churlish Victorians on both sides of the Atlantic (Moore and Bulwer among them) were candid about these "emotional dividends," thereby revealing that the gap between social ideals and political strategies could be very wide indeed, and that misanthropy—seemingly provoked by ever-greater numbers of social causes—cast an increasingly wide net. In 1869, four years after the Civil War, the Baltimore-based *New Eclectic Magazine* ran a short piece called "Laus Iracundiæ" (Praise the Irascible). "The times demand 'good haters,'" the article concludes with bitter irony, the author complaining that liberalism makes it

FIGURE 01.3 *The Grand "March of Intellect"* (May 20, 1828).
George Cruikshank. *Scraps and Sketches* (London, 1830).
Courtesy the University of Wisconsin–Madison Special Collections.

fashion[able] to abuse the great men of the Reformation age, for what
is called their intolerance and bitterness towards adversaries. Our
moderns affect a great advance upon their manners, and are quite in-
tolerant of their intolerance, and fierce in condemnation of their
fierceness. The only thing which seems to be bad enough to excite the
ire of these *nonchalant* gentlemen, is the ancient zeal for the truth.[56]

Ridiculing "the pious horror of some male or female 'Miss Nancy,'" the
author insists that "if the pole of repulsion be but feebly shunned, we
shall expect the pole of attraction to be languidly sought. Hatred tran-
quilly worded, is no more to be confided in than love coldly uttered"
(524, 525). A person who hates poorly lacks other passions, apparently,
and can't be trusted. Impatient with Victorian piety, the author wanted
to return, with Bulwer, to a "ruder age" when misanthropes were misanthropes, without apology.[57]

Maladjustment or Revelation?

Such articles intensified, rather than quelled, the specter of motiveless rage,
demanding new explanations for extreme hatred. Could a misanthrope

FIGURE 0I.4 *Selection of English Heads* (1849). Paul Gavarni.
Gavarni in London: Sketches of Life and Character (London, 1849).
Courtesy Northwestern University Library Special Collections.

love individuals while loathing humanity in the abstract? And could writers still forge clear distinctions between the virtuous and the damned?

Christianity for centuries had tried to instill contempt for worldly goods and ties, and the Book of Romans states (as do other parts of the Bible), "Love worketh no ill to his neighbour: therefore love is the fulfilling of the law" (13:10). But Victorian preachers found it increasingly difficult to reconcile worldly disdain and fellow feeling. In "National Apostasy," the Reverend John Keble warned congregations about "the malevolent feeling of disgust, almost amounting to misanthropy, which is apt to lay hold of sensitive minds, when they see oppression and wrong triumphant on a large scale."[58] In *Hatred of the World*, by contrast, the Reverend Francis Brothers took a more radical line, suggesting that hatred itself displays Christian integrity:

> A strong, universal, and an ever-deepening hatred of the world is essentially the sign of a disciple. It is not to be laid down as of *this* thing or *that* thing, but the "soul" which "hangeth upon GOD" watches with an increasing jealousy whatever may sooner or later separate it from the love of CHRIST. The world is the enemy of GOD: if therefore we love the world, we are the enemies of GOD. If for doing "that which is *lawful and right*" the world hate us, it shall turn to us for a testimony that we are not of the world; for the world would love its own.[59]

While Brothers's adjectives ("strong," "universal," "ever-deepening") highlight the growing complexity of nineteenth-century hatred, his final noun in the first sentence quoted here could as easily be "misanthrope" as "disciple." Brothers assumed his congregations would hate in Christian ways—with God's guidance—but the difference in his sermon between misanthropes and disciples is negligible. Certainly, both sets of figures could argue that, figuratively speaking, they were "not of the world."

When put in secular terms, devoid of conventional moral bearings, this issue became more urgent, raising doubts about whether persons were fully in command of their behavior, and what should happen to them when they lost self-control. Enlightenment tenets represented the individual as the seat of consciousness aspiring rationally to knowledge, freedom, and happiness. But these tenets never resolved whether persons were oriented toward their own maximum pleasure or the greater happiness of all, and, partly for that reason, eighteenth-century writers and philosophers wrote extensively about misanthropy. Classifying people-haters as either bitter or disillusioned—as torn, that is, between rejecting and reforming society—such writers viewed misanthropy as a fulcrum between selfishness and altruism. They returned obsessively to this topic, trying to align characters and citizens on one or the other side of the divide.

But as nineteenth-century theories of satisfaction and sociability gained subtlety, these distinctions became harder to sustain. Was individualism a sign of man's hunger for improvement or an impulse signaling only greed? If nature were in fact indifferent—even hostile—to the plight of humanity, should society mirror its ruthless bid for survival or protect citizens from greater harm? When individuals were incapable of governing their actions, moreover, rational bases for behavior seemed wrongheaded, and many Victorians—indebted to their Enlightenment forebears—concluded that the irascible needed medical and even psychiatric attention. In his 1835 *Treatise on Insanity*, for example, James Prichard warned about the dangers of "moral insanity," which he defined loosely as "a *moral perversion*, or a disorder of the feelings, affections, and habits of the individual."[60] As Christopher Herbert observes, "This condition amounts very precisely to a collapse of what we may call the *cultural* structure of the individual, and is definable, though Prichard does not highlight this point, only by reference to the moral, affective, and behavioral norms of a surrounding community."[61] So while writers like Dickens tried to combine misanthropy and social critique, Prichard's and others' desire to sever these links points to a growing quandary for those representing misanthropy in its "benevolent" forms.

In his study of Victorian anomie, a sociological term referring largely to the myth of boundless human desire, Herbert shows that Prichard wasn't alone in associating rage and insanity with moral delinquency. Other, ingenious arguments spread rapidly at the time, making comparable claims about the cause and moral depravity of misanthropy. When C. P. Bronson published in 1855 his study of *Stammering: Its Effects, Causes, and Remedies*, he tied speech disorders to a host of "analogous nervous diseases," including "Spasmodic Asthma and Croup, Hysteria, Insanity from despondency, peculiar weaknesses of both males and females"—and "Misanthropy."[62] Although this last connection seems baffling to us today, Bronson yoked stammering to people-hating by viewing both as involuntary disorders stemming from an "impaired . . .

authority of the will" (131). Since in his eyes misanthropes can't stop hating humanity, and hatred as such is illogical, then misanthropy is best termed a "nervous disease." Bronson's recommendations for the afflicted included slow eating, avoidance of salt and fatty substances, and regularity in habits. "Cultivate an agreeable state of mind," he urged, "and cherish none but agreeable feelings towards all" (151).

Because to many Victorians a "disagreeable" state of mind implied mental illness, this diagnosis was in fact unsurprising. As John Conolly had remarked two decades earlier, "When the passion [of anger] so impairs one or more faculties of the mind as to prevent the exercise of comparison, . . . the reason is overturned; and then the man is mad."[63] "We see many madmen," he continued gravely and rather ominously,

> whose malady consists in their peculiar excitability to anger, and in
> the impossibility of correcting the judgments of their angry state. . . .
> The commencement of the correction of their angry judgment is the
> commencement of convalescence. Until they can do this, however
> reasonable they may be on all other subjects, on this they are mad.
> When they can do it, they are mad no longer. (227–28)

Conolly was lecturing at University College, London, when he published this claim, and his book became a classic textbook in nineteenth-century psychiatry. Anger is for him not only "peculiar" but also a sign of insanity. As the individual, he reasoned, is directed only toward its own good, departures from this state of mind necessarily imply madness. Conolly apparently had not read Hazlitt's account of "the pleasure of hating," in which rancor isn't opposed to reason but is instead a sign of its reach. But while in the 1820s and 1830s the picture was certainly more complicated than Conolly implied, his and similar judgments eventually won the day.

Well aware of these changing judgments, physiological psychologists such as Herbert Spencer, George Henry Lewes, and William Benjamin Carpenter debated between the mid-1850s and late 1870s whether consciousness regulated will or stood at the mercy of it. Their contributions are important secular alternatives to determinism, as well as related providentialist arguments that Victorian fiction regularly touted.[64] What these intellectuals did not doubt was the need—following Comte—to advance a "religion of humanity" defining individuals relative to society. As Eliot, Lewes's partner, declared in *Felix Holt, the Radical*, "There is no private life which has not been determined by a wider public life."[65] Yet while this grand assertion is apparently commonsensical, Eliot's novel repeatedly shows where its characters' inner lives depart from— and even violate—their social roles. Her narrator amplifies the "irrational vindictiveness" surfacing in not only Harold Transome and Matthew Jermyn's bitter fight over the ownership of Transome Court but also a political demonstration that goes violently awry, because of those "who loved the irrationality of riots for something else than its own sake" (339, 319). This "something else" is a complex desire for revenge that Eliot can neither sanction nor completely discredit, and it points—as we'll see—to a fascinating tension in her claims about fellowship and sociability.

Finding determinism too limited a theory of behavior, then, many Victorian thinkers (including Eliot herself, in much of her fiction and nonfiction) sought a more nuanced model—a "community of interest" is her metaphor in "Birth of Tolerance"—that could mitigate the diffusive effects of individualism and rapid industrialization.[66] Endorsing her project, Lewes argued in the first volume of his *Problems of Life and Mind*, first series, as elsewhere:

> Man apart from Society is simply an animal organism; restore him to his real position as a social unit, and the problem changes. It is in the development of Civilization that we trace the real development of Humanity. The soul of man has thus a double root, a double history. It passes quite out of the range of animal life; and no explanation of mental phenomena can be valid which does not allow for this extension of range.[67]

Superficially, Lewes argues that humanity's "real development" lies in cultivating civilization, but he also asserts intriguingly that human desires and fantasies are not entirely reducible to society, and must therefore be studied as "a double root, a double history."

The Victorians were of course fond of cataloging social distinctions, using nature to dignify social hierarchies and to naturalize labor relations. To take a well-known example, George Cruikshank's *British Bee*

Hive (1840; revised 1867; FIGURE 01.5) puts the Queen and Royal Family, Parliament, the Law, and the Church at the top of the "hive," the professions in the middle, and trade and labor near the bottom. The foundations of the whole rest on the Bank of England plus the Army and Navy. Because Cruikshank represents the hive as self-contained, he doesn't portray life or persons outside it (see also FIGURE 01.6, Cruikshank's Regency satire of "The Load Borne by the British Public" during wartime). Lewes was thus voicing received wisdom when arguing, somewhat optimistically in the third series of *Problems of Life and Mind*, that "men living always in groups co-operate like the organs in an organism. Their actions have a common impulse and a common end. Their desires and opinions bear the common stamp of an impersonal direction. Much of their life is common to all."[68] Still, his metaphor of humanity's "double root"—part "animal," part "social"—didn't resolve this dichotomy in Victorian literature and philosophy. Both discourses instead revealed where social identity fails to eclipse our "animal" counterpart, as is clear in works as different as Stevenson's *Strange Case of Dr Jekyll and Mr Hyde* and Browning's *Ring and the Book* (Guido is called "part-man part-monster").[69] These works probe a faultline in identity that science and psychology—relying heavily on rational explanations for human behavior—were ill equipped to resolve. Indeed, as we'll see throughout this book, the best Victorian minds unearthed impulses that put individuals in conflict, not harmony, with society. Moreover, as the next section shows, the culture sparked strong reactions against full-blown misanthropy and "antisocial" hatred, damning many characters to suffering, penury, and even premature death.

The Rise of Positivism and Psychology

Auguste Widal's midcentury study *Des divers caractères du misanthrope, chez les écrivains anciens et modernes* helps explain why the Victorians drew these conclusions. Reviving antecedents to understand misanthropes, it psychologized them with a vengeance. In attempting to recover a history of "true, moral, philosophical, and forgivable" people-haters since antiquity, Widal invoked Socrates' argument about

FIGURE 01.5 *The British Bee Hive* (1840; rev. 1867).
George Cruikshank. Process engraving. *Courtesy the Victoria
and Albert Museum, London.*

FIGURE 01.6 *The Load Borne by the British Public*
(December 15, 1819). George Cruikshank.

misanthropy's links with immaturity, but treated these links as indicating types, not passing moods.[70]

Widal can't get going, however, without noting vexing psychological exceptions to his thesis. "Misanthropy, resulting from pride and an exaggerated sense of self-love, is," he says, "immoral, and therefore reprehensible [*condamnable*]" (5). Like Widal, many Victorians couldn't help superimposing their beliefs on historical examples, judging them increasingly by their own psychological standards. Consequently, Widal pronounces as regrettable egoism what in earlier centuries were portrayals of justified hatred. Spencer described a similar reevaluative process when noting how his contemporaries gave social and political meaning to formerly theological terms. "In the old divines," the sociologist asserted, "*miscreant* is used in its etymological sense of *unbeliever*; but in modern speech [c. 1862] it has entirely lost this sense. Similarly with *evil-doer* and *malefactor*: exactly synonymous as these are by derivation, they are no longer synonymous by usage: by a *malefactor* we now understand a convicted criminal, which is far from being the acceptation of *evil-doer*."[71]

On what philosophical foundations did these secular judgments rest? One of several important guides for the Victorians was Comte's *System of Positive Polity*, . . . *Instituting the Religion of Humanity*, first translated in 1851, which argued that "in human nature, and therefore in the Positive system, Affection is the preponderating element" (1:10). While conceding that turning self-love into social love is "the great ethical problem," since the first trait is "deeply implanted" in us, Comte insisted that "social sympathy is a distinctive attribute of our nature" (73, 18, 11). He could thus argue—in ways influencing Victorian intellectuals like Lewes and Spencer—that "recognising our subjection to an external power," now viewed in political, not metaphysical, terms, helps make "our self-regarding instincts . . . susceptible of discipline," and thus of social value (18). Comte wanted his "System of Positive Polity" to promote altruism, a noun he coined from the Italian *altrui* ("to or of others") and a phrase in French law, *le bien, le droit d'autrui* ("the well-being and right of the other").[72] It was Lewes who introduced Comte's term into English when publishing *Comte's Philosophy of the Sciences* in 1853, and partly because of Comtean philosophy, the word *community* is almost incapable today of supporting negative connotations.[73]

Still, renegade thinkers upset these communitarian theories by spurning their underlying claims about reciprocity and the individual's willingness or capacity to harmonize with society.[74] "On Human Nature," by Arthur Schopenhauer, says that "to the boundless *egoism of our nature* there is joined more or less in every human breast a fund of hatred, anger, envy, rancour, and malice, accumulated like the venom in a serpent's tooth, and waiting only for an opportunity of venting itself."[75] In 1853, on Eliot's clock as assistant editor, the *Westminster Review* presented Schopenhauer to the British intelligentsia, the same year in which Comte's neologism "altruism" was introduced into the English language.[76] And though Schopenhauer viewed as inevitable humanity's "fund of hatred, anger, envy, rancour, and malice," several intellectuals surpassed him in positing a gratuitous hatred, stemming from pleasure in others' suffering, rather than from a more justifiable bid for survival.

Max Stirner had alluded to this "surplus" rage in the mid-1840s. Like his compatriot, he condemned the frequent stupidity and tyranny of group thought, viewing communitarianism as more coercive than individualism. In his neglected study *The Ego and Its Own*, Stirner usefully explained why "we no longer say 'God is love,' but 'Love is divine.'"[77] "Love is to be the *good* in man, his divineness, that which does him honour, his true *humanity*," he claimed sardonically, characterizing such benevolists as Ludwig Feuerbach, whom he was fond of attacking (47; original emphases). Stirner hoped to undermine what this argument about love surreptitiously presumed: "Love is what is *human* in man, and what is inhuman is the loveless egoist" (47; original emphasis).

Stirner believed that our well-being consists not in conforming with society, since "we two, the state and I, are enemies," but, more broadly, in *"repelling the world"* (161, 25; original emphasis). To be free, humans must "dissolve" their identities and spurn existing ties, "becom[ing] so completely unconcerned and reckless . . . so altogether indifferent to the world that even its falling in ruins would not move" them (26, 25, 22; original emphasis). As no compromise or reform was possible in his eyes, Stirner turned rejection and betrayal into imperatives. "The world must be deceived," he declared bluntly, "for it is my enemy. . . . I *annihilate* it as I annihilate myself" (26, 262; original emphasis).

Not every nineteenth-century writer viewed these claims as mad. Among midcentury texts, Dostoyevsky's *Notes from Underground* represents this philosophy *in extremis*, with similar disdain for consensus and conformity. The novella begins with an extraordinary declaration: "I am a sick man. . . . I am a spiteful man. I am an unpleasant man."[78] The friendless "antihero" boasting this claim then lies to the reader, claiming he loves exhibiting "supreme nastiness" in public, whereas disaffection really governs his outlook (16). After asking rhetorically, "Can man's interests be correctly calculated?" the narrator says that philosophers weighing human actions invariably neglect another type of satisfaction, a "prompting of something inside [ourselves] that is *stronger* than all [our] self-interest" (30; my emphasis). "The point is not in a play on words," he adds, "but in the fact that this ['irrational'] good is distinguished precisely by upsetting all our classifications and always destroying the systems established by lovers of humanity for the happiness of mankind" (31). Once we doubt that self-interest is society's rational foundation, related assumptions crumble. If individuals are drawn to forms of enjoyment causing them harm, then society clearly can't be geared toward only its collective fulfillment.

By the time Freud wrote *Civilization and Its Discontents*, shortly after he'd published an essay on Dostoyevsky, the damage stemming from this "interference" seemed irreparable.[79] Freud argued that society, in trying to protect us from what we want (ultimately, an end to internal tension), instills in subjectivity a profound malaise, while providing "an *occasion* for enmity" rather than, as Comte and Lewes dearly hoped, a viable defense against it.[80] Attempts to bolster society or to protect individuals from harm are at bottom futile, Freud implied, for nothing can protect humanity from itself. To the biblical injunction "Love thy neighbor as thyself," Freud asked: "Why should we . . .?"[81]

Anticommunitarianism and Victorian Schadenfreude

Few Britons apparently could take the argument this far. Nor could they match Dostoyevsky's and Stirner's disdain for cant *and* communities. Though Carlyle is certainly our best judge of the former, according to the *Spectator* even his "misanthropy seems to us to fall short of anything that can properly be called prophetic."[82] Instead, having shorn misanthropes of eighteenth-century idealism, many Victorians sided with the likes of psychiatrist John Conolly and physician Nordau, arguing that if man's "double root" were social and animal, then hatred signaled a reversion to presocial barbarism. They extended, that is, the psychological reach of misanthropy, driving a wedge between the normal and the pathological to imply that misanthropes got what they deserved.

Reflecting self-critically on his youthful melancholy, Thackeray's narrator in *The History of Henry Esmond* consequently insists that the problem stemmed from his vanity and assumptions about hostility in others. "The world deals good-naturedly with good-natured people," he claims naïvely, "and I never knew a sulky misanthropist who quarrelled with it, but it was he, and not it, that was in the wrong."[83] Such perspectives didn't stop Thackeray from mocking other writers and much of his own society, but like several other Victorian novelists, including Anthony Trollope, he felt able to attack hypocrisy without spurning humanity.[84] Indeed, when Thackeray threw misanthropy into the mix, as *Henry Esmond* shows, he did so as something to condemn (given its ties to malice), rather than to cultivate. A year before publishing this novel, he lambasted Swift's *Gulliver's Travels* for its "gnashing imprecations against mankind," urging readers to skip Gulliver's fourth voyage, because it is "filthy in word, filthy in thought, furious, raging, obscene."[85]

Thackeray helped intensify the splitting effect I mentioned earlier, whereby love or reason reforms misanthropes, but antiheroes prove beyond redemption. Some Victorians even augmented this last idea by representing figures that seem to hate gratuitously. For instance, in the memorable opening quatrain of Browning's "Soliloquy of the Spanish Cloister," first published in *Dramatic Lyrics*, the speaker growls with spite:

> Gr-r-r- there go, my heart's abhorrence!
> Water your damned flower-pots, do!
> If hate killed men, Brother Lawrence,
> God's blood, would not mine kill you![86]

The speaker's exuberant hatred prevents us from dismissing his fantasies and siding with either Brother Lawrence or, for that matter, the other monks. For the poem to work, it's necessary that Brother

Lawrence be pathetically (even annoyingly) unaware of the hatred he inspires. We know too little about the speaker to call him misanthropic, but that's one of Browning's points. Although circumscribing the speaker's hatred might comfort readers, it would weaken the corrosive glee that Browning's poem excites. That we enjoy being party to such hatred, without needing to affirm it ourselves, yields a fascinating ethico-religious compromise, given the work's Catholic context. How, we are left wondering at the poem's end, could we despise so readily a monk whose sole "faults" include making small talk, tending his plants fastidiously, and swallowing his orange juice in one gulp, not three? What disposes us to trust the feverish hatred of a man we couldn't distinguish from Adam?

One answer to these questions, which I amplify in chapter 5, is that Browning grasped the subtle links joining schadenfreude, narrative excitement, and readerly satisfaction. The fantasies on which his and others' fiction draws don't simply train minds for self-abnegation and sociability, as some Victorians alleged, but point to forms of excitement in others' suffering that belie self-control. These effects certainly struck many Victorians as degrading and immoral, depending on their tastes and convictions. Writing on "moral evil" in 1879, one writer declared: "Adopt what theory of human depravity you will, modify your statements as you please, still you have on your hands the fact of what must be admitted to, *through some peculiarity of nature*, the deflection of the whole race from the right way, and the true aim of life."[87] Yet the point here, which many Victorian writers grasped, is that this "deflection" wasn't exceptional, but really a well-trod path.

I'll conclude with one of many possible examples: James Fitzjames Stephen, Virginia Woolf's uncle, advocating "gratifying the feeling of hatred—call it revenge, resentment, or what you will—which the contemplation of [criminal] conduct excites in healthily constituted minds."[88] Granted, this hatred struck Stephen as appropriate because it seemed to dissipate with the outlawed behavior he condemned. He even asserted, against a growing body of opinion opposed to capital punishment, that "the feeling of hatred and the desire of vengeance abovementioned are important elements of human nature which ought in such cases to be satisfied in a regular and legal manner"—as, for instance, in public executions, which England didn't outlaw until 1868.[89] (Executions continued thereafter in prisons, long after most of Europe had abolished capital punishment, and they didn't officially end until 1965, with the Murder [Abolition of Death Penalty] Act. Even then, the death penalty technically remained until 1998 for treason, piracy, and the murder of a member of the Royal Family.) But Stephen's caveat "in such cases" wasn't so easy to enforce, not least because—witnesses of public executions often affirmed—"excite[ment]" surpassed these sanctions, springing from elements of fantasy and imagination rather than from the law only. Invoking Dickens's and Thackeray's commentaries on executions (Dickens calling the assembled multitude "odious"), Gay writes vividly: "Mobs of spectators, often numbering into the thousands, drunk with alcohol no less than with the occasion, cheered or jeered the condemned felon, and got into fist fights. Hawkers peddled crudely printed poems, nearly all of them barefaced inventions, describing the crime about to be expiated or retailing the criminal's last words. Pickpockets plied their trade under the eyes of the police."[90]

The crowds relishing these scenes often were so drunk that the word *hangover* eventually was coined to describe their excess and its aftereffects. Quite frequently, children also witnessed these executions, signaling yet another gap between their lived reality and the rhetoric of innocence that many cultural guardians promulgated on their behalf. Indeed, despite the opprobrium accompanying "feeling[s] of hatred" in the wider culture—and the embarrassment, disgust, and even shame that many experienced when encountering them in person and in print—the public's excitement and delight in vengeance expose an unruly, contrary pattern in the culture that isn't easily repressed or explained away. Given this behavior and the fantasies it unleashed, it's unsurprising that a large number of writers and philosophers came to view such antisocial sentiment as widespread and even structurally inevitable. Pointing repeatedly to a near-insoluble antagonism between individuals and society, Bulwer, Dickens, Charlotte Brontë, Browning, Eliot, and Conrad (among others) increasingly resisted the idea that self-abnegation could bring their works to adequate or even satisfying closure.

As will emerge, these writers help explain why imaginative fiction strays from communitarian precepts and magnifies how precariously altruism outshines less noble impulses. I call these impulses "depsychologizing," somewhat awkwardly, because they betray conventional Victorian arguments about will and self-control, pointing to the perverse allure of destruction and eschatology—the disturbing satisfaction of imagining humanity's extinction or one's own annihilation by impersonal forces. That such fantasies recur in some of our most cherished Victorian novels and poems makes these works more volatile and less predetermined than many have assumed. It also requires that we read them differently, paying more attention to the social and ethical problems they unearth than to the sometimes pat notes on which they seem to conclude.

Summing Up: Victorian Enmity

Exploring these lively tensions, the following chapters are broadly chronological, beginning with Bulwer's first novel, *Falkland* (1827), and ending with the "evil, . . . contempt and hate" that bedevil Razumov in Conrad's *Under Western Eyes* (1911).[91] In arranging the book this way, I hope to show how misanthropy—and hatred, more generally—acquired new meanings in the works of single authors, and thus in several generations of Victorian writers. Extending the argument and focus of *The Ruling Passion* and *The Burdens of Intimacy*, my previous books, *Hatred and Civility* investigates why crises about pleasurable aggression recurred when the Victorians' faith in religion and sociability often failed.

As I elaborate in the following readings, especially of Dickens's *Martin Chuzzlewit* (chapter 2) and Eliot's *Romola* (chapter 4), this book dwells especially on the novel's complex relation to hatred, as this literary form not only copied and recast many social problems in the nineteenth century, but also educated readers in the vagarious paths of characters' and their own fantasies. For instance, at a well-known moment in Eliot's *Adam Bede*, the narrator, observing that "Hetty [Sorrel] had never read a novel," asks, How "could she find a shape for her expectations?"[92] The question has far-reaching implications: Novels give voice and form to a host of expectations. They teach us what to want from life, ourselves, and other people—and they show us, both directly and indirectly, whom to hate, and what we can and can't do with that emotion.

If I seem to overemphasize this point and to eclipse all contrary evidence, let me refine it, as I shall in the chapters to follow. Like many of Eliot's works, *Adam Bede* tries to promote a Wordsworthian ethic, developing "fibre[s] of sympathy" to help our hearts "swell with loving admiration at some trait of gentle goodness in the faulty people who sit at the same hearth with [us]" (180–81). And to the degree that this ethic helps us overcome our fury at Hetty for murdering her infant, and at Arthur Donnithorne for recklessly seducing her, the ethic appears sound. But to grasp this novel's full complexity, it's necessary to invert this scenario, because the actions represented are what create a need for authorial intervention. Within the fictional conventions adopted by Eliot, that is, nothing less than this intervention would have let her convey "loving admiration at some trait of gentle goodness" and still conclude the novel with any plausibility. Reading Eliot's fiction against the grain doesn't of course eclipse her interest in compassion, but it shows why this ethic became so fragile in her later works, barely containing the rancor flourishing in *The Lifted Veil, Romola, Felix Holt, Middlemarch*, and *Daniel Deronda*.

Overall, then, it's impossible to detach beneficence from Eliot's widespread interest in narrative antagonism and self-confrontation, and it would be naïve to imagine otherwise. What inspires fiction—and what fiction inspires in us—is rarely so tidy or well behaved. The surplus content of such works, including the affect exceeding narrative control and closure, is my concern throughout. Like Hazlitt, Freud, and many others, I am arguing that nineteenth-century literature educates us in a range of fantasies, including imaginative scenarios that are frequently amoral. As such—and perhaps quite usefully—one of the first things to vanish, briefly or conclusively, from the best Victorian fiction is the thin veneer of altruism protecting us from other people and ourselves.

CHAPTER ONE

Bulwer's Misanthropes and the Limits of Victorian Sympathy

> The age then is one of *destruction*! disguise it as we will, it must be so characterized; miserable would be our lot were it not also an age of preparation for reconstructing. —Bulwer, *England and the English*

Sympathy and Hatred

TWENTY-ONE YEARS OLD, intent on writing a "History of the British Public," Edward Lytton Bulwer feared in 1824 that the destruction of social values, including sympathy, would spawn widespread misery. Time and experience only intensified his concern. Later doubting that the "age of . . . reconstruct[ion]" would redress cultural misery and re-form, he revised his precocious argument. In April 1863, Bulwer, aged sixty, published a scathing critique of "The Modern Misanthrope" in *Blackwood's*, claiming Victorian intellectuals donned their "masked misanthropy" with "equal suavity and equal scorn."[1] "Contempt so serene and immovable is," he said, "the philosophy of hate—the intellectual consummation of misanthropy" (477).

Meditations on hatred and the limits of Victorian sympathy, rarely measured and often wildly contradictory, pervaded Bulwer's career. By associating misanthropy with sincerity and social critique, he nonetheless highlighted the erosion, in Victorian fiction, of eighteenth-century arguments about sympathy and fellow feeling. While the culture at large gradually severed sympathy from misanthropy, tending also to pathologize the latter, Bulwer generally resisted this move, reviving idealist strains of eighteenth-century misanthropy as integral to debate and social change. In his work, misanthropy evolved alongside discussion about sympathy, as a means of social criticism.

Similar preoccupations characterize Bulwer's political career. When he first entered Parliament as the Whig-Liberal member for Lincoln, he supported the 1832 Reform Bill and May 1838 resolution to abolish Negro apprenticeship in the West Indian colonies (the latter was, essentially, a continuation of slavery). After the 1832 Bill became law, he was "credited by many, not least himself, with having done as much as anyone to secure its passage."[2] He seemed motivated by sincere fellow feeling. Yet according to *The New Timon*, Bulwer's long 1846 poem, misanthropes were "Law's outcast on the earth" taking "proud refuge from a world's disdain."[3] How, then, could he credit these figures with heroism and still commit himself to practical reform?

Although few scholars today engage this nexus of ideas, Bulwer's writing continues to have surprising relevance. His essays thicken recent interest in antagonism and anticommunitarianism—voiced by such disparate thinkers as Giorgio Agamben, Étienne Balibar, Jacques Derrida, Ernesto Laclau, Claude Lefort, Carl Schmitt, and Slavoj Žižek[4]—by comparing Victorian misanthropes with their Augustan, Renaissance, and Hellenic counterparts. While many Victorians believed social progress would diminish "irrational" hatred, Bulwer overturned this expectation and associated misanthropy with moral and political reform. He was also something of a Victorian weather vane, having an acute grasp of changing tastes and mores. Comprising thirty novels, roughly three dozen stories, nine collections of execrable poetry, and fourteen plays (some of them commercially successful), his literary output spans Romantic idealism in the mid-1820s and world-weary cynicism in the 1870s. As John Sutherland adds, with forgivable overstatement, Bulwer "can plausibly claim to be the father of the English detective novel, science fiction, the fantasy novel, the thriller, and the domestic realistic novel."[5] Beyond even this, he was the second most widely read novelist in Victorian England—Dickens alone outsold him—and the Germans "worship[ed]" his "Shakespearean" art.[6] So whether or not we agree with him (and countless derisive reviewers did not), Bulwer secured a large audience for his shifting ideas and concerns. His fiction doesn't proceed in tandem with his philosophical perspectives, but at its most bitter it voices intelligent disdain for social injustice, giving us heroes who—like their author—view the world with instructive distrust.

Such, then, is the scope of this chapter, which reads Bulwer's novels and plays against a set of changing claims in his philosophical essays. Bulwer's reflections on sympathy, misanthropy, and social reform were, as we'll see, neither neatly nor securely established. His early essays were especially contradictory. But studying his complex political psychology across his career indicates how sympathy and misanthropy—often melded in the eighteenth century—slowly unraveled in the nineteenth, as an ever-widening gap separated the Victorians' lived experience from their social ideals.

"Modern" Misanthropy

As we saw in the introduction, many of Bulwer's contemporaries thought fellow feeling would diminish "disorders" such as irrational hatred.[7] But since Bulwer initially recast this assumption, representing misanthropy as a precursor to social reform, he highlights what's most specious about the Victorians' rhetoric of sincerity. Turning disingenuous behavior into an art form and allowing sham friendliness to cover repugnance, Bulwer's contemporaries let emotional integrity evaporate from the culture, conceding misanthropes' idealism, allowing its diminishment. He countered that heartfelt misanthropy would broker effective, lasting change.

Bulwer's 1863 essay "The Modern Misanthrope" is thus a watershed in Victorian discussions of hatred and sympathy, for it spotlights the cultural corruption of the latter term in ways Bulwer and several peers (notably Carlyle) had come to resent. The "misanthrope *à la mode* never rails at vice," Bulwer complained; "he takes it for granted as the elementary principle in the commerce of life" (477).[8] Irony and derisive urbanity had become principles of citizenship: the joy of casting aspersion on one's enemies had replaced the peculiar "social career" of the eighteenth century's "amiable man-scorner," a term the Victorians increasingly viewed as oxymoronic (479).

In making this point, Bulwer conceded that scholars might fault him for "employ[ing] the word *misanthrope* incorrectly" (477). "According to strict interpretation," he admitted, "a misanthrope means not a despiser but a hater of men, and that this elegant gentleman [the Victorian misanthrope] is not, by my own showing, warm-blooded enough for hate" (477). Nevertheless, and for reasons that interest me, he persisted in adopting this term, finding it useful to the degree that it no longer epitomized the philosophical stance he admired in former times. In Bulwer's lexicon, *misanthropy* signals humanity's failure to sustain its best ideals, including sympathy and disinterestedness. Consequently, and however counterintuitive it sounds, Bulwer could for many years yoke "benevolent" misanthropy to ideal forms of fellow feeling.[9]

Victorian Sympathy Through the Lens of Augustan and Romantic Misanthropy

Though Bulwer waxed nostalgic about Shakespeare's Timon and Molière's Alceste, viewing their "passionate" denunciation of humanity as a veiled indication of love for society, his strongest intellectual debt was to William Godwin, the Gothic novelist, religious dissenter, and social philosopher whose seminal treatise *Enquiry Concerning Political Justice and Its Influence on Morals and Happiness* advocated liberty from government intervention. Godwin believed strongly in minimal state control and humanity's eventual perfectibility, insisting "government was intended to suppress injustice, [though] it offers new occasions and temptations for the commission of it," including robbery and fraud.[10] He also promoted identification with one's neighbor as a foil to egoism. "Justice requires," he declared, adapting Adam Smith's now-famous proviso in *The Theory of Moral Sentiments*, "I should put myself in the place of an impartial spectator of human concerns, and divest myself of retrospect to my own predilections" (1:xxv).

Since, according to Bulwer, sympathy arises ideally from self-forgetfulness, at first glance he seems to make similar points, prioritizing altruism over egoism. Over time, however, Bulwer challenged Godwin's idea of perfectibility and engagement.[11] And Godwin seemed to realize this, though he claimed to admire Bulwer's *Paul Clifford*. He hinted that the aspiring novelist prized "self-love" over "benevolence," and said it was "of the highest importance to an eminent character" to work out "which side he embraces in [this] great question."[12] Bulwer's principles and his radical espousal of them in fiction were beginning to part company, a problem surpassing immediate biographical concerns. Because it is ultimately self-referring, seeking individual satisfaction before tepidly addressing the plight of others, Bulwer's notion of sociability clashes with conventional altruism. His interest in misanthropy also began to hamstring his political theory, since the former requires symbolic distance from society, along with endless reflection on its practical reform. Thus even as they wrestle with idealism, Bulwer's misanthropes in the 1830s disdain the world's limitations, seeking appropriate outlets for their contempt.[13]

Evidently, something had to give. Either Bulwer's political theory and psychology required greater (and more selfless) participation in society, or his interest in eighteenth-century misanthropy would hamper social participation so greatly that he would withdraw from society in disgust. Veering in later years toward the latter outcome, he began invoking social Darwinism for undemocratic ends, calling progress impossible without enmity and society boring without conflict. Substituting detachment for accountability, such late works as *A Strange Story*, *The Coming Race*, and *Kenelm Chillingly* speculate repeatedly that we might be happiest when left alone. According to Chillingly, too, we should blame the "Academe of New Ideas" for fabricating the notion that "all the working classes of a civilized world could merge every difference of race, creed, intellect, individual propensities and interests, into the construction of a single web, stocked as a larder in common!" (45). Though Chillingly finally overcomes his diffidence toward society, he can't do so without declining all friendships, "surrender[ing] himself to a tranquil indifference,"[14] and telling anyone who'll listen: "The probability is that, some day or other, we shall be exterminated by a new development of species" (*Chillingly* 37).

Ironically, the reasons for this detachment arise in "The Sympathetic Temperament," an essay in which Bulwer tried to explain why the 1860s had made sympathy anachronistic.[15] The essay draws on Seneca and Horace to point up the limitations of Smith's theory. "As we have no immediate experience of what other men feel," Smith had declared, "we can form no idea of the manner in which they are affected, but by conceiving what we ourselves should feel in the like situation. Though our brother is upon the rack, as long as we ourselves are at our ease, our senses will never inform us of what he suffers."[16] Only by controlled use of the imagination do we "enter as it were into his body, and become in some measure the same person with him" (9).[17]

Smith wanted identification to bridge this intersubjective gap, but Bulwer emphasizes its failures. Because the limits of sympathy thwart our interactions with others, Bulwer shows that sociability isn't the answer, but is instead an unavoidable philosophical faultline. As we live in "solitary contemplation," he claims, we must "force [ourselves] to some active interest in common with ordinary mortals" (182). Resembling arguments in his earlier works, this imperative is at bottom selfish: We avoid morbid introspection by tolerating company as a forced choice, and so become better able to cope with alienation and enmity. The man who has forced himself to think about altruism will, Bulwer argued, "be more reconciled to the utter want of sympathy in the process" (182).

Bulwer and Bentham

Such curmudgeonly arguments were not an effect of age; doubts about altruism emerged much earlier in Bulwer's work. In *The Disowned*, he argued that misanthropy was a "blemish," not an "ornament," and said he wanted to correct "a literary error of the age," which was "to link with the romantic and sensitive feelings which interest and engage us, a misanthropical and disdainful spirit—as if they were naturally and necessarily allied."[18] But Bulwer could neither sustain this distinction nor cast the "disdainful spirit" from his work, in which altruism and benevolence are generally quite rare. "There is no chimera vainer than the hope that one human heart shall find sympathy in another," he remarked bleakly in *The Last Days of Pompeii*.[19] In his writing, exasperated hatred stymies altruism, resulting in psychically and politically impotent rage.

As discussed in the introduction, these perspectives arose amid heated debates about sympathy and sociability, including how Bentham pitted "malevolent or dissocial affections" against society's well-being.[20] Bulwer also described this shift in *England and the English*, using his youthful excesses, somewhat immodestly, to characterize the Victorians' wider break with Romanticism: "With a sigh we turned to the actual and practical career of life: we awoke from the morbid, the passionate, the dreaming."[21] So, despite his overidentification with Byron—apparent in *Falkland*, Bulwer's first novel, and from the novelist's probable affair with Lady Caroline Lamb in his mid-twenties, shortly after Byron's death—Bulwer began revising his thoughts on sociability, parting company with Godwin *and* Bentham as he tried directing misanthropy toward more nuanced forms of sympathy.

His break with Bentham and Godwin did not take immediate effect. Bulwer still hoped in 1833 that benevolence would remain "the great prevailing characteristic of the . . . intellectual spirit." "There has grown up among us," he insisted in *England and the English*,

> a sympathy with the great mass of mankind. For this we are indebted in no small measure to the philosophers (which whom [*sic*] Benevolence is, in all times, the foundation of philosophy). . . . We owe also the popularity of the growing principle to . . . the gloomy misanthropy of Byron; for *proportioned to the intenseness with which we shared that feeling, was the reaction from which we awoke from it* [*sic*]. (289–90; my emphasis)

"It is this feeling," he concluded, "we should unite to sustain and to develope [*sic*]. It has come to us pure and bright from the ordeal of years—the result of a thousand errors—but born, if we preserve it, as their healer and redemption" (290). In his early twenties, Bulwer hoped fiction would tilt readers toward sympathy and social responsibility, redeeming society by vanquishing greed and political corruption. It is all the more ironic, then, that his first novel undermines this notion, indicating that "benevolence" was not a feeling he could properly "develope." Let us assess why.

Romantic Morbidity

Falkland appeared in March 1827, when Bulwer was almost twenty-four, but its earliest drafts date to 1824, when, still forming his thoughts on sympathy, he was thoroughly immersed in Byron's "lordly misanthropy."[22] In tracing the internal vicissitudes of Erasmus Falkland's ardor for Lady Emily Mandeville, wife to a Tory politician for whom she feels no passion, Bulwer's first novel adopts a strongly Romantic perspective.[23] Indeed, because it shuns most external points of view, *Falkland* and its protagonist are for structural reasons highly self-involved. "I . . . rendered my vicious hero as thoroughly unamiable as I have shown him to be unprosperous," Bulwer wrote later, "and it is impossible either to sympathize with his character or to commiserate his fate."[24]

The novel shows Falkland's suffering from "morbid . . . melancholy" after he persuades Emily to elope with him, then copes with crushing disappointment when Mr. Mandeville preempts their affair (17).[25] As Falkland waits for Emily he has a premonition of disaster, in which she appears to him as a corpse. (Call it crass foreshadowing, but his fears are well founded: Emily bursts a blood vessel when her angry husband confronts her, and dies from massive hemorrhaging; see also FIGURE 1.1.)

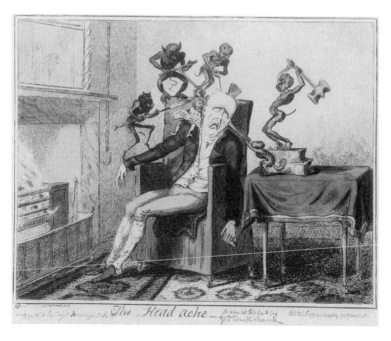

FIGURE 1.1 *The Head Ache* (February 12, 1819), a medical caricature after Captain Francis Marryat. George Cruikshank.
Courtesy the Victoria and Albert Museum, London.

Our primary interest is in Falkland's delirium and guilt after Emily's death. There we learn that since "life is our real night," death is our sole means of gaining enlightenment (221): "There is no Œdipus to solve the enigma of life," says Falkland, and we are fools to expect any other epiphany. The type of misanthropy that Falkland displays may be partly edifying, as it exposes social illusions, but it also resists spiritual redemption and political reform.

Earlier passages in the novel convey Bulwer's disillusionment with social mores. As Edwin Eigner observes, the novel shows Bulwer comparing the world as it is with how it could be, and aspiring to close the gap.[26] The arguments about aggressive selfhood and irksome sociability punctuating his later work also surface crudely in *Falkland*, where yearning for self-completion in another person elevates egoism to a higher plane. While manic philanthropy in this novel does briefly replace misanthropy, it results, paradoxically, in greater disillusionment with society. "Civility," we learn, "is but the mask of design." "In the best actions," adds Falkland in an aphorism worthy of Hazlitt or Rochefoucauld, "there is always some latent evil in the motive" (23; 75).

Given Bulwer's later claims about the limits and dearth of sympathy, Falkland unsurprisingly suggests we cannot live hate-free among other people or, we might add, with ourselves. "When we mix," he says, "we suffer by the contact, and grow, if not malicious from the injury, at least selfish from the circumspection which our safety imposes. . . . It is [only] in contemplating men at a distance that we become benevolent" (27). Contact with others causes suffering; solitude is essential for safety: Falkland comes close to calling society intrinsically pathological and misanthropy not just a path to happiness but a form of wisdom. That the sociable are foolish is an idea, moreover, to which his author was compelled to return.

Personal Inflections

The tangled conceptions of sympathy and misanthropy in Bulwer's early novels were further complicated, for Victorian readers and us, by his notoriously querulous personality and run-ins with rivals. Popularity didn't satisfy Bulwer, leading one critic to speculate that he may even "have taken a grim satisfaction . . . in the fact that he could not find the sympathy he required in this world."[27]

In writing, as in life, he voiced an insatiable demand for praise that often devolved into splenetic denunciations of those who withheld it.[28] And while it's a mistake to conflate his arguments and his personality, it would be naïve to divorce these factors completely, not least because his reviewers endlessly—and gleefully—mistook the first for the second, treating Bulwer's work as a facile extension of his hubristic persona. Finally, the reception of his writing is itself a vital component of nineteenth-century intellectual history, highlighting a mordantly entertaining side to Victorian letters.

In a series of devastating taunts between April 1830 and February 1833, *Fraser's Magazine* dubbed him "Mr. Edward Liston Bulwer," after a real-life comedian. Turning Bulwer's improving misanthropy against him, the journal wrote: "This is bitter bad writing. . . . It is the opening of a puff preliminary. What follows is jejune, base twaddle. . . . [Your writing] is only paltry nonsense . . . which would not have the power of influencing the opinion of a lady's lapdog. . . . [Your p]olitics [are] of the most sneaking kind. . . . All this I have written in the purest affection. I think you a deserving young person, whom nature intended for a footman, and I pity you accordingly, in having missed your vocation."[29]

Egged on by William Maginn, editor of *Fraser's*, an immature Thackeray leapt at the opportunity to mock his rival, christening him "the Knebworth Apollo" and "Bulwig," or, more ornately, "Sawedwadgeorgearllittnbulwig."[30] But despite several publication failures, Bulwer's popularity proved greater than Thackeray's, and when Thackeray grasped this he began leaking compliments, earnestly repenting for his youthful arrogance. In the early 1840s, however, schadenfreude won out, and Thackeray renewed his attacks with gusto. One stanza of "Liston Bulwer's Song," published in *Fraser's*, must suffice as a final example of the journal's outrageous insults:

> Let[itia] Landon declares I'm an ass-
> onant to love and to beauty;
> Cries Mrs. B. "O what an ass-
> ociate in conjugal duty!"

There's Jerdan exclaims I'm an ass-
ayer of poesy's pinions;
And I, too, affirm I'm an ass-
enter to all their opinions.[31]

Striving to combine a career in politics with his voracious literary am-
bition, Bulwer was suffering from acute overwork and periodic bouts of
despair (see FIGURE 1.2, a comic analogue). But despite the taunts of enemies who gloated over his publication failures, the collapse of his marriage to Rosina Wheeler was more damaging and humiliating. The couple's life together was extremely turbulent, soured by public quarrels
and mutual accusations of infidelity. When they finally separated in
April 1836, Rosina hatched a plan for revenge. As her biographer notes,
she "evolved scheme upon scheme to malign and embarrass her husband. Bulwer, the man she had loved, whose every weakness and every
fear was at her mercy, was an easy quarry for her wiles, and she pursued
him with relentless and savage fury until his death."[32]

In the mid-1830s, not surprisingly, Bulwer's letters to his wife change
dramatically in tone. Their mawkish nicknames "Puppy" and "Poodle"
disappear, the former replaced by an E. L. Bulwer who asserts his "UNAL-
TERABLE determination" to separate from "Madam," given her "habitual
contempt," "injurious aspersions," and "gross, and dishonouring vituper-
ation."[33] Thus does Bulwer betray in private correspondence the sentiment he tried to theorize *and* downplay in contemporaneous essays. A letter from Rosina to Bulwer, dated December 14, 1834, offers her
counterpoint: "I also here *most fully* acquit you of being dishonorable
an[d] ungentlemanlike, as ill-treating a wife is, I believe, considered neither. As for what you are pleased to term my 'domestic treachery' in keeping your letters, I have been guilty of equal treachery to myself, as I keep
copies of all my own that I write to you" (417; original emphasis). Around
April 1836 (the letter is undated), she "implore[d]" him not to "attribute to
vindictive or unforgiving feelings *my unalterable* determination of never
again 'cursing your existence with my presence'" (419; original emphasis).

Yet despite—or even because of—the resulting strain, Bulwer persisted in his two careers, sometimes extrapolating from his domestic misery arguments to stoke his essays and scenes to decorate his fiction. "We

FIGURE 1.2 *The Blue Devils* (January 1823). George Cruikshank.
Courtesy the Victoria and Albert Museum, London.

are bound to go on, we are *bound*," he confided to Disraeli, one of his few close friends, in a statement linking his voluminous output to his critics' hostility: "How our enemies would triumph were we to retire from the stage!" "And yet," he continued, "I have more than once been tempted to throw it all up, and quit even my country, for ever."[34]

The Limits of Sympathy

In the midst of all this domestic turmoil, Bulwer published "On the Want of Sympathy." Insisting quite surprisingly that lovers often lack sympathy, he implies that there's little hope for everyone else. Infatuation gives us such "beautiful pliancy," he writes sardonically, that "each nature seems blended and circumfused in each."[35]

Yet we are "fools . . . [to] imagine this sympathy is to endure for ever. . . . TIME—there is the divider!—by little and little, we grow apart from each other. The daylight of the world creeps in, the moon has vanished, and we see clearly all the jarring lines and sharp corners hidden at first from our survey" (108). Since the self-absorption of couples leads ultimately to wretchedness, their disenchantment is but a stone's throw from misanthropy.

Bulwer wrote these words shortly before his bitter separation from Rosina, and clearly knew whereof he wrote: "Mephistophiles [*sic*] himself could not devise an union [*sic*] more unhappy and more ill-assorted!" (106). But the essay highlights a conceptual issue that surpasses his marital woes, and this is our concern. A more general cause of Bulwer's claims is his cherished dream of finding "a counterpart of self," an expectation leaving people incapable of loving differences because we seek only self-replication in others (105). Indeed, when we finally realize what others are like, apparently we shun company altogether. Two remedies soften this conflict, but neither gives lasting comfort. The first lies in self-enforced fellowship: We conquer inertia and loneliness by making "contact with our kind" (109). Crowds become an attractive palliative, and thus an antidote to infatuation, by encouraging "sympathy with that which is *not common* to others" (110; my emphasis). Yet as this emphasis still entails looking for traces of ourselves in other people, the drama of self-replication is diminished, not resolved, by socializing.

This problem increases when we consider Bulwer's second remedy (solitude), which—though it doesn't lead inevitably to misanthropy—dramatizes the limitations of enforced fellowship. By making "our own dreams and thoughts our companion, our beloved, our Egeria[, w]e acquire the doctrine of self-dependence,—self suffices to self. In our sleep from the passions of the world, God makes an Eve to us from our own breasts" (110). One couldn't ask for a more self-referential notion of love. No longer viewed as a cause of crushing disappointment, the "cherished dream" of finding a "counterpart of self" spawns a monadic circuit, in which God restores self-completion and one makes love, in all senses, to oneself.

Perhaps the greatest cause of tragicomedy here is Bulwer's belief that hermetic ideals can ward off suffering. His later essay "On Self-Control" answers the question "What is SELF?" with another question: "What is that many-sided Unity which is centred in the single Ego of a man's being?"[36] Selfhood, as will emerge, is neither centered nor unified in Bulwer's work. Wedded to a fantasy of self-completion, however, he stubbornly concludes that rediscovering alikeness in others stems from our effort at diminishing self-antagonism, rather than fostering sympathy and altruism. Not surprisingly, this yields erratic results. Bulwer's protagonists oscillate wildly between love and hatred, sometimes flinging themselves recklessly at others before nursing grievances in bitter remonstrance. Henry Pelham might praise narcissists as "the dissenters of society,"[37] but Bulwer (with remarkable self-blindness) attacked such traits in others. As he wrote dismissively when reviewing Sir Egerton Brydges's *Autobiography*: "This consequence of a moody and absorbed concentration in self . . . vitiates the whole character: learn to consider yourself alone; make yourself a god; and you deem all who dispute your pretensions little better than blasphemers."[38]

One retort would be that Bulwer punished Brydges—as well as rivals like Tennyson and Thackeray—for traits he disliked in himself.[39] Certainly, it wasn't difficult to goad him: After Thackeray called his poetry "flimsy, mystical, namby-pamby" and described *Lucretia* as "his most appalling and arsenical novel," a distraught Bulwer was on the verge of challenging him to a duel—two friends had to dissuade him.[40] After duking it out with *Fraser's*, moreover, he feuded with Tennyson over the laureate's pension, producing another embarrassing row in the pages of *Punch*.[41] Yet despite their morbid entertainment value, to dwell on these psychobiographical conflicts downplays intellectual tensions in Bulwer's work. Carlyle pointed usefully to an "astonishing . . . contrast [between Bulwer] the man and his enterprise," and Allan Christensen later widened this gap, arguing that "Bulwer ha[d] not really experienced the definite conversion that he [saw] in the intellectual spirit of the nation as a whole"[42]—the move, according to *England and the English*, that "awoke [him and the Victorians] from the morbid, the passionate, the dreaming" state of Romanticism (286). Surpassing biographical concerns, the rifts in Bulwer's work signal how he—and the Victorians more generally—tried redeeming misanthropy by cultivating sympathy.

Solitude and the Divided Subject

"Monos and Daimonos," an allegory reprinted in *The Student*, spotlights this widening gap between hatred and sympathy by describing the plight of the unnamed narrator raised "on a rock" by his misanthropic father.[43] The story's stress on noxious intimacy may have some autobiographical echo, as Bulwer's father had had a powerful aversion to him—a theme Bulwer would repeat in *The New Timon*.[44] But the narrator is deliberately vague about background details: We know only that his mother died when he was an infant, and that the rock on which he lives with his father is not British. His father's decision to "abjure all society" remains enigmatic; and when he dies, the narrator, now eighteen, decides to live with his uncle in London, collecting his inheritance (1:29). London society deems him a savage, however, and after three years' "scorning social life, and pining once more for loneliness," he leaves for Africa and other parts of the world "where human step" apparently had "never trod" (1:33).

After many years alone, the narrator decides to "look upon the countenances of my race once more!" (1:34). But other people are his nemesis. While on a ship bound for England, he encounters "an idle and curious being, full of . . . frivolities, and egotisms," and soon finds he can't escape the man, who "sought me for ever" and "was as a blister to me" (1:35). For the rest of the story, the narrator tries in vain to recover the solitude he gave up. After the ship strikes a rock before reaching England, he swims to a nearby island, believing himself finally alone, but his

> despicable persecutor had escaped the waters, and now stood before me. He came up with his hideous grin and his twinkling eye; and he flung his arms round me,—I would sooner have felt the slimy folds of the serpent—and said, with his grating and harsh voice, "Ha! ha! my friend, we shall be together still!" (1:38)[45]

Thus does the story make company unctuous, an eventual cause of hatred. So too does Bulwer's tale transform the so-called "dæmon of Socrates"—a ministering, indwelling spirit—into a metaphor for internal strife and persecution. Part of a sea change in Victorian conceptions of antagonism, which Bulwer echoed slightly later in *Asmodeus at Large*,

"Monos and Daimonos" highlights an inner force hostile to the subject's well-being.

Bulwer's debts here include Godwin's *Caleb Williams* and James Hogg's *Private Memoirs and Confessions of a Justified Sinner;*[46] another, more oblique debt is surely to Bage's popular *Hermsprong; or, Man as He Is Not*, itself adapting Voltaire's *L'ingénu* and informed by Godwin's *Enquiry Concerning Political Justice.*[47] However, Bulwer's principal debt is to Mary Shelley's *Frankenstein*, and Shelley was, of course, Godwin's daughter. Her memorable scene in the Alps, where Frankenstein confronts his monster, "overwhelm[ing] him with words expressive of furious detestation and contempt," reverberates in Bulwer's story when the "Monos" tries to kill the irksome "Daimonos."[48] But whereas Bulwer's demon merely laughs at the misery he inflicts, Frankenstein's "scoffing devil" vows, when *denied* a companion, that the scientist's "sufferings will satisfy my everlasting hatred" (198, 199). "Let me see," it earlier begs, that "I excite the sympathy of some existing thing" (141).

Though Bulwer's story partly inverts this scenario, it hints at a similarly ghastly outcome: Even after his narrator has "dashed the man to the ground," killed, and buried him, the revenant torments him with demonic laughter (1:43). Desperately repeating a misanthrope's mantras— "Now I shall be alone!" "I shall be alone *now*!" "I am alone at last!" (1:39, 42, 43; original emphasis)—the narrator discovers, as do Frankenstein and Byron's Manfred, why he "canst never be alone."[49] His endlessly thwarted solitude signals both the horror of enforced contact with others and the impossibility of self-unity (see FIGURE 1.3, another comic analogue).

One of the lessons in Bulwer's story is that the subject divided by language can never be "monos," can never be alone, though it continues to dream otherwise. Following the narrator, we begin to doubt the autonomy of this tormentor, which finally is called a "Leech," as if, besides representing a parasite devouring its host, it is also an internal demon goading the narrator toward annihilation (1:47). When contemplating this awful life sentence—imprisoned, effectively, with his own worst enemy inside his head—the man hears from his internal "daimonos" the eerie verdict that he'll never again experience peace. Indeed, after asking a seer, "Must I *never* be alone again?" the narrator learns the answer

Jealousy.

FIGURE 1.3 *Jealousy* (November 1825). George Cruikshank.
Courtesy the University of Wisconsin–Madison Special Collections.

not from the man but from the invisible, undead leech, which "trace[s] one word upon the sand . . . NEVER."[50] Thus does Bulwer's interest in failing sympathy devolve into a powerful suggestion that inner monsters destroy solitude, and that harmony—whether pursued alone, in marriage, or in groups—is illusory, because fundamentally unattainable. Moreover, the extended ending of the later 1835 English edition renders hatred and inner conflict intractable impediments to happiness, for solitude "is only for the guiltless"—those without "evil thoughts." Bulwer implies here that those who are free of guilt are so unusual as to be almost inhuman.[51]

Given his uneasy oscillation in the 1830s between solitude and sociability, Bulwer unsurprisingly went on to write silver-fork fiction laced with irony and distrust. Having transformed his earlier story "Mortimer" into *Pelham*, he composed *Godolphin* and the unfinished *Greville:*

A Satire upon Fine Life. *Pelham* itself bridges *Falkland*'s Byronic motifs and Bulwer's growing interest in crime fiction: We see Falkland's qualities recur in Sir Reginald Glanville, a character whose boundless rage in *Pelham* hastens his death, as if his misanthropic turmoil were enough to destroy him. In *Paul Clifford*, *Eugene Aram*, *Night and Morning*, and *Lucretia*, by contrast, Bulwer's narrators recast individual vengeance, instead condemning swaths of Victorian society under the pretext of trying to reform it. These mid-career novels also let Bulwer have his cake (as literature) and eat it too (as politics), since poverty and social neglect not only absolve their heroes' deep misanthropy, but also frequently are portrayed, somewhat incorrectly, as the factors driving them to crime.

By creating a political reason for people-hating, these novels turn rancor into a type of virtue. Their unflinching assessment of crime apparently improves society by confronting readers with an underclass that, in reality, many would happily have watched hang or have banished to Australia. As Bulwer declared in his 1845 preface to *Night and Morning*, "I set myself to the task of investigating the motley world to which our progress in humanity has attained, caring little what misrepresentation I incurred, what hostility I provoked, in searching through a devious labyrinth for the foot-tracks of Truth."[52] The statement is thoroughly disingenuous: Bulwer, in the next paragraph, turns vehemently on "the ignorant and malicious [who] were decrying the moral of 'Paul Clifford'" (ix). A pretext for his political concern, crime and poverty drive his plots as entertainment, so undermining his reformist project. Focusing on crime also compels him to play up the very elements (chiefly greed and corruption) that at this stage he said he wanted society to eradicate. The ensuing compromise is a key reason the endings of these novels seem contrived, as if their prior, hate-ridden content were always slightly out of kilter with its sanctioned rationale.

Criminal Elements

Part detective novel, part political allegory, and part philosophical treatise on law and determinism, *Paul Clifford* features an orphan raised among shrewd criminals who eventually becomes a dashing—even ethical—highwayman. Borrowing from Gay's *Beggar's Opera* the provocative idea that aristocrats are thieves and that paupers are keeping score of their crimes, Bulwer's novel represents lords, dukes, and even George IV as opportunistic robbers. When Paul Clifford is finally captured in a robbery, moreover, the man later sentencing him to death—Judge William Brandon—turns out to be his father, and he learns about Paul's identity *before* sentencing him. Wrenched by guilt and self-disgust, Brandon commutes the sentence to transportation to Australia, whence Paul easily escapes, eventually living with Lucy, his fiancée, in North America. If the novel is to end happily, Bulwer implies, the couple must emigrate to the New World.

Bulwer's political perspective in the novel at this point still largely derived from Godwin's *Enquiry*, which cautions the rich to expect "reprisals" from the poor, and all to "regard the state of society as a state of war" (1:16). *Paul Clifford* expands its hero's misanthropy into a political claim that society is sanctioned warfare between the "haves" and "have-nots"—terms that Bulwer coined in his later novel *Lucretia*.[53] Additionally, Bulwer's using misanthropy to criticize society differs from the narrower egotistical concerns framing *Falkland*, for like Godwin, he now blames the haves who practice this warfare with guile, enlisting government support to protect their interests against "the rest," who are miserable in dependency (see FIGURE 1.4, dating from 1846, the year *Lucretia* was published). In Godwin's texts, the rich are talentless and lazy; in Bulwer's crime novels they are manipulative criminals.

Paul's misanthropy governs Bulwer's reformist ethic, but it also surfaces in a chapter in which Bulwer is himself settling old scores "in the spirit of English warfare" (xix). Even in this political context, then, Bulwer yokes misanthropy to his own concerns, recasting social issues as personal slights. Paul offers "a misanthropical reverie upon the faithlessness of friends" (1:105), for example, because Peter Mac Grawler, editor of *The Asinæum*, has cheated him—a thinly veiled attack on *The Athenæum*, which had published a negative review of Bulwer's 1829 novel *Devereux* and a few other critical notices. And though Paul insists, midway through *Paul Clifford*, that he "acknowledge[s] no allegiance to society"—indeed, "openly . . . war[s] against it, and patiently will . . . meet its revenge"—Bulwer adds a cautionary footnote, dissociating himself from such extremes: "The Author need not, he hopes, observe,

FIGURE 1.4 *Tremendous Sacrifice!* George Cruikshank.
Our Own Times (London, 1846).

that these sentiments are Mr. Paul Clifford's—not his" (2:146 and
147n.). This is itself an arch allusion to critics' insisting (with some reason) that elements of *Pelham* were autobiographical, an idea Bulwer
strongly denied.

As if underscoring these points, *Paul Clifford* eventually loses most of
its interest in social reform by veering off on a tangent about the hidden
satisfactions that arise from Victorian injustice. Judge Brandon is the
novel's most intriguing character, because his grasp of treachery is impossible to reform. Having a "bitter and malignant spirit" that permits
him, among other things, to sell his own wife and to sentence his son to
death, Brandon distinguishes between "the revenge of hatred" (which
Paul's passionate opposition exemplifies) and "the revenge . . . of contempt," a form of gratuitous cruelty that Brandon cultivates (3:10; also
3:195). "I own I have a bile against my species," he brags to Lord Maulev-
erer, who compliments him on the number of "human pendulums" he has
made from the gallows: "I loathe their folly and their half vices. *'Ridet et
odit'* ['He laughs and hates'] is my motto" (3:157). Ironically, Bulwer's
prose is liveliest when tracking this contempt: "My disdain of human

pettiness rioted in the external sources of fortune, as well as an inward fountain of bitter and self-fed consolation" (3:175–76). So, even as Bulwer seems to redeem misanthropy by aligning it with social and moral reform, his villains (voicing some of his own revenge scenarios) make this outcome implausible. Their "surplus" enmity mars Bulwer's political critique, exposing forms of hatred that belie reform.

The Limits of Reform

Although Bulwer's misanthropy recurs in his novel *Night and Morning* and his play *Money*, pushing sympathy still farther out of the picture, he changed tack once more, inveighing less sardonically against the upper and middle classes when restating his objections to corruption and greed. He turned, that is, to indicting "our sickly civilisation" for its crass materialism, rather than lambasting a diffident aristocracy for its fecklessness and greed. He also implied that the reform of misanthropic protagonists is a spiritual, not political, enterprise (*Night* xiv). In *Night and Morning*, then, "anguish" supplants "the less sacred paroxysm of revenge and wrath" that Philip Morton, the protagonist, feels toward his self-serving uncle (1:72). And the satire governing *Money*, from the year before, abruptly ends when the leading couple's love triumphs over adversity and financial concerns.

Alfred Evelyn, protagonist of this play, may mock the greedy surrounding him, but his ability to parse wealth and happiness ensures, following Bulwer's shifting emphasis, that he ends up with both. According to his eccentric benefactor, Evelyn is "an oddity, like myself—[and] the only one of my relatives who never fawned on me."[54] Dickens made this theme central to his slightly later novel *Martin Chuzzlewit*, and Eliot gave it prominence in *Middlemarch* when Featherstone's relatives wait restlessly for the ailing misanthrope to die. Evelyn tries to cast off similar parasites by pretending to gamble away his fortune, and later marries the only woman (Clara Douglas) whose affection for him remains firm. But since the play partly undermines its own argument about social prominence, the difference between temporary cynicism and lasting misanthropy proves significant. "When I was poor I hated the world," Evelyn admits, whereas "now I am rich I despise it!" (2.2, p. 38). Clara tries to smooth away these wrinkles, claiming Evelyn has exhibited throughout his life "the ardent mind couched beneath the cold sarcasm of a long-baffled spirit" (3.3, p. 73). Yet the only meaningful development in the play is Evelyn's perspective on Clara's constancy; she epitomizes the combined voices of Victorian prudence and sentimentality, shucking off Romantic notions of benign poverty while insisting that love and wealth aren't necessarily incompatible. Regarding hatred, we might say, Bulwer had by this point almost written himself into a corner. All but severing links between misanthropy and social reform, he became increasingly diffident about both elements, uncertain whether either could form a plausible basis for fiction and politics, his central concerns.

Money softens Bulwer's more radical 1830s fiction and the slightly later *New Timon*, then, by replacing confirmed people-haters with cynics capable of putting love above near-ubiquitous depravity. The speaker of the latter poem applauds

> the rare valour that confronts with scorn
> The monster shape, of Vice and Folly born,
> Which some "the World," and some "Opinion," call,
> Own'd by no heart, and yet enslaving all;
> The bastard charter of the social state,
> Which crowns the base to ostracize the great. (16.10–15)

But where in *Money* do we see such steadfast contempt for public opinion? Regrettably, the play enacts the same move from hatred to irony that Bulwer, in "The Modern Misanthrope," viewed as a cause of worrying corruption.

Darkness and Dystopia

These vicissitudes in Bulwer's fiction and political psychology help explain how, much later, he formulated *The Coming Race*, ostensibly a "utopia" but really a novel that makes us averse to sympathy and heartily grateful for social acrimony. Near the beginning of the story, appearing almost a decade after Bulwer became colonial secretary in Lord Derby's conservative government (presiding over the creation of the colonies of British Columbia and Queensland), the American narrator,

Tish, befriends the Vril-ya, a subterranean race that has adapted the inside of the earth to suit its needs. The encounter underground gives Tish enough objectivity to judge humanity, and for much of the novel he compares the Vril-ya's prosperous egalitarianism with the ruthless individualism he experienced aboveground.

The Coming Race fittingly concludes this chapter, because it shows why aggression, thwarting Bulwer's idea of progress and sympathy between roughly 1830 and 1860, was a quality he ended up praising for its antisocial potential. The novel becomes dystopian when Tish recoils in boredom from a society that demands peace. As Bulwer explained to his son about related affairs, satisfying our utopian dreams "would be deadly to us, not from its vices but its virtues. . . . The realisation of these ideas would produce a society which we should find extremely dull, and in which the current equality would prohibit all greatness."[55]

Here, then, is a partial rejoinder to Bulwer's reformist aims and earlier crime novels, which tried to correct injustices against the poor and to render every citizen equal before the law. Though Bulwer's interest in misanthropy expanded once more into a fully political approach to hatred, he retained this emotion as a cherished sign of social friction. Appalled by the results of the Paris Commune, he insisted that socialism was "strife-rot" and that humans were so disposed to competition we would spurn equality if it existed in practice. Apparently we thrive on the very injustice Bulwer had decried in his 1830s' crime novels as promoting misery and mass inequality.

Since both perspectives hinge on the control of aggression, I'll conclude by noting how the Vril-ya unappealingly contain this impulse. According to Zee, "an erudite professor in the College of Sages," humans and several subterranean tribes beyond the Vril-ya live in an "age of envy and hate, of fierce passions, of constant social changes more or less violent, of strife between classes, of war between state and state."[56] The Vril-ya, by contrast, discover "the terrible force of vril" (59)—a force beyond electricity, closer to nuclear energy—which brings "the art of destruction to such perfection as to annul all superiority in numbers, discipline, or military skill. . . . If army [had] met army, and both had [had] command of this agency, it could [have been] but to the annihilation of each" (59).

Publishing his novel when many European countries were zealously expanding their empires—a decade, too, before Herbert Spencer launched his "Anti-Aggression League" in 1881—Bulwer describes tribes rationally ceding their ruling passions. The transitions in his argument may be facile, but as Bulwer's letter to his son indicates, they highlight a cultural and political gulf between the Vril-ya and us. According to Zee, "Man [had been] so completely at the mercy of man . . . that all notions of government by force gradually vanished from political systems and force of law" (59). Voluntary participation in groups and the community replaces coercion. Indeed, what Freud would later call the Oedipus complex fades in this novel into calm, even irritating goodwill, since "there are no hazardous speculations, no emulators striving for superior wealth and rank" (64). The Vril-ya may still have words for "external evil" ("Nan-zi"), disgust ("Poo-pra"), and "falsehood, the vilest kind of evil" ("Poo-naria"), but these are now anachronistic terms indicating what they have left behind. According to Tish's quick phrenological assessment, they have "amazingly full . . . moral organs, such as conscientiousness and benevolence," and small cranial regions given over to combativeness (92, 116).

In most Victorian novels (excepting H. G. Wells's later *Time Machine*, which was much indebted to *The Coming Race*), these traits would indicate admirable development, but Tish can't tolerate the tranquillity because it reminds him of death. Initially fearing he'll corrupt the Vril-ya with his cruder impulses and love for Zee, he finally acknowledges that returning to humanity will help him conquer his "dread of death," though his love for Zee will thereby remain unfulfilled (280). Thus does a horror of death prevail over the lure of intimacy. Like the outcome of Aristophanes' fable in Plato's *Symposium*, Tish lives on earth fully aware of what he's missing, "somewhat disappointed, as most men are, in matters connected with household love and domestic life" (291–92). The statement points to an oddly ambiguous commitment to humanity. Tish now admires—indeed, furtively promotes—qualities that counter the "awful tranquillity" troubling him belowground. Nevertheless, he also grasps why the Vril-ya—precisely in their serenity—will be "our inevitable destroyers" (292). As Chillingly insists in *Kenelm Chillingly*, "the probability is that, some day or other, we shall be exterminated by a new development of species" (37). Paradoxically, our successors over-whelm us with peace rather than by hatred, malice, and guile.

Although the ironic misanthrope briefly vacates Bulwer's 1840s nov-els, then, he returns in a more cynical guise, pointing hopelessly to so-cial problems without much interest in their solution. Chillingly, in E. G. Bell's words, "becomes a contemplative, self-communing nurser of crotchets, a spectator instead of an actor, [and] an old young man."[57] Shorn of idealism, full of bile, and diffident about social reform, Bulw-er's late misanthropes gleefully probe insoluble issues. They punctuate his writing in a guise that Bulwer had always esteemed—as an "amiable man-scorner" ("Modern" 479) who lives alone, disgruntled with hu-manity, knowing all along that everyone is doomed.

CHAPTER TWO

Dickensian Malefactors

The Villain vs. the Recluse

ACCORDING TO THE NARRATOR of *Barnaby Rudge*, "the despisers of mankind . . . are of two sorts. They who believe their merit neglected and unappreciated, make up one class; they who receive adulation and flattery, knowing their own worthlessness, compose the other. Be sure that the coldest-hearted misanthropes are ever of this last order."[1] This statement is true in Dickens's early novel, but it doesn't sum up misanthropy's role in his other works, where hatred and villainy have dramatic, asocial effects. Moments before hanging himself, for example, Ralph Nickleby toasts "the coming in of every year that brings this cursed world nearer to its end. No bell or book for me," he adds, in what is doubtless the best speech in *Nicholas Nickleby*; "throw me on a dunghill, and let me rot there to infect the air!"[2]

Dickens's sentimental misanthropes may declare loudly that they're "neglected and unappreciated," but most abstain from violence, withdrawing temporarily from communities that would corrupt—and even annihilate—their integrity. He styles them as comically self-involved, not as villainous recluses and hateful sociopaths. Among such characters are Mr. Venus, the "harmless misanthrope" in *Our Mutual Friend*, and Nicodemus Dumps ("long Dumps"), an amusing curmudgeon in "The

Bloomsbury Christening" who forewarns his baby godson about life's tribulations.[3] Such men suffer from neglect, and in Venus's case (as his name implies) blossom when their love is requited, but their behavior represents a strategic withdrawal from society, rather than a conclusive break with it.[4] When many Dickens novels end, these misanthropes catch a benign—even infectious—spirit leading them back to other people. Dickens follows Victorian convention in psychologizing them, even turning them into comic legacies of eighteenth-century sensibility and ressentiment.

By contrast, his "coldest-hearted misanthropes" imperil through motivelessness and gratuitous cruelty his interest in self-sacrifice and citizenship. "Disdainful of the company of his fellow-creatures," Tom Codlin in *The Old Curiosity Shop* joins Ralph Nickleby in displaying a "deep misanthropy" that in Dickensian terms rules out ethical engagement with humanity.[5] Although he and comparable antiheroes may refrain from extreme violence, they have little in common with Dickens's lovelorn melancholics. Dickens downplays economic gain as a motive for their villainy, the better to magnify their commitment to personal and collective harm. As John Kucich notes, he diverts them "from an economy of purpose and reward, lifting them into a world of transcendentally profitless combat."[6] Why?

While some haters in Dickens's work (Miss Wade, for example)[7] fall between these stools, signaling the limits of Dickens's categories, hatred of humanity recurs in his writing in psychological and nonpsychological guises, and the latter is my central concern. Such hatred tests his conception of sociability as a realm beyond which groups and communities fall apart in embitterment. Hatred in these instances doesn't ratify society by making the exception prove the rule. As Victor Brombert argued recently, the resulting antiheroism is disturbing, because in its "willful undermining of the idiom of tragedy" it harms "our deep need to bestow dignity and beauty on human suffering."[8] "Hostile to the cult of personality," antiheroism not only thwarts our desire for edification and perfectibility but also compels us to view suffering as a form of anguish for which there may be no meaningful answer or solution.[9]

Dickens used villainous misanthropes to reveal a profound discrepancy between individual drives and socially sanctioned pleasures. In particular, his interest in antiheroic characters destroys psychic and philosophical consistency by breaking with Bentham's utilitarian model, discussed briefly in the introduction. Moving, then, from Dickensian antiheroism to the problems besetting (in ever wider circles) intersubjectivity, familial strife, and social hatred, I'll examine his work in rough chronological order, making clear why his interest in misanthropy recast his social satires, and what is philosophically at stake in this shifting emphasis.

Instead of endorsing Bulwer's association of misanthropy with sardonicism, Dickens unraveled this expectation, indicating that his villains finally evade such measurable principles. To that end, his "coldest-hearted" misanthropes have no redeeming qualities.[10] Amoral in outlook, the cause of their hatred generally unexplained, they're incapable of sharing the world with others, which partly defines my interest in them. Opacity also shrouds the cause of their contempt. We know only that their desire for retribution is stronger than their desire for freedom, which puts them at odds with "the calculative consistency" of utilitarianism, "the dominant ethical programme of the nineteenth century."[11] Flaunting their repugnance for personal and social reform, they override social ties with gratuitous behavior, which in turn helps Dickens offset radical evil from his lovelorn misanthropes' harmless self-regard. Indeed, his malefactors are so devoid of conventional motivation that they become susceptible to metonymic caricature, as when Rigaud's gestures in *Little Dorrit* prove absurdly artificial and Carker's teeth designate his rapacity in *Dombey and Son*.

Since motiveless violence is difficult to condone, Dickens's conception of villainy blocks identification, leaving its agents vulnerable to severe retributive impulses. For reasons that I'll assess, given his satires of social hypocrisy, Dickens insists that such asocial behavior is irremediable and must be eliminated. Punishment isn't enough. The violent deaths of Daniel Quilp and especially Carker—the latter's body ripped apart by a railway train, then thrown to the winds—expunge their hostile impulses in scenes that still carefully probe their intensity.

Preceding a chapter titled "Several People Delighted . . ." and written with deliberate syntactical ambiguity, Carker's death is sufficiently protracted to make him conscious of his impending agony:

> [Carker] heard a shout—another—saw the face change from its vindictive passion to a faint sickness and terror—felt the earth tremble—knew in a moment that the rush was come—uttered a shriek—looked around—saw the red eyes, bleared and dim, in the daylight, close upon him—was beaten down, caught up, and whirled away upon a jagged mill, that spun him round and round, and struck him limb from limb, and licked his stream of life up with its fiery heat, and cast his mutilated fragments in the air.[12]

In Dickens's moral scheme, as the passage illustrates, Fate punishes evil in a corrective impulse almost as violent as the people it eradicates. In *Our Mutual Friend*, indeed, we learn that "Evil often stops short at itself and dies with the doer of it; but Good, never" (105). By this sleight of hand, Dickens makes an otherwise corrosive, contaminating evil relatively self-contained, implying that it needn't tarnish other characters or his narrators. Nevertheless, at other times he ascribed part of his own severity to "the attraction of repulsion," an "invisible force" binding him imaginarily to not only murder and death but also the agents—Bill Sikes, Tulkinghorn, and Jonas Chuzzlewit, among them—who can't abstain from violence.[13] "Still he was not sorry," the narrator says, recounting Jonas's murder of Montague Tigg in *Chuzzlewit*. Through indirect speech and a rare moment of interiority, he establishes almost eerie familiarity with Jonas's murderous aims: "He had hated the man too much, and had been bent, too desperately and too long, on setting himself free. If the thing could have come over again, he would have done it again. His malignant and revengeful passions were not so easily laid."[14]

The narrator captures Jonas's cruelty and contempt for old age, but avoids explaining "his malignant and revengeful passions," leaving in doubt why they galvanize him. The same holds for all such malefactors: The real cause of their hostility recedes into elements of identity that Dickens stops short of psychologizing. First introduced to us as a form of human "vermin" (16), Rigaud seems to hate only good people. Besides noting his joy in terrifying Mrs. Flintwinch and in revenge against a society imprisoning him, we'd be pressed to explain why. Carker, too, may be repellent, and Quilp "a study in sadistic malice," but what inspires their behavior—beyond their shared pleasure in tormenting the weak and defenseless—baffles us.[15] We know only that such abusiveness must end.

The severity with which Dickens treats such violence implicates us as readers. Because Carker's gruesome death seems meant to equal the joy he received in humiliating others, his swift punishment should satisfy readers who are "virtuously disgusted" by such antiheroes.[16] Indeed, one form of relief we experience from moral corruption is the pleasure of witnessing a shoddy specimen of humanity dismembered and "cast [into] mutilated fragments." This isn't our sole satisfaction in completing *Dombey and Son*, but the narrator's extreme description presses us to consider what it means to defeat one form of vindictive cruelty with another. Why else did witnesses at public executions cheer with approval when people hanged, as Dickens noted with alternating contempt and fascination when, in July 1840, forty thousand people (himself among them) watched the murderer François Courvoisier die?[17] Why else, too, do some North Americans today follow zealously the plight of inmates on death row, counting down the final seconds of the prisoner's life so joyfully that they might almost be ushering in a new year?

The Family of Man

Let's return briefly to the early 1840s, though, to invoke before displacing biographical concerns. At the start of his first six-month trip to North America, in early 1842, Dickens was basking in his newfound celebrity. The ordeal of fame soon began to tell, however, as he found Americans' aggressive interest in him intrusive and, ultimately, disgusting. He resented being an object for vast crowds, who peered at him as if he were inhuman. "If I turn into the street," he complained to John Forster from New York, "I am followed by a multitude. If I stay at home, the house becomes, with callers, like a fair. . . . I go to a party in the evening, and am so inclosed [*sic*] and hemmed about by people, stand where I will, that I am exhausted for want of air. I dine out, and have to talk about everything, to everybody."[18]

His revulsion peaked at Niagara Falls, where, instead of reading about Americans' sense of awe in the visitors' books, he saw comment after comment that was merely fatuous. "If I were a despot," he wrote Charles Sumner, "I would force these Hogs to live for the rest of their lives on all Fours, and to wallow in filth expressly provided for them by Scavengers who should be maintained at the Public expence [*sic*]. Their drink should be the stagnant ditch, and their food the rankest garbage; and every morning they should each receive as many stripes [whippings] as there are letters in their detestable obscenities."[19]

Five months after returning from North America, Dickens began *Martin Chuzzlewit*, a satire informed by his experiences abroad, though the novel isn't reducible to them. Several chapters representing Tapley's and young Martin's episodes in America condemn the country's obsession with money, ostentatious culture, and indifference to poverty. According to the narrator, life—especially in North America—is ruthless and deeply inhumane: "Such things [as infant mortality] are much too common to be widely known or cared for," the narrator complains with devastating understatement. "Smart citizens grow rich, and friendless victims smart and die, and are forgotten. That is all" (601).

As many Britons and North Americans lived at the time in appalling conditions, with cities like London beset by overcrowding, disease, and "cess lakes," most of these characterizations are painfully accurate. Dickens read Edwin Chadwick's *Report on the Sanitary Condition of the Labouring Population* (1842) shortly after it appeared, and, like Henry Mayhew, Friedrich Engels, and Elizabeth Gaskell, confirmed its wretched summary of urban poverty whenever he visited England's poorest slums, factories, and prisons.[20] Over the course of the nineteenth century, the population of London alone swelled from roughly one million to four and a half million, while the city's average age of mortality at midcentury fell, incredibly, to twenty-seven (twenty-two for the working classes); life expectancy in the capital—and in England and Wales generally—didn't improve substantially until the last quarter of the nineteenth century (see FIGURES 2.1 and 2.2, respectively John Thomson's photograph *London Nomades* and Gustave Doré's study *Bluegate Fields*).

FIGURE 2.1 *London Nomades*. John Thomson.
Street Life in London (London, 1877–78).
Courtesy the Victoria and Albert Museum, London.

FIGURE 2.2 *Bluegate Fields.* Gustave Doré.
London. A Pilgrimage, with Blanchard Jerrold (London, 1872).
Courtesy Musées de Strasbourg.

Since it was common for families of seven or eight to live in one room (which also doubled as a workplace for its many occupants), it was often necessary, according to a cringing inspector in 1856, that when a death occurred "the living . . . eat, drink and sleep beside a decomposing corpse, overheated by a fire required for cooking, and already filled with the foul emanations from the bodies of the living and their impure clothes."[21] As Peter Ackroyd asserts in his excellent biography of Dickens, "No Londoner was ever completely well, and when in nineteenth-century fiction urban life is described as 'feverish' it was a statement of medical fact and not a metaphor" (384).[22] At the end of 1847, roughly half a million Londoners were infected with typhus fever, a figure excluding the vast number of people already dead from typhoid (a separate affliction), cholera, tuberculosis, scarlet fever, diphtheria, scrofula, and smallpox. Such was the extent of disease and poverty that Dr. Simon, working extensively to reform public health, described "swarms of men and women who have yet to learn that human beings should dwell differently from cattle—swarms to whom personal cleanliness is utterly unknown; swarms by whom delicacy and decency in their social relations are quite unconceived."[23]

Dickens wasn't referring to such "swarms" and "cattle" when he fantasized whipping North America's human "hogs" and "fellow swine," and I'm not reading him as a sociologist. But it's necessary to remember this fantasy and context when we examine his satire of Victorian selfishness hobbling sociability. As he remarked in the preface to *Chuzzlewit*'s first cheap edition, published several years later, in 1849, the novel aims to show "how Selfishness propagates itself; and to what a grim giant it may grow, from small beginnings" (39). Like Bulwer's, his account of antisocial behavior is also conceptual, the novel advancing a sophisticated perspective on self-regard that with devastating effect makes reciprocity and intersubjectivity almost inconceivable. This encapsulates my interest. "At every turn! . . . Self, self, self," laments old Martin: "Every one among them for himself" (*Chuzzlewit* 868; also 95). "What is missing here, and throughout *Martin Chuzzlewit* for the most part," adds J. Hillis Miller, in a brilliant reading of the novel, "is any intersubjective world. There is no world of true language, gesture, or expression which would allow the characters entrance to one another's hearts."[24]

Through its mock genealogy of the Chuzzlewits, the novel thematizes this dearth of sympathy in its opening chapter.[25] Yet after a probing inquiry into murder, fraud, criminal psychology, poverty, and solipsistic hatred, the novel ends with a flood of sentiment so richly exuberant that the narrator asks six times if such joy amounts to folly. Though he considers these questions rhetorical, producing the amusingly dismissive answer—"If these be follies, then Fiery Face go on and prosper! If they be not, then Fiery Face avaunt!" (905)—is innocent pleasure sustainable when reciprocity seems *constitutively* impossible?

Dickens, in the early 1840s, insisted that it is. Characters like Tapley and Tom Pinch triumph over adversity, representing tenacious—if demure—examples of loyalty. Near the beginning of *Chuzzlewit*, the narrator even claims: "No cynic in the world, though in his hatred of its men a very griffin, could have withstood these things in Thomas Pinch" (147). He's referring with mock-epic bathos to Tom's incomparable satisfaction in eating a stale sandwich (the Pecksniffs' thoughtful leftovers). Yet despite its comic aim, the statement is inaccurate, even woefully mendacious. Virtual parodies of resilient innocence, Tom and his sister—"pleasant little Ruth!"—are recipients of gratuitous abuse in a world almost indifferent to their beneficence and well-being (672). As Miller notes, they represent "the unexpected theme of the impasse to which total unselfishness leads. . . [:] that the man who is wholly unselfish ends with nothing but the esteem of those around him, and the privilege of serving them" (121).

Miller's is a productively harsh way of judging such modest virtue. Despite old Martin's triumphant restoration of order at the end, it's wholly improbable that the simpleminded Pinches would prevail over the unscrupulous Chuzzlewits. Even John Westlock is pallid beside such scoundrels as Seth Pecksniff and Sairey Gamp, who has insight enough to insist, in these now-famous words, "we never knows wot's hidden in each other's hearts; and if we had glass winders there, we'd need keep the shetters up, some on us, I do assure you!" (534–35). As Gamp's self-involvement exemplifies a type of nonreciprocity driving the novel's moral and social vision, she compels us to reassess the characters' presumed autonomy and capacity for intersubjectivity, a topic I shall consider as a symptom of familial and social hatred.

Aspects of this enmity survive the narrator's final attempts at eliminating them. Indeed, the novel's preoccupation with malice and glee remains intractable, a problem the conclusion can't resolve. During the final cleanup, the narrator even hints that part of old Martin's misanthropy is feigned to test his grandson's affection for Mary Graham (888). This is a tepid explanation for the old man's justified fury, especially when "family forces" have left him in a "state of siege" (105). What ensued was "a skirmishing, and flouting, and snapping off of heads" (106)—a type of internal corrosion stemming from rancor, to alter the metaphor, that wears away subjectivity until all that remains, as Gamp foresaw, is individuals' petty satisfactions and cruelties.

Because it destroys meaning and symbolic relations, this depletion of subjectivity has profound antifamilial effects. In collective terms, "the family forces" eventually dissolve into a "jealous, stony-hearted, distrustful company" (107). And like Martin's marauding relatives, Jonas waits impatiently for *his* father's (Anthony's) death. In mockery that Chuffey pretends not to hear, he voices an extraordinary hostility to old age, giving full rein to normally repressed oedipal hatred. If we considered Dickens only indignant about such cruelty (or wholly in control of his fictions' meaning), we might call these and other scenes realizations of the common Victorian metaphor "the battle of life," which he helped popularize.[26] But as we saw earlier when invoking his "attraction [to] repulsion" and interest in executions, Dickens was captivated by the demonic energy and asocial drives fueling characters like Jonas, Krook, Headstone, and especially Quilp, so it's necessary to consider the philosophical implications of these scenarios.[27]

Time and again (despite the country's already severe mortality rates), *Chuzzlewit* announces that the old don't die fast enough, as if those waiting to inherit must either pounce at the right opportunity or, in Jonas's case, attempt patricide. According to the novel, such murderous life envy taints every generation. With remarkable candor, old Martin adds that under such circumstances the elderly are for their brethren "fit objects to be robbed and preyed upon and plotted against and adulated by any knaves, who, but for joy, would have spat upon their coffins when they died their dupes" (92). "But for joy": These relatives are so predatory, he implies, that not even tact can veil their resentment at his protracted energy, an idea we'll see Browning elaborate. The narrator concludes the first chapter by invoking "the Monboddo doctrine touching on the probability of the human race having once been monkeys" (56).[28] But after we've seen the Spottletoes, Pecksniffs, and Slyme and Tigg in action, the analogy seems unfair to apes.

"Why do you talk to me of friends! Can you or anybody teach me to know who are my friends, and who my enemies?" (84). Given Martin's assessment of his relatives, such remarks turn intergenerational hatred into a fault line splintering the Chuzzlewits' lineage and cooling the warmth of "Fiery Face" at the novel's end (905). As old Martin insists, again voicing the psychological cause of his misanthropy, "Brother against brother, child against parent, friends treading on the faces of friends, this is the social company by whom my way has been attended" (92).

Since the novel's opening chapter blends satire and allegory, advancing "a kind of master-summary of the family of man," the narrator views such treachery and parasitism as a universal tendency that society tends to encourage rather than quell.[29] The Pecksniffs and Spottletoes display traits to which all humanity is susceptible, that is, but to which Victorian society, with its love of wealth and status, is especially prone. In Dickens's representational scheme, the nineteenth century is propelled toward mutual depredation exactly as it imagines itself transcending nature entirely. If "mankind is evil in its thoughts and in its base constructions" (373), as the narrator later claims, then it's understandable old Martin would "fle[e] from all who knew me, and taking refuge in secret places [would] live . . . the life of one who is hunted" (92–93). Because of his "contempt for the rabble," the only social tie he can imagine, early on, is one in which he thwarts others' expectations of remuneration after his death (223, 93). What he wants, paradoxically, is a consensual dearth of sympathy.

Hatred and Self-Regard

Although *Chuzzlewit*'s satire on selfishness compounds Dickens's problems in concluding the novel, we can't explain his difficulties by invoking the novel's somewhat chaotic material (a standard criticism of the work). Nor can we follow other critics and specify the novel's thematic problem in creating altruism out of widespread selfishness. Because the novel's interest in self-regard shapes its overall perspective on character and intersubjectivity, it's impossible to separate characters' traits from their relation to society. As most of them are drawn conceptually to isolation, that is, thematic modifications, such as the removal of old Martin's prejudice, make the narrator's final stress on sociability unconvincing. The novel's very structure derails that move.

Let's approach the thematic issue, however, in order to displace it. For in doing so we'll see how thwarted intersubjectivity in the novel becomes a powerful metaphor for wider concerns like stymied collectivity. One of the skills old Martin tries to renounce, apparently in wisdom, is reading his relatives' unconscious motivations. In the end, he considers this scrutiny to be as selfish as the behavior it delights in exposing:

> "There is a kind of selfishness," said Martin: "I have learned it in my own experience of my own breast: which is constantly upon the watch for selfishness in others; and holding others at a distance by suspicions and distrusts, wonders why they don't approach, and don't confide, and calls that selfishness in them. Thus I once doubted those about me—not without reason in the beginning—and thus I once doubted you, Martin." (884)

Superficially, this form of address—from Martin Senior to Junior—bolsters interpersonal, generational, and narrative connections, but it also severs other ties and prolongs the novel's rancorous dynamic, for Martin's reflection quickly swerves into a rant against Pecksniff. Because little substantively improves at the end, the novel's rebuke to humanity— its justification for misanthropy—confirms why characters would shun one another, aspiring ideally to autarky. Having detailed such extreme hatred, the novel faces near-insurmountable difficulties in representing once-sworn enemies starting to trust one another. Interpreting an earlier moment in the novel, Miller reminds us that "most of the characters are unwilling to consider such reciprocity, and instinctively try every means they can find to do without other people" (123).

Why is this avoidance "instinctive"? By emphasizing the novel's interest in selfishness, rather than its comparable concern about hatred,

Miller surprisingly can't say. He reads the novel's conclusion as a gesture toward reciprocity and collective integrity, with Dickens indicting antisocial behavior. Yet, arguably, this is only half true: The novel's focus on familial embitterment overwhelms its later stress on sympathy. Despite his brilliant reading of the novel's dearth of intersubjectivity, then, Miller surely begins from the wrong premise. As many characters strive to *avoid* reciprocity, it's hasty to imply that they've wanted all along to participate communally (see FIGURE 2.3). The novel disqualifies this optimism, replicating forms of violence and division even as it seems to eradicate them.

Put bluntly, Miller leaves insufficient room for the novel's interest in disaffection. Assuming that the characters' bids for autonomy are only briefly warranted, he supports the novel's facile conclusion, which jars with its early pronouncements on the characters' solipsism. Because of Dickens's model of thwarted intersubjectivity, that is, they're *unable* to form such ties, rather than merely *disinclined* to do so. Compare this with Miller's point: "There is no help for it," he claims, referring to Nadgett the spy, an early incarnation of Detective Bucket in *Bleak House*. "Each man must seek some kind of direct relationship to other people, a relationship which recognizes the fact of their consciousness, and makes it an integral part of the structure of his own inherence in the world" (127). The imperative in this sentence is odd, given Miller's cogent argument, four pages earlier, about instinctive avoidance. Nevertheless, he concludes that the characters try to cultivate "authentic individuality," healing their self-division and the community's flagrant vices (139).

There is, I contend, "help for it," but only if we're prepared to view "help" as strong opposition to the noxious effects of "family forces" (*Chuzzlewit* 105). Impressive as a type of ideal, Miller's argument downplays that language and satire hamper "authentic individuality"; and he simplifies Dickens's acute understanding of characters' unconscious aspirations, whereby, at least in fantasy, "inherence in the world" obtains not by emulating Tom Pinch, as Miller noted, but by triumphing over one's enemies, even shockingly—as in Jonas Chuzzlewit's case—by trying to kill one's father.

Let me stress, once more, that although Dickens traverses this fantasy, he doesn't tolerate its outcome. Indeed, he condemns such extremes

FIGURE 2.3 *Our Next-Door Neighbours.*
George Cruikshank. *Sketches by Boz: Every-Day Life and
Every-Day People* by Charles Dickens (London, 1836–37 ed.).
Courtesy the University of Wisconsin–Madison Special Collections.

when he might have harnessed Jonas's hatred by depicting milder forms of antisocial behavior. In the opening chapters of *Chuzzlewit*, for example, the desire for autarky is for the novel one of few viable paths to survival. Subjectivity, the narrator implies, is so precarious—so vulnerable to assault from predatory relatives—that we should view it as a defensive war against the world. According to this model, which Dickens develops in later works, antisocial sentiment is understandable, though not exactly desirable. Friendship and love occur—if at all—only after this elemental battle has taken place. The following section represents this battle by taking a brief but necessary detour through the work of Dostoyevsky, one of Dickens's near-contemporaries and brilliant readers.

The Antihero

Though *Nicholas Nickleby* and *The Pickwick Papers* appeared in Russian in 1840 (*Oliver Twist* and *Barnaby Rudge* followed the next year, and *Chuzzlewit* in 1844), Dickens secured his reputation in Russia with the translation, in mid-1847, of *Dombey and Son*. As many critics have observed, he had a profound effect on Tolstoy, Gogol, Belinsky, and Dostoyevsky (born nine years after Dickens), who saw in his accounts of society a fascinating oscillation between restoration and disintegration.[30] During the five years that Dostoyevsky spent in penal servitude in Siberia for his limited role in the Petrashevsky circle, a group comprising radical idealists opposed to the czar, he read *David Copperfield* and *The Pickwick Papers* in Russian. Twenty years later, having published *The Insulted and Injured* and *The House of the Dead* and traveled to Paris and London, he wrote *Notes from Underground*, often viewed simplistically as the gateway to such mature works as *Crime and Punishment* and *The Brothers Karamazov.*[31]

"I am a sick man. . . . I am a spiteful man. I am an unpleasant man."[32] With these words, Dostoyevsky's friendless cynic recounts how, as a civil servant, he loved exhibiting "supreme nastiness" (16). "When people used to come to the desk where I sat, asking for information, I snarled at them, and was hugely delighted when I succeeded in hurting somebody's feelings. I almost always did succeed" (15). But the narrator's self-evaluation isn't reliable. Apparently, he lies to us "out of spite" when supplying this opening anecdote: "I was simply playing a game with [these] callers; in reality I never could make myself malevolent" (16).

The narrator lacks the will, apparently, to retaliate when others wrong him, yet he can't resign himself entirely to inaction. His life consists in alternately splenetic and voluptuous forms of self-torment, rendering him abject (17). Evincing a "morbid irritability" stemming partly from his unexpressed hatred of others, he "resentfully sulk[s] in the background," seething to himself (51, 52).

Too pure a hatred of others apparently would rob Dostoyevsky's antihero of the pleasure of self-recrimination, generating a type of grandiose contempt for others that he would find nauseating. Yet for many years he has "carried on a campaign" against an officer, an enemy he can't intimidate. This begins one evening when the officer, finding the dejected narrator in his way, takes him by the shoulders and lifts him aside, as if he were "an insect" (52). Although the narrator claims he's recklessly courageous, this time he is stymied, humiliated.

The resentment flourishes for want of an outlet. The narrator composes a story slandering the officer, but when a journal rejects it, the author's "rage positively choke[s]" him (54). He writes a letter begging the officer to apologize for his rudeness, but challenging him to a duel if he refuses. The narrator tells these details self-mockingly, yet similar pique mushrooms into attempted murder in Dickens's *Our Mutual Friend*, published the same year, when Eugene Wrayburn scorns Bradley Headstone's accomplishment in becoming a teacher. Wrayburn survives Headstone's later attempt on his life, but Headstone is so deranged by this point that he finally kills himself and Rogue Riderhood. Though Dostoyevsky's narrator keeps a fraction more perspective, he writhes in torment whenever the officer brushes him aside. After years of self-rebuke, he exults one day when they squarely collide, the narrator refusing to yield. The officer walks on, scarcely noticing, but the narrator "return[s] home completely vindicated. I was delighted. I sang triumphant arias from Italian operas" (58).

This well-known anecdote is relevant for understanding not only Dostoyevsky's and Dickens's work, but also all arguments about hatred and civility in this book. As my introduction explained, the anecdote gives Dostoyevsky's narrator a rationale for asking, "Can man's interests be correctly calculated?" (30). After referring to such satisfactions as wealth, freedom, and prosperity, he notices that philosophers omit from consideration another impulse, a "prompting of something inside [ourselves] that is stronger than all [our] self-interest" (30).

Neglecting this satisfaction apparently nullifies the above elements of pleasure, rendering them "nothing but sophistry" (31). Indeed, in a move anticipating Freud and Jacques Lacan, the narrator highlights a form of counterintuitive enjoyment that's satisfying in proportion to the ontological damage it causes.[33] "The point is not in a play on words," he insists, "but in the fact that this ['irrational'] good . . . upset[s] all our classifications[,] . . . always destroying the systems established by lovers of humanity for the happiness of mankind. In short, it interferes with everything" (31).

Dostoyevsky's interest in what "destroys" utilitarianism and related social arrangements parallels Dickens's depsychologizing account of malefactors, twinning radical opposition to society with an equally extreme capacity for self- and collective harm. As this satisfaction has quasi-revolutionary effects in Dostoyevsky's novella, whose punning title positions the iconoclastic and misanthropic somewhere "beneath" normalcy (*podpo'lie*, "underground," can mean dissidence, shelter from social harm, and death),[34] I'll advance this parallel briefly in implicit commentary on Dickens's contemporaneous work.

In a move influencing aspects of Western literature and philosophy, Dostoyevsky's narrator views the decision to pursue this satisfaction as inimical to culture and custom:

> It is indeed possible, and sometimes *positively imperative* (in my view), to act directly contrary to one's own best interests. One's own free and unfettered volition, one's own caprice, however wild, one's own fancy, inflamed sometimes to the point of madness—*that is the one best and greatest good*, which is never taken into consideration because it will not fit into any classification, and the omission of which always sends all systems and theories to the devil. (33–34; second emphasis mine)

In short, Dostoyevsky's narrator establishes an ethical relation to the unconscious, which in its indifference to Victorian culture's staid precepts frees individuals from frequently unjust social imperatives. Yet while it's difficult to exaggerate the influence of these well-known claims on subsequent forms of nihilism, existentialism, and radical psychoanalysis,[35] it's necessary to assess the relative strength of these antisocial impulses as they recur in contemporaneous Victorian fiction. As the next two sections show, such writing may lack the philosophical clarity of Dostoyevsky's remarkable novella, but it sometimes depicted comparable scenes and arguments with equal intensity.

Dickens and Disaffection

"I am a disappointed drudge," explains Sydney Carton, in *A Tale of Two Cities*. "I care for no man on earth, and no man on earth cares for me."[36] Though lacking the edginess of Dostoyevsky's antihero (whom he uncannily echoes), Dickens's protagonist points similarly to a gap between individual drives and socially sanctioned pleasures, such that the former exceed the latter, leaking into more-complex terrain. For much of the novel Carton is almost immobilized by ennui, his nightly drinking confirming an apparently unshakable morbidity. Love for Lucie Manette shatters his complacency, generating a desire for self-sacrifice, but under conditions that ordinarily would spawn greater futility: She's all but engaged to Charles Darnay, whom she eventually marries. Instead of despairing that his love is largely unrequited, however, Carton awaits a chance to confirm Lucie's estimation of him. The moment comes when, resembling the imprisoned Darnay, he substitutes himself for the condemned man and sacrifices himself in what Dickens calls "an act of divine justice."[37]

Although *A Tale* portrays this moment as valiant, my summary of the novel highlights a psychological paradox that other works by Dickens—chiefly *Chuzzlewit* and *Our Mutual Friend*—put more skeptically. Love in *A Tale* is more an extension of egoism than a means of voiding it. The pleasure of self-sacrifice is necessarily—though not exclusively—self-serving. Carton doubtless secures an honorable reputation for posterity and makes an undeniable difference to Darnay and Lucie, but as he's "half in love with easeful Death," in Keats's phrase, Lucie is partly a sublime means of fulfilling his destiny.[38] In this ambiguous light, she's a prop for a mission half perceived—Carton's well-documented desire for self-dissolution—rather than a means of aborting his purposelessness. "I have had unformed ideas of striving afresh, beginning anew, shaking off sloth and sensuality, and fighting out the abandoned fight," he tells her in a crucial passage. Yet even here his language is ambiguous, signaling a desire to break with the past ("beginning anew") by reconnecting with some unfinished business ("fighting out the abandoned fight").

"A dream, all a dream," he continues, "that ends in nothing, and leaves the sleeper where he lay down, but I wish you to know that you inspired it" (181). Unlike Macbeth, whom he partly echoes, Carton finds peace, not anguish, in annihilation. Since we can't isolate his drive to sympathy from this "dream," the material effects of sacrifice increase, rather than diminish, the satisfaction of the internal drama. Elements of Carton's altruism paradoxically extend his preexisting illusion, whereas the gratuitous rage of a character like Ralph Nickleby almost could succeed, in the earlier novel, in destroying this fantasy.

As at the end of *Chuzzlewit*, Dickens and many of his critics would defend Carton's illusion. Indeed, because the latter's self-sacrifice touches on heroism, it might seem wrongheaded to hint that a preceding commitment to death tarnishes valor with suicide. Still, Carton's—and the novel's—final words are inconclusive, binding with a semicolon two statements answering related but nonidentical aims (sacrifice and self-dissolution): "It is a far, far better thing that I do, than I have ever done; it is a far, far better rest that I go to than I have ever known" (404).

Starker outcomes in other Dickens novels implicitly comment on these permutations. In *Great Expectations*, Bentley Drummle's diffidence to humanity is in most respects identical to Carton's. Pip calls him "a sulky kind of fellow . . . proud, niggardly, reserved, and suspicious" (192, 203). Drummle exemplifies what I would call an aversion to—or even nondisposition for—sociability that runs throughout Dickens's work, which characters can't overcome by fiat. Accordingly, Drummle slinks around as if he were subhuman, even prehistoric:

He would always creep inshore like some uncomfortable amphibious creature, even when the tide would have sent him fast upon his way; and I always think of him as coming after us in the dark or by the back-water, when our own two boats were breaking the sunset or the moonlight in mid-stream. (203)

The analogy isn't gratuitous, as Drummle does indeed haunt Pip and menace his dreams. Winning the support of Jaggers, who christens him "the Spider," he marries Estella, casting both in marital hell until he's killed flogging a horse. But as Drummle temperamentally has much in common with Carton—for long stretches of time, both live under a "cloud of caring for nothing" (*A Tale* 179)—why does Dickens give them such different fates? Owing to their resemblance, Drummle might (like Carton) have found salvation in self-sacrifice; and Carton (like Drummle) could easily have maintained "a fixed despair of himself," remaining "silent and sullen and hang-dog" (180, 169). These comparisons point to a chiasmus in Dickens's work, extending the distinction in *Barnaby Rudge* between sentimental misanthropes and those whose hatred pushes them beyond redemption. Carton's misery opens a saving path to sympathy that Drummle's torment disables, even voids. Dickens intriguingly makes misanthropy worthy of sympathy in *A Tale*, but a precursor to complete embitterment and death in *Great Expectations*. As in previous works, then, but especially at this moment in his literary career, misanthropy is central to his fiction and its underlying philosophy, representing the fulcrum on which his conception of sociability turns.

Leaving Society

Although the passage from *Barnaby Rudge* with which I began this chapter underscores the importance of this fulcrum as Dickens established his career, hatred's effect on his communitarian spirit intensified in scope, shifting from lovelorn misanthropes, such as Carton, to "cold. . .-hearted" antiheroes like Drummle. In even later works, however, Dickens continued representing characters that hate humanity, but (in ways resembling Bulwer) tipped the emphasis toward wholesale indictments of societies, as corrupt forces violently overwhelm his solitary misfits.

As we saw earlier, signs of this tension appear in *Martin Chuzzlewit* and recur prominently in the later *Bleak House*, given Tulkinghorn's temperamental differences with the aptly named Lawrence Boythorn. But the tipping point in Dickens's fiction arguably is on the cusp of the 1850s and 1860s, when he published *A Tale of Two Cities* and *Great Expectations*. Hence, in the 1858 short story "Going into Society," a character's querulous relation to society finally devolves into a powerful narrative indictment of the latter. Though Chopski (Major Tpschoffki), an ambitious dwarf, tries entering "select" London Society to pass among the wealthy, his plans come to nothing: soon destitute, his fortune stolen, he returns to his former life "soured by his misfortuns [*sic*]."[39] According to him, Society performs the same circus tricks that he once cultivated, and knowing this brings his disaffection close to misanthropy: "They'll drill holes in your 'art, Magsman, like a Cullender," he tells his interlocutor, "and leave you to have your bones picked dry by Wultures, like the dead Wild Ass of the Prairies that you deserve to be!" (229–30).

Given its ambivalence about society—set off by Chopski's pun on *art* and *heart*—the story is also a precursor to *Our Mutual Friend*, a novel that in this respect is really Dickens's darkest work and crowning achievement.[40] The Veneerings, Podsnaps, and especially the Lammles epitomize the circus act that Chops dismisses. They're also endless recipients of Dickens's narrative contempt: Mrs. Podsnap displays a "quantity of bone, neck and nostrils like a rocking-horse," and Lady Tippins's throat has a "certain yellow play" that resembles "the legs of scratching poultry" (21, 23).

These de-anthropomorphizing comparisons recur throughout the novel, recalling earlier allusions to human vermin, cattle, hogs, monkeys, and spiders. Reversing the position of men and animals relative to culture and nature, such comparisons also gnaw at dignity. Whereas Dickens's early illustrator and (generally) close friend Cruikshank presented Victorian society as benign, industrious, and well regulated in his "British Bee Hive" (discussed in the introduction), his own analogies in *Our Mutual Friend* are consistently degrading. Comparing a "perfect piece of evil" like Rogue Riderhood to "a roused bird of prey," the novel tirelessly displays what is "half savage" about humanity (358, 14, 13).[41] Indeed, these comparisons are so noticeable—and unflattering— that one of Dickens's own characters alludes to them, as if imitating readerly discomfort, and recommends that they cease (98). They don't.

As these descriptions surpass the novel's real and false aristocracy, Dickens's satire of "Society" frequently balloons into a bitter indictment of all communities. When for instance Lightwood and Wrayburn visit London's Docklands to identify the drowned body of ostensibly John Harmon (actually George Radfoot), they pass "where accumulated scum of humanity seemed to be washed from higher grounds, like so much moral sewage, . . . pausing until its own weight forced it over the bank and sunk it in the river" (30). While the anger in this passage is unmistakable, its source is unclear (see FIGURE 2.4, a sketch adapting Richard Beard's daguerreotype *The Sewer-Hunter*). The judgment rests with the collective subject of "seemed," which potentially embraces the two diffident gentlemen, the "Society" with which they're often reluctantly associated, and even the narrator. The point is, we cannot be sure.

This generalized hostility may explain the narrator's allusions to "us smaller vermin" and the "crawling, creeping, fluttering, and buzzing creatures, attracted by the gold dust" of Noddy Boffin (118, 208). But the object to which *vermin* once referred (a villain like Rigaud) now refers to society in its entirety. Indeed, the ensuing elemental bestiary in *Our Mutual Friend* lies broadly between humanity and dust, the latter being in two senses the goal of life, as the novel reminds us with devastating irony. So, despite the narrator's bid to clean up—and even sublimate—Harmon's Dust Mounds, his preoccupation with slime, waste, and death helps erode an early nineteenth-century belief in perfectibility (see FIGURE 2.5, Thomson's photograph *Flying Dustmen*). Though it voices contempt for Wrayburn's eventual marriage to Lizzie Hexam, "Society" gorges on what Boffin's workers recover from old Harmon's Mounds.

Underscoring the irony of this perverse ecology, *Our Mutual Friend* forges a partnership of sorts between Mr. Venus and Silas Wegg, one of its antiheroes. Wegg is perhaps best known for combining egregious disloyalty with easy familiarity, even condescension, toward perfect strangers. Yet since his treachery fuses an impulse to appropriate others' lives (self-aggrandizement shielding him from recognition of his pathetic stature), his anticommunitarianism is more complicated than Quilp's or Rigaud's. Better integrated into society, he nicely represents its shameless duplicity and dark "plotting" (187).

FIGURE 2.4 *The Sewer-Hunter*. Richard Beard. Sketch made
from daguerreotype. *London Labour and the London Poor*, vol. 2,
The London Street-Folk, by Henry Mayhew (London, 1851).
Courtesy Northwestern University Library Special Collections.

Most characters in the novel are either as opportunistic as Wegg or as
desultory as Venus—indeed, by the end misanthropy tarnishes almost
everyone *but* the novel's now reformed "harmless misanthrope" (297).
Lizzie and Harmon go separately into hiding, the latter holding exemplary status as a wandering Cain, less despite than because of his inno-

FIGURE 2.5 *Flying Dustmen.* John Thomson.
Street Life in London (London, 1877–78). *Courtesy the Victoria
and Albert Museum, London.*

cence. "I have no clue to the scene of my death," he tells himself in a remarkable passage; a "spirit that was once a man could hardly feel
stranger or lonelier, going unrecognized among mankind, than I feel"
(360). The narrator calls this "communing with himself," something
other characters do, often unconsciously, at moments of profound despair and vulnerability (367). Besides Harmon's eventual marriage to
Bella, and Wrayburn and Lizzie's concluding love, this may be, remarkably, the closest the novel comes to nonantagonistic intimacy.

When Charley Hexam threatens to betray Headstone to the police, as
well, a "desolate air of utter and complete loneliness [falls] upon [the lat-
ter], like a visible shade" (692). Notwithstanding Wrayburn's joy in
goading him, an internal voice exacerbates Headstone's murderous consciousness more effectively than could any legal authority. Apparently,

Headstone "irritated [his condition], with a kind of perverse pleasure akin to that which a sick man sometimes has in irritating a wound upon his body" (535). Such Dostoyevskian insights recur frequently in the novel, underscoring Dickens's break with Bentham, for whom psychic negativity was illogical and socially irresponsible. Moreover, despite his solitary existence as a reclusive lock-keeper, Riderhood paradoxically is anything but alone. When asleep, he experiences "an angry stare and growl, as if, in the absence of any one else, he had aggressive inclinations towards himself" (617).[42] These inclinations surpass extreme guilt and self-recrimination, and thus—as I argued earlier—conventional forms of psychology, the narrator emphasizing that "nothing in nature tapped" this character (617). Still, remarkably, when Riderhood is brought back from the brink of death, the narrator calls his resistance to life *un*exceptional. "Like us all, every day of our lives when we wake," the narrator admits, "he is instinctively unwilling to be restored to the consciousness of this existence, and would be left dormant, if he could" (440). Our commitment to death and contempt for consciousness are stronger than our interest in life (an idea Browning develops), and this outcome collapses most ontological distinctions between Dickens's "waterside character" and us. Self-extinction may be our ultimate goal, but even paltry company in this novel is preferable to facing our conscience. Society, however, has other concerns.

Our Mutual Friend's most thoughtful sign of this tension is so subtle it's likely to wrong-foot us: Wrayburn realizes that his marriage to Lizzie is incompatible with his continuing participation in Society.[43] Although his choosing love would bolster sentiment in an earlier Dickens novel, Wrayburn makes this decision solemnly, weighing and then rejecting what membership in Society entails. Considering the novel's interest in ubiquitous hatred, significantly neither its antihero nor its reformed misanthrope voices the intelligent disdain concluding Dickens's last complete novel; instead, one of its erstwhile citizens does so. "But it cannot have been Society that disturbed you," Lizzie cautions. Wrayburn gently corrects her: "I rather think it *was* Society though!" (792).

CHAPTER THREE

Charlotte Brontë on the Pleasure of Hating

Reader! when you behold an aspect for whose constant gloom and frown you cannot account, whose unvarying cloud exasperates you by its apparent causelessness, be sure that there is a canker somewhere, and a canker not the less deeply corroding because concealed.
—Brontë, *Shirley*

Passionate Antipathy

WHETHER CONCEALED OR EXPLOSIVELY MANIFEST, hatred underwrites citizenship in Charlotte Brontë's fiction. None of her protagonists discovers what it means to be sociable without feeling "an almost insuperable repugnance" for other people.[1] Such aversion surpasses interpersonal conflict, proving endemic to her fictional communities. And though the moral education of countless Victorian protagonists lies in their renouncing such extreme feeling, few novelists of the time state so eloquently or stubbornly that our obligations to others are a burden we long—but generally fail—to relinquish. Representing aggression as inseparable from society, Brontë intensified the demands that many nineteenth-century characters endure when living with distant, sometimes heartless relatives—a common trope from the eighteenth century that, as we've seen, Bulwer and Dickens helped popularize in the nineteenth. Since Brontë's protagonists suffer greater hardships while holding tenaciously to their principles, their struggle with renunciation is more traumatic and socially revealing.

Although it's now commonplace to say Brontë used "abnegation of self" to both radical and conservative effect, few critics have addressed her novels' preoccupation with hatred or claimed that this trait determines her characters' relation to the world.[2] Highlighting instead the obstacles thwarting these protagonists, critics more often turn her fiction into a form of protest while finding ways to reconcile her heroines to women's limited opportunities. This curtails Brontë's interest in hostility, viewing her work as redemptive in aim and merely a therapeutic extension of her life. Such perspectives tether art to biography, asking that we resolve the enigmas of Brontë's fiction by invoking what Sandra Gilbert and Susan Gubar have called the "oscillation between overtly 'angelic' dogma and covertly Satanic fury that would mark the whole of her professional literary career."[3] Inspired by this approach, critical debate seesawed for years between Brontë's transgressive impulses and containment strategies, without coming to rest on either.

In *Repression in Victorian Fiction*, John Kucich appeared to break the ensuing deadlock, arguing that Brontë often viewed repression expansively, turning self-control to her characters' advantage. "The fluid structure of Brontëan desire," he wrote, "has as its end an emotional destabilization that thrives on this ambiguous conjunction" between expression and repression. One of Kucich's interests is Brontë's "positive relationship to interpersonal or social power," yet he surprisingly joined historicists in claiming that she ultimately tried to "empty" sexual relations of "social content," placing all "patterns of relationship in her fiction . . . transparently . . . within a solipsistic dynamic of desire."[4] This emphasis accepts the Romantic strain of individualism flourishing as hatred in Brontë's novels, but it sequesters her protagonists. The hostility that Kucich views as productive self-antagonism, given its antirepressive character, also turns the aggression of Brontë's protagonists into politically impotent rage.

Brontë is adept at explaining why her protagonists try to shun other people. Neighbors in her fiction are frequently real or potential enemies who thwart happiness more often than they encourage it. Moreover, her novels are haunted—sometimes overwhelmed—by forms of enmity that are surplus to society and irreducible to political causes. Kucich is thus slightly at odds with Brontë when claiming that "her angle of vision always returns to the narrow sphere of the personal and romantic" (39). His argument about Brontë's "pretensions to social commentary" ironically reinforces the myth of stubborn individualism adhering so easily to all the Brontës, ridding their works of context while turning their characters into model outcasts. While in this respect Brontë studies has yet to escape the transgression-containment deadlock, the fiction itself points in another direction.

Charlotte Brontë's initial descriptions of hatred in *Shirley* develop from *Jane Eyre* and *The Professor* a perspective on the rift impeding an individual's full incorporation into society. But because her account of misanthropy is not exclusively Romantic and frees hatred from murder and suicide, her fiction breaks conceptually with her sister's emphasis in *Wuthering Heights*, where the phrase "a perfect misanthropist's Heaven," appearing in its opening paragraph, sets the scene for Heathcliff's and Hindley Earnshaw's near-limitless rancor.[5] Unfettered hatred also circulates in Charlotte Brontë's novels as resentment and passionate antipathy. Failing repeatedly to truncate this affect, her plots also make clear that aggression is a permanent feature of her imaginary societies.

This tension between hatred's expression and curtailment is intriguing, leaving us to establish whether it implies retreat from the world, direct confrontation with it, or a partial break with the conventional bonds representing membership in it. As Brontë's notion of citizenship is frequently inseparable from aggression, freedom logically consists in her protagonists' spurning their neighbors. Because her invocations of personal duty modify her protagonists' troubled relation to their communities, moreover, Brontë sometimes implies that these characters would be happiest if they could dissolve their ties completely. Before I amplify these claims in close readings of *Shirley* and *Villette*, let me briefly discuss the prominence of hatred in Brontë's earlier work.

Assessing the heroine Jane Eyre in 1848, the *Christian Remembrancer* opined, "Never was there a better hater." The journal then tried to sum up Brontë's argument: "All self-denial is but deeper selfishness."[6] The assessment isn't entirely wrong. Two-thirds through the novel, Jane calls herself an "outcast . . . who from man could anticipate only mistrust, rejection, [and] insult"; and she endures forms of peculiar glee from Mr. Brocklehurst and Mrs. Reed, the latter taking her irrational hatred of Jane to the grave.[7] Many critics add that Jane's marriage to Rochester is far from a triumphant substitution of harmony for conflict. According to Nina Auerbach, it is "less a synthesis of the two worlds [passion and reason, Nature and Calvinism, and so on] than a partial conquest of one world by the other."[8]

Though Brontë critics often represent *Villette*, her last novel, as both a retreat from the world and a sublime fulfillment of the hostility surfacing in *Jane Eyre*, the idea of a "partial conquest" complicates any suggestion that a neat developmental line joins these novels. Indeed, to posit this line is to ignore *Shirley*, which comes between them, and *The Professor* (formerly "The Master," published posthumously in 1857), which Brontë wrote first, in 1846. As William Crimsworth recounts his upbringing at the start of *The Professor*, in an unanswered letter to an "old school acquaintance" to whom he professes no affection, his description of family life is littered with phrases such as "mutual disgust," "determined enmity," "persevering hostility," "gratuitous menace," and "symptom[s] of contumacity."[9] Because of the "irreparable breach" separating Crimsworth from his uncles, after his father's death he decides to ask his brother, Edward, for financial assistance, trying thereafter to live without betraying "the sense of insult and treachery [that] lived in me like a kindling, though as yet smothered coal" (141).

"In the peculiar centrifugal prose of [Crimsworth's] story," writes Heather Glen in a valuable introduction to the novel, "self itself appears to be held together by violence."[10] While this point is almost indisputable, it applies to most of Brontë's works. In *Shirley*, for instance, violence governs—indeed, characterizes—the novel's interest in group bonds. Surpassing *The Professor*, *Shirley* does more than interrupt the reputed continuity between *Jane Eyre* and *Villette*; for significant reasons the novel fails to limit hatred to the private realm. *Shirley*'s conception of interiority and exteriority makes this restriction impossible, thereby signaling Brontë's thoughtful political intervention.

Whenever *Shirley* voices a generic hatred of people—and it does so frequently—a rift develops between the novel's public and private realms. Instead of providing an overarching explanation for the conflicts arising in each register, the novel uses misanthropy to expose their arbitrary and perhaps insoluble design.[11] *Shirley* tries halfheartedly to re-

solve the political strife and communal hatred accompanying the Luddite revolts in 1811 and 1812, harmonizing what Brontë—following
Thackeray—called "the warped system of things."[12] But the opening
chapters set in motion a chain of events the narrator cannot curtail without manipulation and cant. Indeed, the scope of hatred in *Shirley* logically belies a tidy ending. As the narrator declares in the second chapter,
"The throes of a sort of moral earthquake were felt heaving under the
hills of the northern counties. But, as is usual in such cases, nobody took
much notice" (62).

Misanthropy is a part of this "moral earthquake," as it raises profound
questions about the characters' responsibility to others, and is the vehicle by which the narrator pushes awkwardly for emotional and political
reform. *Shirley*'s bid to make Robert Gérard Moore a better landowner
and employer accompanies Caroline Helstone's efforts to determine
whether he has enough sympathy to be a viable husband. One can't be a
good husband, the novel implies, while despising one's workforce. (*Villette* is more provocative in suggesting otherwise; M. Paul is adept at
pursuing Lucy Snowe while raging at his colleagues and pupils.) To this
extent, Moore's increasing generosity toward his employees proceeds
hand in hand with the discovery of his love for Caroline. "I have seen
the necessity of doing good," he says sententiously in "The Winding-
Up," the ambiguously titled final chapter; "I have learned the downright
folly of being selfish" (597). With almost parodic simplicity, the novel
implies that social reform obtains from this change of heart, and it does
so in language almost as mechanical as the mill consolidating Robert and
Caroline's future wealth: "Now, I can take more workmen; give better
wages; lay wiser and more liberal plans; do some good; be less selfish:
now, Caroline, I can have a house—a home which I can truly call
mine—and *now*—" [. . .] "And *now*," he resumed—"now I can think of
marriage; *now* I can seek a wife" (594; original emphases).[13] Though
Moore could almost be parroting social expectations here, the novel's interest in hatred clashes conceptually and rhetorically with his plans.

With its great stress on reform, *Shirley* superficially echoes countless
Regency, Georgian, and mid-Victorian novels—notably Bulwer's *Pelham* and Thackeray's *Pendennis*—that style marriage as an effect of acquired altruism and public munificence. The moral equivalent of

Austen's *Emma* for men, these novels view diminished selfishness as an axiom of personal maturity. This isn't to ignore the narrative violence involved in forging this equivalence; the publication history and countless revisions of *Pelham* alone indicate the cultural forces shaping, perhaps manipulating, such reform. But *Shirley* is more complicated, its earliest pronouncements on marriage and anticommunitarianism sufficiently bleak to undermine subsequent efforts at personal and political reform, thus anticipating *Villette*'s complex antisocial impulses. "If there is one notion I hate more than another," proclaims Malone in chapter 2, "it is that of marriage: I mean marriage in the vulgar weak sense, as a mere matter of sentiment; two beggarly fools agreeing to unite their indigence by some fantastic tie of feeling—humbug!" (56). While at the end of *Jane Eyre* Jane views marriage as a type of compromise formation stitching Rochester and her into a larger social fabric, the same gesture is really an empty promise in *Villette* and it carries a cynical edge in *Shirley*, serving almost as a parody of the two weddings that conclude Austen's *Pride and Prejudice* and *Sense and Sensibility*.

Despite sounding some of the anger reverberating in *Jane Eyre*, *Shirley* (first titled "Hollow's Mill") often frames this sentiment as political strife subject to personal bias. The novel thereby highlights forms of antipathy surpassing its interest in the Luddite revolts. These resulted from the Orders of Council, an economic blockade against Napoleon, and the mill owners' drive to mechanize at the expense of their labor force. But the novel's interest in antagonism exceeds this context: Characters in *Shirley* sustain only transitory relationships to their love objects, underscoring powerfully their isolation, especially when trying to establish reciprocal affection and strong social ties. When the novel stages a double wedding, the plot therefore feels contrived, untrue.

Considering this tension, G. H. Lewes was surely right to lament that in *Shirley* "all unity, in consequence of defective art, is wanting. . . . The authoress never seems distinctly to have made up her mind as to what she was to do; whether to describe the habits and manners of Yorkshire and its social aspects in the days of King Lud, or to paint a character, or to tell a love story. All are by turns attempted and abandoned."[14] Lewes meant the observation as a rebuke, and Brontë certainly took it as one, responding tartly: "I can be on my guard against my enemies, but God

deliver me from my friends!" But Lewes underscored her formal difficulties in connecting "Yorkshire," "character," and "a love story."
"*Shirley* cannot be received as a work of art," he insisted; it is "faulty,"
"unnatural," a "curious anomal[y]."[15]

Though many critics acknowledge the novel is less compelling than
Jane Eyre and *Villette*, there's no real consensus as to why. Some conclude that Brontë eschewed harmony and conveyed society in fragments, so as better to record its political turbulence. One thing is clear:
The novel creates this effect when trying to make political strife dove-
tail with its marriage plot.[16] As Lyndall Gordon observes, "The workers' attack on [Moore's] mill . . . is seen from the perspective of two
women [Shirley Keeldar and Caroline] hiding themselves at a distance
from the action, and this comes to be the perspective of the novel as a
whole."[17] Disconcertingly, the novel refracts political turmoil through
realms, like "privacy" and female consciousness, that ostensibly had
nothing in common with this strife.

Shirley's diffusion also stems from its lack of a single protagonist, the
formal repercussions of which become clear when the novel ends. The
narrator's oddly laconic conclusion makes little effort to bind the marriage plot with the hatred flourishing in the opening chapters. For instance, her suggesting that the reader supply the right moral exacerbates
her noncommittal statement "I suppose Robert Moore's prophecies"
about the end of the blockage against Napoleon and the consequent rise
in trade "were, partially, at least, fulfilled" (599). The conclusion tries to
show that people's plans mesh with political events, but the narrator
can't resist suggesting that the results are entirely satisfactory to no one.
With this "partial . . . fulfil[ment]," some gratification is wanting, implying that the marriage plots are neither reducible to personal harmony
nor especially congenial to a society that at times seems indifferent to
such ritualized bonding. *Shirley*'s feminism even hints that marriage extends the novel's fascination with enmity. Antisocial impulses, we might
say, have a palpable, resilient life in this novel.

Most important, Brontë's unique turn to third-person narrative in
Shirley clashes with the novel's unusual method of undermining objectivity. The narrator often weakens the external point of view, thereby
augmenting the novel's vacillation between inward and outward life.

When describing the Yorke family, for example, she destroys its fragile domestic harmony by whisking us forward twenty years and telling us, bluntly, that one of the Yorkes' daughters will die young. "Mr. Yorke," interrupts the narrator, asking a rhetorical question the reader alone hears: "If a magic mirror were now held before you, and if therein were shown you your two daughters as they will be twenty years from this night, what would you think? The magic mirror is here: you shall learn their destinies—and first that of your little life, Jessy" (167). In Hardyan fashion, Yorke is next seen visiting Jessy's grave, before witnessing the "virgin solitude" to which his other daughter, Rosie, apparently has emigrated. "Will she ever come back?" the narrator asks almost tauntingly (168). But Yorke never leaves his living room; the reader alone travels in this peculiar time machine. The narrative snaps back to the present with an abrupt knock at the door, leaving Yorke none the wiser about the future and the reader sensitive to the heartless vagaries or facile logic by which the narrator arranges her characters' fates. At such moments, the narrator not only questions providentialist belief, but also makes clear that nature and society—indifferent to the plight of individuals— aren't entities in which we find lasting happiness.

Branwell, Emily, and Anne Brontë were alive when Charlotte Brontë began composing *Shirley*, in the summer of 1848. By the time she'd completed the second volume, however, all three siblings had died—Branwell suddenly, and Emily and Anne over the course of several months, during which Charlotte "effaced for the time [her] literary character" and nursed both sisters.[18] After Anne died in May 1849, Brontë began composing the novel's third volume, adding countless allusions to suffering and grief. According to its author, completing the novel was painful but helpful, a temporary defense against loss. But even in this extreme instance, biographical details do not have complete explanatory power. *Shirley* sounds a powerful conflict in society, and the resulting hostility throws every citizen into radical isolation. Gordon put this well when noting that Caroline's unspoken love for Moore "festers in a stagnant existence. . . . The explosiveness of the book is not primarily the actual attack on the mill, the broken windows, and the wounded; it ferments in the destructive force of feeling that may not be stated."[19] This is surely why Caroline tells Shirley that love "is so tormenting, so rack-ing it burns away our strength with its flame" (265). Still, according to this insight, women see more acutely into social "system[s]" than do the men who attribute to them "soft blindness." "The most downcast glance has its loophole," the narrator adds, "through which it can, on occasion, take its sentinel-survey of life" (273).[20]

What acute observers see at such moments is a form of hatred that, despite springing up between individuals, isn't limited to them. *Shirley* dwells obsessively on the way this hatred not only impedes contact but also is a pretext for it, as if the conditions promoting intersubjectivity, and thus sociability, were in the novel inseparable from a desire to destroy all remaining chances of communication. "Misery generates hate," the narrator insists, referring to the unemployed weavers' limitless contempt for the ruthless mill owners (62).[21] When violence ensues and Moore's frames are broken, he and Helstone determine "with a sense of warlike excitement" to "hunt down [the] vermin" and "punish the miscreants" (63, 73, 57). The cycle of vengeance turns full circle, ending only when Moore—discovering goodwill in the final chapters—declines redress for the bullet that almost kills him.[22]

But the primary cause of this violence remains enigmatic, unfathomable—a strange circumstance, especially in a Condition-of-England novel. *Shirley* invokes all the likely factors: the workers' desperate poverty and hunger; Moore's haughty contempt for their plight; his "scorn of low enemies, [and] . . . resolution not 'to truckle to the mob'" (118); the fear of competition goading him relentlessly; and even his contempt for Tory nationalism, owing partly to his half-Belgian origins. However, the novel can't settle on a single answer and finds all such factors wanting. *Shirley* discredits the Luddites' opposition to economic "progress," for example, while sharply criticizing bourgeois values.[23]

The novel thereby echoes the "Gospel of Mammonism," which Carlyle published six years earlier, in *Past and Present*: "We call it a Society; and go about professing openly the totalest separation, isolation. Our life is not a mutual helpfulness; but rather, cloaked under due laws-of-war, named 'fair competition' and so forth, it is a mutual hostility" (see FIGURE 3.1).[24]

To some, Brontë's quandary about establishing the real cause of violence betrays her political bias. E. P. Thompson wasn't alone in claiming that the novel, voicing a jaundiced vision of Luddism, is really "a true ex-

FIGURE 3.1 *Thomas Carlyle "Like a Block of Michelangelo's Sculpture"* (1867). Julia Margaret Cameron. Albumen print.
Courtesy the Science and Society Picture Library, London.

pression of the middle-class myth" of the phenomenon.[25] Certainly, the narrator distorts history and diminishes the Luddites' credibility when representing their constituency as "chiefly 'downdraughts,' bankrupts, men always in debt and often in drink—men who had nothing to lose, and much—in the way of character, cash, and cleanliness—to gain" (370). Statements like these help exonerate Moore's desire for retribution (he "hunted . . . these persons . . . like any sleuth-hound" [370]), before representing his abstaining from full revenge as heroic self-restraint. Indeed, all the likely causes of political strife—poverty, hunger, resentment at Moore's profit motive, the gentry's and manufacturers' cavalier disregard for the country's staggering inequalities—warranted mass rebellion, especially during a period unlikely to yield reform or redress. Many of the dramatic insurrections taking place in April 1812 were food riots, designed to force down the prices of potatoes and bread.[26]

But one can't right this picture by alluding to Brontë's values, in part because the novel's vision of near-ubiquitous hatred belies any simple reform. Nor is it enough to celebrate the Luddites as casualties of progress struggling to correct injustice. The novel's account of conflict is more complex and intelligent, in part because it insists that the rationale for violence *always* exceeds the discernible and ineffable conditions provoking it.[27] In this respect, *Shirley* does more than condemn specific forms of violence, and it's worth considering this outcome even if one decides, as many have, that the novel is misleading historically. Arguably, Brontë's departure from conventional history doesn't invalidate her account of politics; it invites us to reflect more carefully on the way we view history and define especially sociality.

The narrator argues that some of the weavers—either blind or indifferent to retribution's long-term effects—find revenge more satisfying than justice. They're prepared to destroy all the renovated mills, and thus almost everyone's chances of employment, if they can bankrupt the manufacturers in the process. Thompson concedes that the novel is accurate in this regard, reproducing an anonymous letter from April 1812, whose writer states: "It is Not our Desire to Do you the Least Injury But We are fully Determin'd to Destroy Both Dressing Machines and Steam Looms Let *Who Will* be the Owners."[28] Given such threats, Moore's question to his workforce may be more searching than cavalier: "Suppose [the mill] was a ruin and I was a corpse, what then?—you lads behind these two scamps, would that stop invention and exhaust science?—Not for the fraction of a second of time! Another and better gig-mill would rise on the ruins of this, and perhaps a more enterprising owner come in my place" (156).

Shirley voices this counterargument neither to support progress at any cost nor to downplay the weavers' grievance, but to make justice compete with the weavers' powerful impulse to destroy the community entirely. The logical corollary of justice here is organized revolt, and the narrator identifies William Farren as its sober representative, "a very honest man, without envy or hatred" (157). As the novel's earlier chapters made clear, however, "endurance, overgoaded, [had] stretched the hand of fraternity to sedition," and *Shirley* explores the extension of this crisis into potential anarchy without dismissing the weavers' anger (62). George Eliot arguably strives for similar effect in *Felix Holt* when her narrator claims, during the novel's riot scene, "Mingled with the more headstrong and half-drunken crowd . . . were some sharp-visaged men who loved the 'irrationality' of riots for something else than its own sake."[29] Although Eliot and Brontë gave this "irrationality" a face bordering on caricature, this doesn't obscure their larger point: In both novels, destruction is as frequently explained by casuistry as by injustice, promoting riot as an activity that invariably comes at the expense of class interest.

Moses Barraclough, a "scamp and hypocrite" in *Shirley*, typifies this corruption of ethical politics into anarchy (46). His very appearance displays the type of antisocial will that Dickens would give Silas Wegg and Eliot would provide John Raffles. Moses—named with keen irony a false prophet—is "distinguished no less by his demure face and cat-like, trustless eyes, than by a wooden leg and stout crutch: there was a kind of leer about his lips, he seemed laughing in his sleeve at some person or thing, his whole air was anything but that of a true man" (153).[30] His misanthropic uninterest in others sours communitarian sentiment, in ways complicating—without discrediting—radical politics.[31] "I'm a very feeling man," he insists, "and when I see my brethren oppressed like my great namesake of old, I stand up for 'em" (155). Brontë's narrator uses this cant to puncture the vision of bucolic paradise that Carlyle, Disraeli, *and* the Luddites invoked as idealized "customs and paternalist legislation":[32] "Or iver you set up the pole o' your tent amang us, Mr Moore, we lived i' peace and quietness; yea, I may say, in all loving-kindness" (155).

Because it distrusts these claims about social harmony, *Shirley* undermines all such myths about communities (including bourgeois ones), thereby veering uncannily close to Barraclough's antisocial impulses. The novel arguably can't define group ideals without identifying a type of misanthropy capable of thwarting them. Granted, the novel stops short of this full undertaking, trying ultimately to narrow the gap between Moore and Farren by recommending that the former treat the latter fairly. But it does so indicating that the cycle of revenge spawns a disturbing economy of its own, whose enjoyment far outweighs productive gains in wealth, thereby crippling any real sense of closure. Moore discovers that the "excitement" he obtains from seeking redress "was of a kind pleasant to his nature: he liked it better than making cloth" (370). Barraclough's followers discover too that attacking Moore "rouse[s] . . . the fighting animal" in all of them (336). As violence exceeds rational causes in this novel, the narrator—pronouncing frequently on human cruelty—seems at a loss to explain its effects. Even Farren admits, "Human natur', taking it i' th' lump, is naught but selfishness" (320). Still, "the aftertaste of the battle" reveals "death and pain replacing excitement and exertion," and Shirley tries "to prevent" such discord, as if she and other women in the novel must ward off this ecstatic bid for victory at any cost (338).

Moore and Caroline confront these impulses in a chapter appropriately called "Coriolanus," when trying to establish why the Roman patrician was banished by his erstwhile admirers. "And what was his fault? What made him hated by the citizens? What caused him to be banished by his countrymen?" asks Moore, before the "battle" in *Shirley* takes place (117). As he reads Shakespeare's tragedy aloud, Caroline insists that Moore "sympathize[s] with that proud patrician who does not sympathize with his famished fellow-men, and insults them" (116). Brontë's narrator clearly means us to learn a historical lesson from this comparison. Yet the recurrence of humiliation—owing perhaps to hubris, "soaring insolence," and what Aufidius calls Coriolanus's "defect of judgement"—suggests that history is blind to cause, offering a lesson about repetition only.[33] Although resentment is situated firmly in history, with most citizens vowing to kill Caius Martius "in hunger for bread, not in thirst for revenge" (1.1.23–24), a point that Brontë partly echoes, the citizens voice sentiments reaching beyond their immediate circumstances, allowing Moore to "revel in the large picture of human nature" that partly escapes the context of ancient Rome and Victorian England (116).[34] With Brontë's female protagonists, we're invited to take this "sentinel-survey of life," in hopes that we too will find an antidote to hatred (273). But the results promise little in the way of resolution, advancing only Moore's flimsy ideals: "I can take more workmen; give better wages; lay wiser and more liberal plans; do some good; be less selfish: . . . I can have a house . . . [and] I can think of marriage" (594).

In *Character of Shakespear's Plays* [*sic*], William Hazlitt, also offering an extended reading of *Coriolanus*'s "large picture," said what many will find unacceptable: Pleasure obtains from power over others. "The whole dramatic moral" of the play, he argued, "is that those who have little shall have less, and that those who have much shall take all that others have left."[35] Hazlitt's book appeared during the years concerning Brontë in *Shirley*, and as she gratefully admitted to William Smith Williams—her first supporter at Smith, Elder, and a friend of Hazlitt's—she read his essays with keen interest.[36] However, Shakespeare's play intrigues Hazlitt for more than its relevance for his own troubled times. According to Hazlitt, *Coriolanus* voices the stark idea that "the insolence of power is stronger than the plea of necessity" (215). This apparently is the reason Coriolanus's loyalty turns on a dime, and why he makes "a plea for enslaving" his own country (215). Indeed, this moment of betrayal—piquant, because it follows a celebration of Coriolanus's allegiance—points up the rancor that fascinated Brontë. She recoiled from Hazlitt's conclusion, however, separating Moore from his propensity to copy Coriolanus, and thereby improbably converting his contempt for others into a hazy notion of sociability. But Hazlitt did not recoil, instead giving full rein to this misanthropic fantasy:

> This is the logic of the imagination and the passions; which seek to aggrandize what excites admiration and to heap contempt on misery, to raise power into tyranny, and to make tyranny absolute; to thrust down that which is low still lower, and to make wretches desperate: to exalt magistrates into kings, kings into gods; to degrade subjects to the rank of slaves, and slaves to the condition of brutes. . . . We may depend upon it that what men delight to read in books, they will put in practice in reality. (216)

This conclusion departs from those who view art as a defense against cruelty, a way of protecting us from what we imagine we need to enact. In *The Scandal of Pleasure*, for example, Wendy Steiner argues compellingly against "the folly of [our] pervasive literalism." "The more practiced we are in fantasy," she writes, "the better we will master its difference from the real."[37] Hazlitt doesn't so much dispute this last claim about fantasy as show how our pleasure in art's "virtual" realm bleeds frequently into other registers. Our experience of art is so intoxicating, he implies, that we seek ways of replicating that excitement in public life. Fantasy propels us into the public sphere, and as it corrupts that sphere with possible fanaticism it erodes a distinction we struggle to maintain between public and private life. We preserve this struggle, Hazlitt argues in a final turn of the screw, because our protection from others depends upon it; our humiliation would otherwise give them exquisite joy. The satisfaction that we obtain from art must therefore also block any chance that we'll become objects of ridicule for other people: "The history of mankind is a romance, a mask, a tragedy," he says, "constructed upon the principles of *poetical justice*; it is a noble or royal hunt, in which what is sport to the few is death to the many, and in which the spectators halloo and encourage the strong to set upon the weak, and cry havoc in the chase though they do not share in the spoil" (216; original emphasis).

Given Hazlitt's spirited interpretation, much is clearly at stake when Moore reads Shakespeare's play and Caroline declares that he "sympathize[s] with that proud patrician who does not sympathize with his famished fellow-men" (116). Moore's identification with the Roman apparently overrides empathy for his own workers, requiring even that he scorn them. Brontë's logic here is Hazlittian, which may be one reason *Shirley* struggles so clumsily to overcome this antipathy, producing social identification devoid of aggression and stable ideals. The novel's concern to end Moore's misanthropy truncates the excitement that Hazlitt says is most infectious in art. Put another way, *Shirley*'s final, awkward bid for emotional and political reform betrays the excitement marking its early chapters.

Life as a War

"The rage to improve the world," Peter Gay writes of Victorian philanthropy, was "usually called benevolence," but was in practice closer to "what Freud called a reaction formation—a defense mechanism that converts aggressive feelings into their opposite and thus masks them."[38] "The most determined anti-aggression," he says, "is often aggressive in origin." Doubtless, we see signs of this conversion in *Jane Eyre*'s St. John Rivers, and note both the "telescopic philanthropy" of Mrs. Jellyby and the fanatical "beneficence" of Mrs. Pardiggle in *Bleak House*, but should we view this "determined anti-aggression" as emanating from Brontë herself? Need my suggestion that *Shirley* partly offset deep suffering (the loss of three siblings) spawn only psychobiographical conclusions?[39]

According to Hazlitt, we should implicate all fiction in this difficulty, seeing our impulse to participate in these virtual worlds as less to escape hatred than to engage it, to remind ourselves of the pleasure we gain from watching others suffer in fiction, and thus why we—with Moore— might also experience a sense of "warlike excitement" when reading the battle scene in *Shirley*. Indeed, because such novels prevent us from forgetting this sensation, they bring to our attention its transformative power. As Hazlitt claims in "On the Pleasure of Hating," "In reading we always take the right side, and make the case properly our own. Our imaginations are sufficiently excited, we have nothing to do with the matter but as a pure creation of the mind, and we therefore yield to the natural, unwarped impression of good and evil. . . . We are hunting after what we cannot find, and quarrelling with the good within our reach."[40]

Given these claims, the resentment flourishing in *Shirley*'s early chapters is best viewed as a deeply historical account of religious conflict *and* as an allegorical pronouncement on forms of enmity. As the novel emphasizes, religious conflict often influences how we look at, and define, history. Yet enmity in history and in *Shirley* neither begins nor ends with religion; this hostility in the novel is merely a pretext by which characters give shape to a type of hatred they could voice independently.[41] What may be historical in such conflicts, the novel comes close to saying, is merely the form of this aggression, the vehicle proving most conducive to hostility's expression.

This point is clearest in *Shirley*'s opening chapters, a microcosm of Yorkshire's wider conflicts. The characters' cynical remarks on marriage stain their community, extending outward in a commentary on the antisocial impulses that debilitate the region, the country, and, finally, the continent at war. How, then, can women find self-fulfillment in a state that seems inimical to their happiness? *Shirley* answers this question by viewing marriage beside a larger dilemma about citizenship, with responsibilities to others, nagging doubts about what constitutes a desirable group tie, and a host of unspoken expectations impeding the autonomy of individuals. Partly because interpersonal enmity glides so easily into community warfare, the novel often implies that group ties aren't worth the effort.

To stress this point, the narrator begins the novel in 1812, close to Napoleon's defeat, with a caustic account of three local curates: Donne, Malone, and Sweeting. *Shirley*'s opening chapter is titled "Levitical," following the Levites—priests of Israel—who "ought to be doing a great deal of good" (39). But the rowdy curates in Brontë's novel are far too busy arguing to bother about anyone's salvation, least of all theirs. They "lie very thick on the hills," the result of an "abundant shower" that's "fallen upon the north of England" (39). Such analogies may be Brontë's mild revenge on Elizabeth Rigby, who dubbed *Jane Eyre* "preeminently an anti-Christian composition."[42] Granted, we may hear an echo of "the angel forms, who"—before Satan's first rousing speech— "lay entranced, / Thick as autumnal leaves that strow the brooks in / Vallombrosa," in *Paradise Lost*, book 1, but Brontë's description is finally devoid of lyricism.[43]

While the three curates argue in her novel, the woman serving them explicitly "hates" them (41). Indeed, by the fourth page of the novel we know that when Mrs. Gale is ordered to slice bread for the "besottedly arrogant" Malone, she has a powerful impulse to stab him, "her Yorkshire soul revolt[ing] absolutely from his manner of command" (42). Lewes called the curates "offensive . . . boors" whom Brontë must have "despised" (164). "What attracts them," the narrator says less dramatically, "is not friendship; for whenever they meet they quarrel. It is not religion; the thing is never named amongst them. . . . It is not the love of eating and drinking." They meet, as their landladies insist, "'for nought else but to give folk trouble'" (40–41). This "trouble" agitates Brontë's language, as though reproducing the near-revolutionary conditions of West Riding in the 1810s, anticipating the later battle over the mill, and replicating the antisocial impulses that throughout the novel define individuals as potential enemies, traitors, and strangers. As Malone becomes progressively drunker and more obstreperous, for example, he "re-vile[s]" Doone and Sweeting "as Saxons and snobs." They in turn "taunt . . . him with being the native of a conquered land." So he "men-ace[s] rebellion in the name of his 'counthry' [*sic*] [and] vent[s] bitter ha-tred against English rule," while they speak of "rags, beggary, and pesti-lence" until "the little parlour [is] in an uproar; you would have thought a duel must follow such virulent abuse" (43–44).

By the time the narrator begins discussing Moore's misanthropy, the term is curiously devoid of personal meaning. At various points of the novel, Yorke, Louis Moore (Moore's brother), and Mrs. Pryor are each described, respectively, as "a misanthrope," "misanthropical," and a "misanthropist" (174, 434, 596). But the terms could readily apply to James Helstone, Caroline's dead father ("a man-tiger" [427]), and Mrs. Yorke—"specially bilious and morose"—whose "natural antipathy" to sensitive people makes her "as much disposed to gore as any vicious 'mother of the herd'" (388). Moreover, in young Martin Yorke, we find "a regular misogamist" [*sic*], aged roughly thirteen, who calls women "proud monkeys" (176, 529). And in the "unamiable" Miss Mann, one of the novel's several aging spinsters, we note a misandrist who finds all men egregiously "selfish" (192).

Given the preponderance of hatred in *Shirley*, this judgment is strangely self-evident. Indeed, the narrator delivers an almost identical verdict at the beginning of the same chapter—"All men, taken singly, are more or less selfish; and taken in bodies they are intensely so" (183). As if overhearing, the protagonists promptly agree. Moore calls "men in general . . . a sort of scum" (111), and Yorke later confirms: "Men are made of the queerest dregs that Chaos churned up in her ferment" (504). These claims establish a predictable tone for the novel's allegorical de-scriptions of mob violence, where "Wrath wakens to the cry of Hate . . . and rises to the howl of the Hyena" (335). As the examples pile up, push-ing forward to a violent climax, they underscore the near-ubiquity of this sentiment in *Shirley*. Given this pervasiveness, what's unique about Moore's contempt for humanity?

He has "two natures," a duality proving instrumental to his moral re-form. Split between "world and business" on the one hand and "home and leisure" on the other, he assigns his middle name, Gérard, to the first category while allowing Caroline to call him Robert, the name designating a man who's "sometimes a dreamer" (258). Moore is riven internally (like Shakespeare's Coriolanus and Browning's Paracelsus) between contempt for others and a fantasy of securing their salvation, but the latter ideal prevails only when the novel allows goodwill to triumph over hostility (and Robert in essence to displace Gérard).

However, Robert Moore as public figure holds little interest for the novel or us. He merely dispels forms of conflict that the narrator previously considered almost insoluble, especially as characters like Helstone and Yorke show "how cordially [they] detest each other" (85). Gérard Moore's "crabbed contumacy" compels us (and apparently Brontë), on the other hand, because it indicates that *beneficence* is an irritating "act" and that Moore's "foreign gall" corrodes "his veins" and all related social ties (68, 100). In this guise he is, like Helstone, indifferent to the hatred he elicits, and prides himself on being "taciturn, phlegmatic, . . . joyless," and friendless (99). Describing his father's and uncles' betrayal by their friends, he insists, "Au diable les amis! . . . Ce mot, ami, m'irrite trop; ne m'en parlez plus" (74–75). Read beside Brontë's later chapter "Coriolanus," the statement echoes the Roman protagonist, who in Shakespeare's play laments:

> O world, thy slippery turns! Friends now fast sworn,
> Whose double bosoms seem to wear one heart,
> [. . .] shall within this hour,
> On a dissension of a doit, break out
> To bitterest enmity. (4.4.12–18)

As in *Coriolanus*, too, Moore's claim that benevolence is a pretense suggests not that selfishness corrupts our essential virtue, but that virtue is, on the contrary, a result of humans' feeble attempts to subdue their greater capacity for harm. Those who lack effort in this regard, imply Shakespeare and Brontë, far outnumber those who strive for precarious altruism.

Lewes missed this point, lamenting that Moore has "something sordid in [his] mind . . . and repulsive in [his] demeanour." "A hero many be faulty, erring, imperfect," he insisted, hobbling Brontë's interest in misanthropy, "but he must not be sordid, mean, wanting in the statelier virtues of our kind" (166).[44]

A critic as intelligent and unorthodox as Lewes here illustrates a profound mid-Victorian resistance to Brontë's bleak vision of society. Still, he correctly surmised that Moore's "duality" presents formal, artistic difficulties for the novel. Struggling to reconcile this protagonist's "two natures," the narrator tells us candidly that Moore is "a wolf in sheep's clothing," not the reverse (170). For this reason, love *cannot* simply prevail over hostility—as it can't in *Coriolanus* (181). How, then, does the novel set about transforming him?

Moore's brother, Louis, appears just as the narrator brings together Robert and Caroline. Paving the way for a double marriage, Louis is clearly necessary for the plot. That several characters nonetheless mistake him for Robert also is useful, for the second brother shares with the first "the character of being misanthropical" (434). As Robert evolves into a considerate employer and lover, a switch occurs in the novel, in which Louis prolongs the austere hatred of which his brother is eventually cured. Like many of Dickens's novels, Brontë's styles misanthropy chiastically, reforming its central protagonist while giving his hatred a fraternal afterlife.

What stops this from being a private, or even a family affair, is Brontë's interest in links between interpersonal and impersonal violence. Indeed, as such violence extends—not replaces—the novel's hitherto ontological understanding of misanthropy, almost no aspect of the social field remains devoid of hatred. Arguably one of Brontë's strongest political points, it emerges from her interest in Shakespearean and Hazlittian rancor.

Let us be clear: For Brontë (as for Hazlitt and Coriolanus) such violence persists *despite*, and not just because of, specific social conditions, a point that clearly irks historicists and materialists like E. P. Thompson and Terry Eagleton. Indeed, although *Villette*—Brontë's last completed novel—describes society ostensibly in times of *peace*, Lucy Snowe, the protagonist, seldom experiences tranquillity, instead viewing her peers, students, employer, and even the man who would be her spouse as menaces from whom she requires sanctuary. In this regard, the novel develops *Shirley*'s meditations on group ties by forging links between company and sorrow. "In public, [I] was by nature a cypher," claims Lucy, though this suggestion of anonymity and facelessness is exacerbated, not resolved, by her moments of profound solitude.[45] When over a school vacation Lucy is almost alone for seven weeks, she likens herself to a hermit who must "swallow his own thoughts . . . during these weeks of inward winter" by "mak[ing] a tidy ball of himself, creep[ing] into a hole of life's wall, and submit[ting] decently to the drift which blows in and soon blocks him up, preserving him in ice for the season" (348).[46] Poignantly, during other holidays Marie Broc (the cretin) is her sole companion.

While *Villette* describes such isolation with exquisite beauty, the novel is far from rendering its protagonist a simple victim of others' cruelty; nor does it voice a mandate that she live reclusively. Yet the novel helps us see why hatred remains integral to Brontë's conception of subjectivity and citizenship. For reasons that we deduce easily, Ginevra Fanshawe calls Lucy "Diogenes," "Timon," and "the Dragon"; to even facile Ginevra, she's a "dear cynic and misanthrope," alternately obsessed with and disgusted by "the whole burden of human egotism" (575, 450). These are perhaps fresh allusions to Carlyle, whose Diogenes Teufelsdröckh ("Devil's Dung") responds to the question "Why am I not happy?" by writing that the universe "was all void of Life, of Purpose, of Volition, even of Hostility."[47] But Lucy can't accept this last clause. "If life be a war," she says, re-enlivening a military metaphor and giving voice to a sentiment recurring throughout *Villette*, "it seemed my destiny to conduct it single-handed." This realization provokes her into asking, with superb clarity, "But, oh! what *is* the love of the multitude?" (381, 539). For important conceptual reasons, none of Brontë's four novels can answer this question, an outcome that's extraordinary, given the pressure of novelistic conventions facing Brontë.

Since Lucy is endlessly harassed by "strange inward trials, miserable defections of hope, intolerable encroachments of despair" (350), privacy is no sanctuary in *Villette*; and her engaging with others proves a source of disappointment and difficulty. Although we're used to reading the novel's revised ending as indicating Lucy's ardent desire for reunion with M. Paul, even the happier conclusion is reticent in confirming this, indicating only that it must "leave sunny imaginations hope" (596). Lucy's happiness consists in expecting closeness, we infer, but the narrator can't repress the idea that M. Paul's death would give her just what she wants: a school to run, a home to enjoy, and the benefits of deferred intimacy.

Like *Shirley* and Brontë's other fiction, *Villette* shows us the warped effects of sustained egoism, while telling us we can't escape the intractable qualities that time and history "impress" on us, to borrow one of Lucy's terms (341). In this respect, the novel echoes *The Professor*'s suggestion—voiced by Crimsworth—that narcissism regrettably is the basis for affection and group ties: "No regular beauty pleases egotistical human beings so much as a softened and refined likeness of themselves" (57). Perhaps, Crimsworth implies, we're drawn to confirm our worst faults, especially in love, in ways replicating them throughout society. As we've seen, this idea is unyielding and strangely emancipatory in Brontë's fiction, for narcissism in these novels slightly unravels the social tie and leads to a productive betrayal of social conformity that disentangles her protagonists, as much as conditions will allow, from unpleasant circumstances. As Max Stirner would corroborate in his near-contemporaneous study, *The Ego and Its Own*, "The freedom of man is . . . freedom from *persons*" (105; original emphasis). One reaches this extreme not only by self-assertion, the desire not to mimic others, but also by an impulse to avoid the subservience that Hazlitt earlier described.

Although Brontë enjoyed Hazlitt's work, we've no record of whether she read Stirner. In their bleakest formulations, however, her novels advance, then partly discredit, arguments similar to those of both thinkers, leaving her protagonists suspended among several false alternatives. They are stymied by personal and political history, bereft of credible social ideals, and still compelled—mostly—to live among others in conditions that they haven't fully chosen. Perhaps for this reason, the idea that sociability is "a bilious caprice" is strangely edifying after all. Let us now see how Eliot—and especially Browning and Conrad—develop this idea.

CHAPTER FOUR

George Eliot and Enmity

Friendliness is [like] a steed . . . : it will hardly show much alacrity unless it has got the thistle of hatred under its tail. —Nello in *Romola*

Fantasies Betraying Fellowship

IN *THE LIFTED VEIL*, one of Eliot's least-known works, the protagonist's misery begins the moment he finds out what other people are really thinking. Afflicted with a "superadded consciousness," Latimer discovers that his clairvoyance exposes his friends' duplicity, not their generosity.[1] Although these revelations initially make him cautious, he ends up so disheartened that he indicts human treachery. Because of his "microscopic vision," he witnesses "all the intermediate frivolities, all the suppressed egoism, all the struggling chaos of puerilities, meanness, vague capricious memories, and indolent make-shift thoughts" that others hatch, often at his expense (14).[2]

Eliot might have distinguished here between Latimer's friends and his lover, Bertha Grant, but the latter—with her "barren worldliness" and "scorching hate"—turns out to be the worst culprit of all (19, 20). Yet though Latimer can predict the pitiable state of their future marriage— "She was my wife, and we hated each other"—he feels beforehand a "wild hell-braving joy that Bertha [will eventually] be mine" (20). Acknowledging this paradoxical satisfaction, his yearning destined to result in mutual unhappiness, Latimer worries that the reader will find him unsympathetic: "Are you unable to imagine this double consciousness at work with me, flowing on like two parallel streams which never mingle their waters and blend into a common hue?" (21). The question could as easily stem from an author concerned that she's exposing an aspect of humanity her readers might prefer remain veiled. The final blow to Latimer's joy—a poignant victory for the supernatural world, given the novella's interest in clairvoyance—falls when he learns that Bertha is planning to poison him. Not surprisingly, this knowledge corrodes all remaining fellowship in the tale, leaving the protagonist a confirmed misanthrope: "The relation between me and my fellow-men was . . . deadened" (35–36).

Finding no limit to perfidy, *The Lifted Veil* is doubtless Eliot's bleakest work. As Latimer sees "repulsion and antipathy harden into cruel hatred, giving pain only for the sake of wreaking itself" (32), the sensitive intellectual finally disbelieves in affection, viewing most of his friends as covert enemies. But though critics may agree that ill will and even sadistic meanness flourish in this and other works by Eliot, they're less certain about the effect of these qualities on her fiction, not least because she's renowned for believing literature should foster "deep human sympathy."[3]

Granted, Eliot would sometimes chafe against this persona, telling Lady Burne-Jones with exasperation just a few months before she died: "I am so tired of being set on a pedestal and expected to vent wisdom."[4] But as Benjamin Jowett noted just a few years earlier, she "wanted . . . an ethical system founded upon altruism. . . . Her idea of existence seemed to be 'doing good to others,'" and the judgment—at least as a principle of intent—is doubtless correct.[5] Thomas Noble has since called this Eliot's "doctrine of sympathy"; Bernard Paris (echoing Comte), her "religion of humanity."[6] Throughout Eliot's fiction and essays, letters and journals, there's overwhelming evidence for these claims. Indeed, when her publisher, John Blackwood, objected that *Scenes of Clerical Life* was "written in the harsher Thackerayan view of human nature," Eliot responded firmly, even tartly: "I should like *not* to be offensive—I should like to touch every heart among my readers with nothing but loving humour, with tenderness, with belief in goodness."[7] Unambiguous once more as an aspiration, the statement nonetheless sidesteps Blackwood's concerns and leaves unresolved, antisocial conflicts in her fiction.

Despite Eliot's "doctrine of sympathy," enmity not only haunts her work but also undermines her fictional endings and thrives at the expense of her moral philosophy. One could respond that her religious humanism would be fatuous and naïve if it represented the world without hostility, and that Eliot merely guides us toward more selfless behavior. But both rejoinders simplify her fiction's moral and aesthetic complexity and slip too quickly into doctrinal approaches to literature. Although Eliot was immersed in intellectual debates, her novels aren't simple illustrations of the principles that concerned her. Nor, despite the acute suffering she endured, are her essays, journals, letters, or experience complete or even viable guides to her fiction. Eliot's stress on compassion—voiced repeatedly in her essays—is thus an inadequate remedy for her novels' concern with enmity.

In many episodes in her work, hatred obliterates reparative compassion;[8] it does so, because Eliot represents the former emotion in quasi-impersonal terms, as a force extending beyond individual and social control. This poses formidable problems for her novelistic communities, which Eliot's narrators sometimes mask by adopting forms of providentialism that she elsewhere discredits. All the same, and despite the timely death of villains, misanthropes, and egoists, the underlying issues don't disappear, but bedevil her fictional couples and communities (see, relatedly, FIGURES 4.1–4.3 from Paul Gavarni's midcentury studies, *Les Invalides du sentiment*, and FIGURE 4.4, his 1873 plate *Croquis*).

Representative scenes in *The Mill on the Floss*, *Silas Marner*, *Romola*, *Middlemarch*, and *Daniel Deronda* show that converting enmity into fellow feeling requires more than faith, insight, or goodwill from Eliot's characters. It asks, first, that they sacrifice both self-interest and the joy they would experience in thwarting others. Second, they must resist an impersonal form of enjoyment that, surpassing such relations, threatens to destroy them entirely. Later passages from *The Mill on the Floss* and *Middlemarch* will confirm the latter idea, but perhaps the best example of satisfaction tied to betrayal arises in *Romola*, when Baldassarre confronts Tito Melema, his treacherous son, with a plan to avenge him in murder: "I saved you—I nurtured you—I loved you. You forsook me—you

FIGURE 4.1 *Les femmes? . . . un tas de serpents* (1851).

FIGURE 4.2 *J'ai voulu connaître les femmes.*
Ça ma coûte une jolie fortune . . . je n'en sais rien! (1851).
Paul Gavarni. Sketches. *Les Invalides du sentiment* (1851).
Œuvres choisies de Gavarni (Paris, 1944).
Courtesy Northwestern University Library Special Collections.

FIGURE 4.3 *Je n'ai plus la terre de Chênerailles, ni mes bois . . .* (1851).
Paul Gavarni. Sketch. *Les Invalides du sentiment* (1851).
Œuvres choisies de Gavarni (Paris, 1944).
Courtesy Northwestern University Library Special Collections.

FIGURE 4.4 *Croquis* (1873). Paul Gavarni. Sketch. *Gavarni: l'homme et
l'Œuvre* (Paris, 1873; plate from 1925 edition). *Courtesy Northwestern
University Library Special Collections.*

robbed me—you denied me. What can you give me? You have made the world bitterness to me, but there is one draught of sweetness left— *that you shall know agony.*"[9] Although several critics have discussed aggression in Eliot's work, few have discussed the "sweetness" of retaliation and its misanthropic effects. Correcting that tendency, this chapter examines the conceptual rather than merely thematic repercussions of this extreme, weighing its impact on her fictional communities and interest in compassion.[10]

Unwarranted Altruism

Eliot's characters find it easier to renounce self-interest (a standard Victorian duty) than to sacrifice their joy in thwarting others. Even Dorothea Brooke's earnest sacrifice results in accusations that she's displaying a "fanaticism of sympathy," as if submitting to Casaubon's repulsive egotism has perverse rewards of its own.[11] Dorothea and Gwendolen Harleth in *Daniel Deronda* can't adapt the maxim "Do as you are done to," moreover, as this would replicate disastrous hostility, but at just the right moment fate relieves them of their obnoxious husbands.[12] In doing so, fate lets both women question past assumptions; they are unnerved to discover, as does Latimer in *The Lifted Veil*, that striving for altruism may have stopped them from considering whether their neighbors, friends, and spouses actually deserve it.[13]

Since Eliot's characters can't determine easily the source of their glee, these predicaments offer valuable lessons, if not always moral guides. As the narrator of *Deronda* explains, "the embitterment of hatred" is usually "as unaccountable to onlookers as the growth of devoted love."[14] Persistent and enigmatic, enmity flourishes in Eliot's fiction, but it doesn't sum up her perspective, and the apparent inconsistency derives from more than her unwillingness to end her novels on a sour, hateful note: Her narrators discern structural impediments to fellowship, as well as the psychic cost of living among other people. *The Lifted Veil* highlights this difficulty when describing other people's hitherto "veiled" treachery. *Deronda*, by contrast, extends this treachery to include the person judging it in others. "Within ourselves our evil will is momentous," Deronda concedes to Gwendolen, "and sooner or later it works its way outside us" (699).

Highlighting a corrosive edge to Eliot's well-known interest in sympathy, these and many other statements impede (without destroying) her characters' aspirations to selflessness. Indeed, given its somber recognition of what characters must overcome or repress to be of any value to other people, Eliot's last novel turns the defeat of egoism into an ethical demand. "Our gain is another's loss," says Deronda, sounding one of the novel's dilemmas, "—that is one of the ugly aspects of life. One would like to reduce it as much as one could, not get amusement out of exaggerating it" (337). Certainly, the novel does try to reduce this "ugly aspect." Yet it can't promote sociability or "scourging of the self" by fiat (767), the narrator realizing that characters' fantasies and wills belie self-management and tidy integration into communities. Another reason compassion fails when Eliot's narrators apply it to the social realm is that the suffering of others is reassuring, even perversely comforting. Asks Deronda, ruefully: "Who has been quite free from egoistic escapes of the imagination picturing desirable consequences on his own future in the presence of another's misfortune, sorrow, or death?" (710).

Most of Eliot's novels are equally astute when noting the unwelcome persistence of enmity and its ensuing moral problems. Appearing just nine months after *The Lifted Veil*, *The Mill on the Floss* portrays a dimension of hatred so unrelenting that it contributes to Edward Tulliver's financial ruin and eventual death. Because of this hatred, Mr. Tulliver urges Tom to record in the family Bible a curse against John Wakem, his father's creditor: "I wish evil may befall him. Write that."[15] Nor is Wakem lacking in "parenthetic vindictiveness" (340), and the narrator is adept at explaining why: "To see people who have been only insignificantly offensive to us, reduced in life and humiliated without any special efforts of ours[,] is apt to have a soothing, flattering influence: . . . by an agreeable constitution of things, our enemies, somehow, *don't* prosper" (340; original emphasis).

Our attachment to this glee is so tenacious, the narrator implies, that the hypocrisy scarcely veiling it is constitutive of human affairs. When a person whom we revile suffers, we take comfort in the fantasy that "Providence, or some other prince of this world, . . . has undertaken the task of retribution for us" (340). In extreme cases, the hypocrisy itself is a source of joy. Tulliver's misfortune gives Wakem added piquancy, *because* the latter masks his ill will as sympathy: "To see an enemy humiliated gives a certain contentment, but this is jejune compared with the highly blent satisfaction of seeing him humiliated by your benevolent action of concession on his behalf" (340). This "jejune . . . satisfaction" best flourishes when it arrives unbidden at another's expense. Wakem enjoys the satisfaction that Latimer exposed but couldn't eradicate in *The Lifted Veil*.

Despairing that his misery fuels Wakem's happiness, Tulliver recklessly exchanges years of "irritation and hostile triumph" for the pleasure of attacking his enemy (458); the humiliation of renting Dorlcote Mill from Wakem exacerbates his festering "paroxysm of rage" (373). Common sense tells us the fight would be futile, surely worsening his family's predicament and perhaps culminating in his own sickness and death. But since Tulliver's thinking follows a different rationale here, "the sight of the long-hated predominant man down and in his power threw him into a frenzy of triumphant vengeance" (460). Such acts are in principle so psychically rewarding, the narrator suggests, that we would pursue them even if we knew beforehand that they would ruin our health and kill us.

The combined excitement and futility of such "triumphant vengeance" can overwhelm the homiletic strain of Eliot's fiction, asking us briefly to identify with another's worst—indeed, death-ridden—instincts. At such moments, Eliot's plots blend with her characters' mania, as if harnessing our peculiar pleasure in watching characters destroy themselves. This problem recurs when *Romola*'s narrator faithfully details Baldassarre's bid for revenge and Mirah despairs at Lapidoth's "gambling appetite" in *Deronda*—an appetite that "in its final, imperious stage, . . . seems [to signify] the unjoyous dissipation of demons, seeking diversion on the burning marl of perdition" (773). The language here may resemble the Old Testament, but Eliot is too shrewd to seek metaphysical answers for these conflicts. Similar impulses, concerning gambling, theft, class hatred, and political revenge, have comparable prominence in *Silas Marner*, *Middlemarch*, and *Felix Holt*. The point is less that Eliot found no adequate moral alternative to these appetites (who, frankly, could?) and more that the sympathy her narrators want us to cultivate is itself an accomplice to, rather than a means of erasing, the "jejune . . . satisfaction" we derive from characters' misfortunes.

The *Times* wasn't alone in alluding to this predicament in *The Mill on the Floss*. In May 1860 it called a "majority of the [novel's] characters" "prosaic, selfish, nasty," and observed with irony that Eliot's genius lay in reconciling us to "a world of pride, vain-glory, and hypocrisy, envy, hatred, and malice."[16] The *Spectator* and *Guardian* also noted the first problem but voiced a different conclusion, decrying the novel's interest in passion's "perverted and unwholesome growths," which risk "stealing like a frightful and incurable poison over not merely principle and self-respect, but even . . . faith and honour." "We are safer and happier in knowing [wrongdoing and wrong feeling] . . . at a distance," the *Guardian* sniffed, suggesting that novelists might henceforth follow the advice that Dante imagines hearing from Virgil: "Non raggioniam di lor, ma guarda e passa": "Let us not speak of [these deficiencies], but look and pass by."[17]

Eliot not only strongly disagreed with these claims but lost no time in telling William Blackwood, her editor, that the *Times*'s pronouncement was a horrible mistake. "I have certainly fulfilled my intention very badly," she explained, five days after receiving the review, "if I have made the Dodson honesty appear 'mean and uninteresting.' . . . I am so far from hating the Dodsons myself, that I am rather aghast to find them ticketed with such very ugly adjectives."[18]

While sentiments like these ignore the narrator's powerful remarks about society's hate-ridden currents, critics invoke such letters quickly to dismiss the novel's darker insights. If we need only establish whether Eliot is "far from hating the Dodsons," then apparently we can rest easy. But can we still confirm that fellow feeling predominates in her fiction and, indeed, has enough philosophical clout to do so?

This question brackets more than Eliot's correspondence, and eschews for their conceptual simplicity some of the arguments she advances in her essays. Eliot's best-known allusion to sympathy is doubtless a passage in "The Natural History of German Life," where she calls the arts "mode[s] of amplifying experience and extending our contact with our fellow-men beyond the bounds of our personal lot."[19] In this essay, moreover, the word *altruism* makes only its second appearance in the English language, following Lewes's adoption of Comte's midcentury neologism three years earlier.[20] Describing increased sympathy in her readers as the best outcome of her fiction, Eliot tried to uphold Feuerbach's distinction between "self-interested love" and "the true human love [that] impels the sacrifice of self to another," leaning strongly toward the latter.[21] Many other letters, reviews, and journal entries voice identical concerns, implying that our salvation lies in compassion toward others (if not always toward ourselves).[22]

Yet Eliot's fiction surpasses this vision so often that to tie the fiction to such aesthetic and moral ideals almost guarantees misprision. As the passages I've quoted voice contrarian impulses, including characters' venal attempts at thwarting others, the recipients of such acts seem *justified* in avoiding contact with other people. We might view these passages as simple plot devices upholding a greater principle of fellowship, or claim that sympathy has meaning only if it outlasts a near-devastating contact with antipathy (the more convincing the foe, the stronger is our sense of victory, and so on). But after Eliot's expansive vision of enmity in *The Lifted Veil*, and the resonance of ill will in almost all her other works, these claims oversimplify her fiction and limit her intellectual achievement, which presents aspects of social conflict as insoluble and participation in communities as sometimes irreparably damaging to individuals. Moreover, one needn't conclude that Eliot began writing fiction with an improbably ideal view of human nature, and then recoiled from what her fiction or imagination exposed.[23] I'm suggesting instead that while she stressed the need for compassion, her ethic remains abstract and impersonal, lacking efficacy when it surfaces in her fiction. Since her later novels represent the ensuing damage, partly contradicting her thesis in "The Natural History of German Life," we had best view this and other essays as limited assessments of her narrative effects.

Isolation, a Precondition for Fellowship

Fiction, I argue throughout this book, is irreducible to biographical details and authorial statements. As critics nonetheless insist that these registers are in Eliot's case complementary,[24] let's at least consider where she departed from moral piety. In 1848, Eliot was interested in Carlylean misanthropy and—inspired by the French Revolution—denounced the "miserable reign of Mammon" still flourishing in England.[25] "You will wonder what has wrought me up into this fury," she wrote Charles and Cara Bray and Charles and Rufa Hennell; "it is the loathsome fawning, the transparent hypocrisy, the systematic giving as little as possible for as much as possible that one meets with here at every turn. I feel that society is training men and women for hell."[26] Three years later, in her review of Robert William Mackay's *Progress of the Intellect*, she protested: "Our civilization, and, yet more, our religion, are an anomalous blending of lifeless barbarisms, which have descended to us like so many petrifications from distant ages."[27]

While these remarks have only limited interpretive power and are sometimes inconsistent, the fury they convey surpasses that inspired by social injustice. The year Eliot wrote the Brays and Hennells about England's "lifeless barbarisms," she discussed wanting to rid herself of "all the demons, which are but my own egotism, mopping [*sic*] and moving and gibbering"; the false complacency of "some religionists and ultragood people"; and her personal "repugnance" for "a horrid savage of a man," a neighbor in St. Leonard's, East Sussex, and the surrounding "women [who] are such fawning hags."[28]

Distraught that her closest siblings and some friends rejected her after she decided to live unmarried with Lewes (who couldn't procure a divorce), and chafing at the exposure resulting from *Adam Bede*'s popularity, including widespread speculation about its authorship, Eliot was mostly unhappy while writing *The Lifted Veil*, *Brother Jacob*, and *Silas Marner* in 1859 and 1860. Gordon Haight describes her and Lewes as living like outcasts in Blandford Square, London; and Eliot refers to her interest in "renouncing all social intercourse but such as comes to our own fireside."[29] While enduring vicious attacks in the press,[30] she told her close friend Barbara Leigh Smith: "For myself I prefer excommunication. I have . . . my freedom from petty worldly torments, commonly called pleasures, and that isolation that really keeps my charity warm instead of chilling it, as much contact with frivolous women would do."[31] An impasse arises here between Eliot's rhetoric of fellow feeling and the elements of revulsion that seem to cancel it in her fiction. As before, however, one must question how far this and other letters govern our interpretations. Eliot sent this letter while composing the first half of *Marner*; seven weeks later she mailed John Blackwood the novel's first thirteen chapters. Yet in turning to this novel, we'll see how far it exceeds its author's biographical and didactic concerns.

Marner and Mockery

Isolated and betrayed, mocked and robbed, Marner can tolerate his neighbors' cruelty only by dedicating himself to regaining his stolen wealth and by loving Eppie, his adopted daughter. Before he's robbed in Raveloe, however—in the process losing his entire fortune—Marner is banished from a religious community in Lantern Yard. William Dane, his closest friend, sets him up for a robbery that he himself commits. In doing so, William not only exploits his friend's cataleptic fits, which put him in a trance, but also snags Marner's fiancée, Sarah. Evidently, with friends like these . . .

Marner does end happily, but only in a brief afterword explaining that Eppie marries. By the end of the novel proper, the protagonist's well-being consists largely in his deflecting Godfrey Cass's paternal claims on Eppie. Moreover, as Alain Barrat notes, "the hero . . . never obtains total redress: he cannot find the minister or any member of his religious sect to expose his unfair treatment."[32] This injustice gels with another factor—Marner's inability to accept the full extent of his friends' and neighbors' treachery—arguably the primary reason he flourishes in Raveloe, fifteen years later. "Stunned by despair," Marner suffers briefly "the anguish of disappointed faith" arising from a "shaken trust in God and man" (14; see also FIGURES 4.5 and 4.6, Julia Margaret Cameron's remarkable photographs of the nonmisanthropic scientist and astronomer Sir John Frederick Herschel). When the Lantern Yard community fails to clear Marner of a crime he didn't commit, he exclaims in misery: "There is no just God that governs the earth righteously, but a God of lies, that bears witness against the innocent" (14). But sustained reflection on this treachery proves unbearable and, finally, impossible: Two days after his banishment the outcast takes "refuge from benumbing unbelief, by getting into his loom and working away as usual" (14).

FIGURE 4.5 *Sir John Frederick Herschel* (1865).
Julia Margaret Cameron. Wet collodion.
Courtesy the Science and Society Picture Library, London.

We might picture Eliot's writing this novel in radical isolation, rebuked by her siblings and former admirers, but a psychobiographical reading of the work loses traction here. Unlike with Eliot, Marner's failure to understand enmity is ironically a reason that his "simple" love returns; he imbibes taunts without fury. "Condemned to solitude," he tries to avoid incurring scorn from his new neighbors, "his life narrowing and hardening itself more and more into a mere pulsation of desire and satisfaction that had no relation to any other being" (9, 20). He even manages, in a strikingly beautiful phrase, to "reduce his life to the unquestioning activity of a spinning insect" (17). But his solitude, though satisfying, derives

FIGURE 4.6 *Sir John Frederick Herschel* (April 1867).
Julia Margaret Cameron. Albumen print.
Courtesy the Metropolitan Museum of Art, New York.

from incomprehension rather than deliberate misanthropy. A stronger intelligence, we infer, would grasp that treachery is bound to recur. And it does—for as Deronda understood, individuals thrive on their neighbors' suffering. "Our tenderness and self-renunciation seem strong," adds Latimer in *The Lifted Veil*, "when our egoism has had its day . . . after our mean striving for a triumph that is to be another's loss" (32–33). Thus Eliot's stress on fellowship has paradoxical effects: Trying to diminish characters' autonomy, the novels install a type of noxious propinquity that drives them farther apart. "This strange world [was] made a hopeless riddle" to Marner, the narrator explains, and the riddle worsens when Dunsey Cass steals all his savings (19).

Sociability in this novel stems paradoxically from Marner's limited grasp of treachery; he doesn't realize that his peculiar trances are enough to *invite* persecution, "mockery," and "scorn" (6). (As we saw in the introduction and will revisit in the next chapter, a similar dynamic has innocuous Brother Lawrence provoke fierce contempt in Browning's "Soliloquy of the Spanish Cloister.") At other times, the villagers' belief that Marner's catalepsy will harm them is oddly to his advantage. "It was partly to this vague fear," we're told, "that Marner was indebted for protecting him from the persecution that his singularities might have drawn upon him" (9). The novel relies on Marner's "trusting simplicity" to sustain its illusion of sympathy, its image of enduring neighborliness (10). That this illusion often fails in the novel exposes more than petty iniquity. The characters' reckless egoism leaves a hole in the novel's communitarian system.

Betrayal shadows all experiences of community in *Silas Marner*, rendering sardonic the narrator's insistence in *Middlemarch* that "sane people did what their neighbours did, so that if any lunatics were at large, one might know and avoid them" (9). When even mild aberration is a pretext for persecution, only fools would shun conformity.[33] The idea modifies, without discrediting, Eliot's insistence, in "Birth of Tolerance," that "community of interest is the root of justice; community of suffering, the root of pity; community of joy, the root of love."[34] What *Marner* complicates, however, is the notion that "community of interest" is transparent and universally beneficent; the novel does so by twice pitting its protagonist against villagers who sincerely believe they're promoting this ideal.

Although in *Marner* this opposition isn't wholly malign, the same is not true in Eliot's later fiction. Moreover, that Raveloers shun Marner as a threat and the devout in Lantern Yard banish him as a thief and infidel signal alarmingly how unforeseen motives (say, William Dane's and Dunsey Cass's) combine with collective stupidity to derail the "community of interest." The result transforms this formerly benign entity into one that's utterly devoid of justice, pity, and love. Instead of being exceptional, Dane's and Cass's acts are really inseparable from competing fantasies tugging at the novel's pitiable collective wisdom. Complicating matters further, *The Mill on the Floss* indicates that characters draw hidden satisfaction from such injustice even as they profess to abhor it. So, given all these factors and Eliot's commitment to peopling *Silas Marner* with simple villagers, it's unsurprising that she intervenes, enlightening the ignorant and punishing most of her miscreants (Dunsey Cass drowns, but Dane gets off scot-free). Not surprisingly, too, the novel retreats into parable and myth, where providentialism has more force.

When Silas appears to cure Sally Oates's heart disease and dropsy, Raveloers do change their minds, presuming that his "supernatural" powers are now beneficent. The community happily exchanges hostility for medical treatment. But though the comic effects of their superstition are undeniable, the cynical edge of their self-interest blunts any suggestion of lasting goodwill: "Silas now found himself and his cottage suddenly beset by mothers who wanted him to charm away the hooping-cough [*sic*], or bring back the milk, and by men who wanted stuff against the rheumatics or the knots in the hands" (18). Because he refuses to drive "a profitable trade in charms," he turns "one after another away with growing irritation" (18, 19). Infamy fosters annoyance, and Marner is punished for his candor. Indeed, when the community suspects he's withholding medicinal skills, it rejects him more harshly than before. "Thus it came to pass," the narrator declares, "that his movement of pity towards Sally Oates, which had given him a transient sense of brotherhood, heightened the repulsion between him and his neighbours, and made his isolation more complete" (19). The same aggressive reaction recurs when the community "produces" a culprit responsible for stealing Marner's gold—the man in question has "a 'look with his eye'" and "a swarthy foreignness of complexion which boded little honesty" (61). Though significant, this scapegoat motif can't explain what's going on here.

Impersonal Glee

Because of their flourishing rancor, Raveloe and Lantern Yard are decidedly postlapsarian in character—far from being Wordsworthian arcadias. While Godfrey and Dunsey replicate Cain and Abel's fraternal antagonism, their hostility festers, weakening "the ties and charities that bound together the families of [their] neighbours" (51, 125).[35] That Dunsey leaves Godfrey's horse "pierced with a hedge-stake" illustrates more than callous indifference or deliberate cruelty (35); it signals his unwillingness to sacrifice what the narrator calls "impersonal enjoyment" surpassing conventional pleasure, which culminates in limitless glee at the expense of others (30). Commenting on this problem, she explains that Dunsey's impulses are "grandly independent of utility," while surely wondering what punishment would rival his reckless joy (35).[36] To this extent, Eliot joins Bulwer, Dickens, and Charlotte Brontë, spotlighting utilitarianism's conceptual deficiencies in theorizing links between impersonal satisfaction and fragile sociability.

Marner resembles other Eliot novels in telling us that these impulses don't surface haphazardly but motivate entire communities in ways beyond remedy. For example, when Marner—discovering that his gold is stolen—appeals frantically to his neighbors, the dynamic fueling Tulliver's and Wakem's hatred in *The Mill* partly returns, albeit more mildly: "The repulsion Marner had always created in his neighbours was partly dissipated by the new light in which this misfortune had shown him" (77). Misfortune dissipates repulsion: The idea is nicely paradoxical, implying that reparation can't proceed without hostility, and tragedy alone softens our hatred of others.[37] *Adam Bede* barely touches on this dynamic when the eponymous hero voices a milder alternative: "Trouble's made us kin" (464).

Marner's calamity clearly makes his neighbors happy, but why is his misfortune the sole means of fostering banter on their part and timid amity on his? Though nothing less seems capable of integrating him into the community, this reliance on disaster undermines the happy note on which the novel ends, altering the principle of fellowship that Eliot signposts in her essays. *Marner* touches here on extrasocial factors such as "impersonal enjoyment" and "jejune . . . satisfaction," making clear that no amount of moralizing or historicizing can get us around their effects. Accordingly, we surpass the narrator's initial claim that Marner's catalepsy and marginal profession cause his woe (9). "I suppose one reason why we are seldom able to comfort our neighbours with our words," she adds later, "is that our goodwill gets adulterated, in spite of ourselves, before it can pass our lips. We can send black puddings and pettitoes without giving them a flavour of our own egoism; but language is a stream that is almost sure to smack of a mingled soil" (77–78).

Language is duplicitous, the narrator's mixed metaphor implies, because it veils neither our delight in our neighbors' suffering nor our fervent wish that envy paralyze them when contemplating our lives. This much seems psychologically "true." But as in *Deronda* and even *Adam Bede*, this enjoyment is impersonal; language mediates our relation to other people, and these signifiers aren't simply ours to command. Disputing that we're the agents of speech, for instance, Jacques Lacan argued that "a society founded in language" transforms what it means to be "a collection of individuals."[38] He adds, "Reference to the experience of the community . . . settles nothing. For this experience assumes its essential dimension in the tradition that this discourse itself establishes."[39] *The Mill on the Floss* calls this discourse "soothing," because it helps us represent our enemies as "reduced in life and humiliated" (340). Since this soothing experience is also surplus to meaning, as Eliot and Lacan differently convey, it escapes reference and individual control, posing difficulties for Eliot just when she's most didactic.

The Mill on the Floss, we recall, insists that our willingness to credit "Providence, or some other prince of this world" with our "jejune . . . satisfaction" is a ruse (340): We imagine that our fantasies alter the destiny of other people. But this is an infantile notion of fate, and the novel refuses to countenance it, instead laying bare the individual and collective delusions that inform it.[40] In *Marner*, by contrast, the narrator challenges without fully discrediting such providentialism.[41] She echoes a form of psychological conceit, popular with Godfrey Cass and Nancy Lammeter, that attributes wealth and happiness to externally correct behavior. "When we are treated well," the narrator summarizes archly, "we naturally begin to think that we are not altogether unmeritorious, and that it is only just we should treat ourselves well, and not mar our own good fortune" (119). Godfrey manipulates this logic for unethical gain when he delays telling Nancy that Eppie is his child.

Voicing Marner's shaken trust in God and humanity, the narrator likewise observes that after Dunsey Cass steals Marner's gold, the weaver contemplates whether "a cruel power that no hands could reach . . . had delighted in making him a second time desolate" (44). Because most forms of justice in this novel rest on contingent forms of sociability, the narrator's perspective on fate, chance, and moral punishment arguably is as equivocal as in the above passage detailing Godfrey's casuistry. Jerome Thale observes of the former scene: "What [Marner] has lost is not a creed but a sense of the world."[42] Justice therefore must arise not through religious belief, since the novel partly discredits this, but through a careful reordering of social and psychic reality—a reordering in which Godfrey, Nancy, and others are thoroughly, even cynically, adept. A form of group illusion determines the result, yet the novel can't detach this illusion from the ignorance and bad faith fueling Marner's misery. Given the "chasm in [Marner's] consciousness" that enmity produces (110), the novel hints several times that the ensuing trauma is irreparable.[43]

Put bluntly, Marner's rising fortunes at the end of this novel can't credibly imply that he's more "meritorious" than Nancy Lammeter or Godfrey Cass; to do so would reward Marner for assumptions of which the narrator wants to rid the casuists. Just as shoddy treatment by others is but one instance in this novel of near-ubiquitous moral turpitude, so greater happiness can't axiomatically obtain from "quiverings of tenderness" and "awe at the presentiment of some Power presiding over" our lives (111). Yet because the novel wants to renew secular belief in the redemptive power of these "quiverings," burying all contrary evidence in a specious claim that fellowship overrides malice, *Marner* is least satisfying when it concludes. Readers closing the book midway wouldn't learn that fellowship compensates for much at all. They might even entertain the contrary—and perhaps more salient—idea, prevalent in *The Lifted Veil*, that malice stems from rash trust and unwise friendship.

Ironically, the novel's most sophisticated statement about heedless joy nudges us toward this conclusion. After listing Godfrey's favorite pastimes—"sporting, drinking, card-playing, or the rarer and less oblivious pleasure of seeing Miss Nancy Lammeter"—the narrator remarks:

> The subtle and varied pains springing from the higher sensibility that accompanies higher culture, are perhaps less pitiable than that dreary absence of impersonal enjoyment and consolation which leaves ruder minds to the perpetual urgent companionship of their own griefs and discontents. (30)

The more one rereads this complex sentence, the more the narrator's "perhaps" sounds ironic. Her allusion to "higher sensibility" and "higher culture" isn't prim, but instead voices concern that "ruder minds" lacking in "impersonal enjoyment and consolation" relish even cruder forms of entertainment. Receiving this enjoyment—especially at another's expense—apparently is more rewarding than morbid introspection. Life without our neighbors' suffering would be unimaginably dreary. Further, Eliot's narrator doesn't claim that those enjoying a "higher sensibility" are immune to this consolation; she even implies that their "subtle and varied pains" derive from complex efforts at disguising this delight by expressing it in culturally appropriate ways, as *The Mill on the Floss* cleverly reminded us.

Eliot understood well that "the passions and senses decompose, so to speak."[44] Simple disdain for moral ambiguity can't revoke these impulses or diminish their effects. The most we can expect from her vulnerable protagonists is a form of stoic resignation that is powerless against others' treachery. What this means is that Eliot's sophisticated grasp of "irrational" pleasure places her characters at the mercy of others' inexhaustible cruelty. And when her narrators intervene, meting out rewards and punishments according to a discredited providentialism, her fiction betrays its best psychic and philosophical insights.

Enmity in Eliot's fiction arises almost inevitably from proximity to other people and their not-so-secret schadenfreude. Hatred and joy are thus inseparable from the pleasure-inducing antipathies that haunt her fiction. As the examples of Dunsey Cass and Lapidoth attest, these qualities contaminate each other, leaving us sometimes incapable of differentiating them. *Marner* does more than explain why we should distrust our neighbors; at moments, it sanctions the impression that misanthropy would make us safer—because more skeptical and resilient—citizens.

The Contours of Revenge

Although the gap between Eliot's beliefs and her fiction's antisocial strains highlights her difficulties in resolving the latter, we shouldn't underestimate her efforts at expunging these impulses near the end of her novels. Despite—or because of—its fervent revenge motif, for example, *Romola* concludes with such emphatic union that Eliot refashions her imaginary community to destroy its rancid elements. After detailing

Baldassarre's retributive fantasies and desire to murder his treacherous son, Eliot's narrator downplays any generalized outcome arising from Romola's careful advice to Bernardo del Nero, her godfather: "Trust nobody. If you trust, you will be betrayed" (452). Still, the novel follows so closely Baldassarre's hope of retaliation that Romola's fear seems plausible and almost universally applicable.

Neither Baldassarre nor the novel finds peace without exposing Tito's betrayal, a situation compelling both to unmask his elaborate deception. The narrator must of course detach her moral search for truth from Baldassarre's extreme motives, but with whom does the reader side? Considering Eliot's remarkable accounts of Grandcourt's, Tulliver's, and Dunsey Cass's nemeses, we could easily stray from the author's line. Eliot cannot also unmask Tito without giving us at least some satisfaction that is at odds with fellow feeling.

Unlike in *Marner*, *The Mill on the Floss*, and *Daniel Deronda*, too, Baldassarre's pursuit of Tito in *Romola* is formally inseparable from the novel's ability to conclude. In plot terms, this means that his yearning for catharsis must be one we *partly* share if we're to reach the final chapter. We may recoil from Baldassarre's frenzy, his "ecstasy of self-martyring revenge" (234); the narrator also thwarts much of the catharsis accompanying the murder. But she doesn't help matters by calling the scheme to accomplish this act "exquisite" (268, 336), so putting in play all the adjective's meanings—as "ingeniously devised," "accurate, careful," and "of such consummate excellence, beauty, or perfection, as to excite intense delight or admiration."[45]

There's no mistaking the narrator's unease at this outcome and, indeed, her efforts at warning us that nothing good can come of it. She tries preempting Baldassarre's yearning by saying his "hunger and his thirst were after nothing exquisite *but*" this retribution, a statement sounding circular and self-defeating, given the novel's interest in his ardor (336). The narrator's caveat nearby also is thoroughly ambiguous: "If baseness triumphed everywhere else, if it could heap to itself all the goods of the world and even hold the keys of hell, it would never triumph over the hatred which it had itself awakened" (336). The idea is similar to that in the *Spectator*, cited in the introduction: "There is nothing in intelligence of itself to extinguish hate . . . , and to understand accurately may only make you understand more clearly the hatefulness of the person hated."[46] But learning about this problem almost midway through Eliot's novel might make us wonder whether her narrator's statement discredits hatred or merely explains its resilience.

As Baldassarre seeks the "one draught of sweetness left [him]—*that [Tito] shall know agony*," it's imperative that the latter *not* die during this confrontation—that the novel place obstacles between Baldassarre and this "sweetness" to prolong its intensity (308; original emphasis). This heightens complicity between the novel and Baldassarre, leaving the narrator on even shakier moral ground. Consider her perspective in the following passage, which reproduces then scrutinizes Baldassarre's interior monologue:

> "Curses on him! I wish I may see him lie with those red lips white and dry as ashes, and when he looks for pity *I wish he may see my face rejoicing in his pain*. It is all a lie—this world is a lie—there is no goodness but in hate. . . ."
>
> But Baldassarre's mind rejected the thought of that brief punishment. His whole soul had been thrilled into immediate unreasoning belief in that eternity of vengeance where he, an undying hate [*sic*], might clutch for ever an undying traitor, and hear that fair smiling hardness cry and moan with anguish. But the primary need and hope was to see a slow revenge under the same sky and on the same earth where he himself had been forsaken and had fainted with despair. And as soon as he tried to concentrate his mind on the means of attaining his end, the sense of his weakness pressed upon him like a frosty ache. (270; my emphasis)

Owing largely to Eliotic fellow feeling and Victorian assumptions about links between rancor and ill health, the novel depletes Baldassarre just when his chances of securing vengeance are best assured. As we'll see in the next chapter, on Browning's poetry, such hazy outcomes let the Victorians retain apparent moral purity while reading in fascinated, guilty suspense.

Eliot's compromise is significant, if predictable. She lets the murder occur—granting the protagonist, reader, and novel long-deferred satisfaction—but dampens any untoward excitement the act might spawn.

We never hear, by the free indirect speech for which she's famous, how Baldassarre *feels* after achieving his aim. When he "presse[s] his knuckles against [Tito's] round throat," following the latter's important recognition of his killer, the narrator exclaims, "Let death come now!" (548). It's difficult to disagree, not least because, at this late stage, part of us hopes Baldassarre succeeds. Except for the hidden reader, though, the scene occurs without a witness, which stifles any lasting sense of vindication. The narrator hurries on to describe another scene in Florence, in which Savonarola confesses before he too is tried and executed. By the time we return to the first scene, Baldassarre has died. Terminating his jubilation, this "fitting" expiation of villain and villainy requires that a third party—a hapless farmer—stumble across the scene a few hours later. Later still—a critical narrative interval, quelling the climax even further—the bodies are identified and the meaning of revenge pieced together by bewildered onlookers.

Eliot vacillates, then, between narrative excitement and moral probity. Despite trying to do justice to both registers, she quashes any psychic rationale for Baldassarre's revenge, discrediting it with malice. Quietly scorning the energy her narrator surreptitiously harnesses, she leaves us almost as hamstrung as Edward Tulliver.

Neighbors in Middlemarch

Lest we imagine that these interpersonal tensions arise only from Eliot's concern to depict credible villainy and that the problem dissipates when the villain dies, let's consider the powerful implications of these tensions for her fictional communities. At this more abstract level, Eliot's ethic of fellowship becomes precarious and difficult to control. In *Middlemarch*, the last Eliot novel I'll examine, enmity among characters is inseparable from what it means to be a citizen and neighbor. The malice impeding Tertius Lydgate and Nicholas Bulstrode implicates the entire community, to the detriment of collective advances in medicine. Of course, this increases the risk that greater numbers of Middlemarchers will die from cholera, typhoid, and other infectious diseases, yet the community's desire for vengeance—inflamed by Bulstrode's insufferable rectitude and Lydgate's talent and arrogance—

overrides such logical concerns. Long before Bulstrode's past becomes public knowledge, Lydgate privately admits to Dorothea: "Half the town would almost take trouble for the sake of thwarting him" (439).[47] Still, Eliot's narrator would have us believe, when all is revealed and Lydgate seems implicated in murder, that Dorothea's unflinching faith in him will bring the town to reason. Her loyalty is an unlikely bulwark against the community's zest for retaliation.

Destroyed by avarice and dishonesty, Bulstrode is brought to account by John Raffles, a maverick so far beyond conventional forms of justice, and so oblivious to the rights of others, that he surpasses anything resembling a "return of the repressed." Consequently, the revenge motif in Eliot's novel is again out of kilter, exposing more than it feasibly can correct. As false piety screens Bulstrode's immoral conduct, the novel needs an agent capable of shattering his hypocrisy; the abstract providentialism overseeing *Silas Marner* pales beside such sophisticated dissimulation.

Raffles's "eagerness to torment" Bulstrode apparently is "almost as strong in him as any other greed" (614). But though Raffles overshoots the mark, destroying the "host" that succors him, the narrator's stress on "almost" here is intriguing. The desire for retribution, which *Romola* probes at length, is in *Middlemarch* poisoned at the outset by bile. It's as if Eliot is so concerned that we'll side with the vengeful Middlemarchers that she dampens their (and our) indignation by tarnishing the latter with Raffles's blackmail, scavenging, and alcoholism. (Relatedly and conveniently, Casaubon dies before Dorothea confronts him over the fate of his research, which leaves her unsullied by anger but also emotionally muzzled. Casaubon dies heartsore, but can't connect this unhappiness with his egoism and conceit.)

Eliot's narrator does, however, make one important concession with Bulstrode. When Raffles returns to him at Stone Court, almost destroyed by drink and—Victorian readers surely inferred—his furious revenge, Bulstrode feels almost comparable malice. With "scorn hurrying like venom through his system," he fantasizes that "the will of God might be the death of that hated man" (623, 697), so permitting Eliot's narrator to advance a provocative irony: The man whose evangelical arrogance patronizes most of Middlemarch reveals that the "God" vindicating his purity extends his basest projections.

The implications of this moral corruption are more widespread than the narrator's success in uncovering evil, a relatively simple task. For what's to stop us from universalizing Bulstrode's ruse and representing God as the imagined agent of our collective yearning, the entity that in the Old Testament punishes miscreants and swaths of godless enemies—those failing to heed the illusions that we invest with absolute certainty? How can Eliot—and, by implication, monotheism in all its forms—condemn the first fantasy as idolatrous monomania while resisting the logic of its application to all systems of belief and prayer? Eliot certainly tries to parse irreverence and iconoclasm from sanctioned faith, but *Middlemarch* is too complex and subtle to sustain this frequently questionable distinction. In the end, Bulstrode's fantasies render him almost indistinguishable from Raffles, and thus similar to a host of other characters in the novel, including the predatory relatives waiting like vultures for Featherstone to die. Taken to its logical conclusion, this similitude tarnishes Eliotic fellow feeling, adding a menacing undertone to Bulstrode's ignominious exit from the community.

Since Bulstrode's killing Raffles deflects the community's hostility, it's fitting that Eliot compare his and his wife's hurried departure from Middlemarch with Pilgrim's and Faithful's trial as enemies of Vanity Fair in Bunyan's *Pilgrim's Progress*. The jury in Bunyan's allegory includes Mr. Love-lust, Mr. Live-loose, Mr. Enmity, Mr. Lyar, Mr. Cruelty, Mr. Hate-light, and Mr. Malice (103).[48] There's rich irony in the narrator's likening the Bulstrodes to Bunyan's victims, but the punishment of Harriet Bulstrode-as-Faithful is even more notable. In Bunyan's allegory, Faithful is sentenced to death, then brutally killed: "First they Scourged him, then they Buffetted him, then they Lanced his flesh with Knives; after that they Stoned him with Stones, then prickt him with their Swords, and last of all they burned him to Ashes at the Stake."[49] Bunyan made Faithful a martyr, of course, but Eliot represses most of this violence by turning the Bulstrodes into pariahs. Her allusion to this scene in *Pilgrim's Progress* nevertheless pinpoints the collective recrimination that her commitment to fellowship eventually must stifle.

One could view her backward glance at Bunyan as a nod to the Victorians' steady substitution of vengeance by law, but that's only half the story, not least because Bulstrode-as-Pilgrim is an almost obscene analogy. If this is progress in terms of collective restraint, then it indicates how easily Christian faith can lapse into elaborate casuistry. Moreover, as in *Romola*, Eliot's narrator seems split among incommensurate registers. Given Bulstrode's grotesque self-righteousness, it's worth asking whether the novel could have reached this sense of justice *without* introducing and expunging Raffles.

Although *Middlemarch* alludes only to the jury in *Pilgrim's Progress*, Raffles indicates how treachery and cruelty, mutually involved, ripple through Eliot's communities. Indebted to Casaubon for financial assistance, for example, Ladislaw soon realizes that "his dislike" of his cousin

> was flourishing at the expense of his gratitude, and spent much inward discourse in justifying the dislike. Casaubon hated him—he knew that very well; on his first entrance he could discern a bitterness in the mouth and a venom in the glance which would almost justify declaring war in spite of past benefits. (360)

A "venom in the glance . . . would almost justify declaring war": If the novel weren't intent on highlighting Casaubon and Ladislaw's mutual contempt, setting it against Bulstrode's later "war" with Raffles, we could dismiss the remark as hyperbole. But spite tarnishes intersubjectivity. We witness a model of intimacy here, prevalent as we've seen in Dostoyevsky's and Dickens's work, that's contingent on another's humiliation, even annihilation. We can't limit this problem to Eliot's villains, for it bleeds conceptually into all her social arrangements and is formally inseparable from her notion of sociability.

Apparently, Casaubon feels "deprived" of an earlier belief in his "superiority": "His antipathy to Will did not spring from the common jealousy of a winter-worn husband: it was something deeper, bred by his lifelong claims and discontents" (360). The narrator uses this acrimony to generalize about our peculiar readiness to despise those to whom we feel indebted:

> That is the way with us when we have any uneasy jealousy in our disposition: if our talents are chiefly of the burrowing kind, our honey-sipping cousin (whom we have grave reasons for objecting to) is likely to have a secret contempt for us, and any one who ad-

mires him passes an oblique criticism on ourselves. Having the scruples of rectitude in our souls, we are above the meanness of injuring him—rather we meet all his claims on us by active benefits; and the drawing of cheques for him, being a superiority which he must recognize, gives our bitterness a milder infusion. (360)

Though some confessional self-accusation may inform the narrator's characteristic "we," the "milder infusion" of bitterness is of course ironic, pointing to the lesser of two evils: Casaubon has neither "scruples of rectitude" nor a reason finally to *refrain* from "the meanness of injuring" Ladislaw. Such bitterness flourishes in the codicil to his will, which impedes Dorothea's chances of happiness, while neatly suggesting to Middlemarchers that she and Ladislaw flirted with adultery before Casaubon died. As in *The Mill on the Floss*, when Tulliver rashly assaults Wakem, Eliot's narrator implies that Casaubon's illness stems partly from failed efforts at suppressing his vindictive rage. It's too easy—and mistaken— to view these cases as isolated incidents, so disavowing our satisfaction that the embittered implode from half-vented fury. To many characters in Eliot's fiction, life consists in struggling to make sympathy prevail over what may be a healthier dose of rancor.

"The poet must know how to hate" (qtd. 224), the narrator reminds us, quoting Goethe, before using this wisdom to voice "a hatred which certainly found pretexts apart from religion such as were only too easy to find in the entanglements of human action" (442).[50] "Pretexts *apart from* religion" is again ironic: While religion can be a channel for unexamined hostility, as Feuerbach acknowledged when discussing "the hatred that belongs to faith" (*Essence* 265), it inadequately defends us against other forms of social cruelty. As Eliot's protagonists grope toward happiness, painfully aware of the obstacles thwarting them, the narrator concedes: "There is no general doctrine which is not capable of eating out our morality if unchecked by the deep-seated habit of direct fellow-feeling with individual fellow-men" (619). By this point in the novel we have few reasons for trusting this "deep-seated habit." Indeed, the statement's universality blots the novel's residual optimism by staining religion, philanthropy, and even sympathy with ubiquitous egoism. The narrator of *Felix Holt* similarly concludes: "Our selfishness is so robust and many-clutching, that, well encouraged, it easily devours all sustenance away from our poor little scruples" (454). The more Eliot amplifies these truisms, the harder it becomes to trust her remedies.

Fellow Feeling Redux

In voicing these intractable conflicts, *Middlemarch* complicates a thread from the earlier novels, especially when discussing what it means to be neighborly. The novel also develops an argument we've encountered before in Eliot's fiction—that since violent impulses easily override our "deep-seated habit of direct fellow-feeling," misanthropy is a propensity her characters can't always repress (619). Casaubon is perhaps the best example of a character with traits similar to misanthropic Featherstone's (parsimony, spite, disdain for others' stupidity, and resentment of "rivals" perceived as threats and thieves), but such disparate characters as Joshua Rigg, Raffles, Lydgate, Bulstrode, Ladislaw, and even Fred Vincy display similar traits. When Fred considers what he might inherit from Featherstone, for example, the narrator says "such ruminations naturally produced a streak of misanthropic bitterness" (119), as if Fred were set to inherit more than wealth from his aging benefactor. Raffles, as we've seen, moves beyond even vindictiveness, representing a type of force that in its "purity" is utterly averse to all forms of sociability. Despite representing fellow feeling as an ideal to which most characters aspire, then, *Middlemarch* endlessly catalogs what destroys sympathy (the Garths, Dorothea, and the aptly named Mr. Farebrother are sympathy's only conscientious proponents).

One explanation for this emphasis is the novel's apparent inability to decide if "silent suffering" is admirable or imprudent. Applauded when it prevails in figures like Silas Marner and Adam and Seth Bede, this condition has darker repercussions in *Middlemarch*. As Ladislaw tells Dorothea: "I suspect that you have some false belief in the virtues of misery, and want to make your life a martyrdom" (219–20), a comment surpassing the idea of tolerance and benign humility in *Adam Bede*. Whereas Dinah Morris's meek trust in others' goodness prevails in the earlier novel, others happily exploit the same qualities in Dorothea.

Like Eliot's earlier fiction, *Middlemarch* represents friends squabbling, spouses bickering, friends reveling in envy, and neighbors exulting in their enemies' mistakes. But while *Adam Bede* implied that suffering unites strife-ridden communities (464), *Middlemarch* indicates how poorly we make other people happy (519–20). It does so by confronting our limited tolerance for others' bigotry and pleasure, a theme that recurs prominently in the next chapter. "To most mortals," the narrator declares, "there is a stupidity which is unendurable and a stupidity which is altogether acceptable—else, indeed, what would become of social bonds?" (583–84). If given the chance, we might join Raffles in rescinding them. The problem devolves most painfully on relationships, and thus on marriage. Amplifying Dorothea's domestic misery and Bulstrode's nadir, the novel mercilessly spotlights Lydgate and Rosamond's unhappiness, the "hideous fettering of [their] domestic hate" (667)—a prelude, of course, to Gwendolen and Grandcourt's mutual loathing in *Daniel Deronda*.

Eliot's formidable intellect endlessly discovers weaknesses and forms of coercion in her putative communitarian arguments. As I've indicated, this is but one reason that fellow feeling in her novels clashes starkly with diverse hostile impulses. A superficial response to this dynamic would claim that her fiction amplifies these impulses the better to domesticate them. But this suggestion doesn't take us far enough, leaving too much assumed and too little examined. For a start, the hatred often *is* domestic, and Eliot's sometimes pat conclusions create in her novels an unsatisfying stalemate that smothers—without disguising—the impulses granting them complexity.

Even at their most sympathetic, then, Eliot's novels never forget the unpleasant underside of communities—their superstitions, petty jealousies, and appalling displays of cruelty. Behind her narrators' claims about fellowship, strains of conflict erupt, revealing the fragility of amity, the potential tyranny of groups, and the impersonal force of enjoyment. Mr. Snell can't skirt these problems by declaring fatuously at the end of *Marner*, "When a man had deserved his good luck, it was the part of his neighbours to wish him joy" (182). We might confer this role on our neighbors, but the risks in doing so aren't small. Snell's sentiment is morally satisfying, but the cant it typifies in Eliot's novels is often a pretext for violence.

CHAPTER FIVE

Life Envy in Robert Browning's Poetry

Hatred and Aesthetics

WHEN ROBERT BROWNING first told Julia Wedgwood that he "unduly like[d] the study of morbid cases of the soul," he broached a topic that has intrigued and baffled scholars ever since.[1] An intelligent socialite to whom Browning was attracted and with whom he corresponded frequently between 1864 and 1870, Wedgwood demurred. His subjects were disturbing, she thought, and his characters inartistic. Instead of "belong[ing] to the world," Guido Franceschini, arch villain in *The Ring and the Book*, seemed to her to inhabit a place "where Art finds no foothold."[2]

Dismayed and quibbling, Wedgwood advised Browning to stick to more sanguine topics. She scolded him for spoiling her pleasure and upsetting her expectations: "I fear I shall not find much food in the remaining books. . . . Shame and pain and humiliation need the irradiation of hope to be endurable as objects of contemplation; you have no right to associate them in our minds with hopeless, sordid wickedness."[3] By the time Browning responded, fully seven weeks later, the friendship had cooled.

Wedgwood was an unimaginative reader, but her belief that Guido and his ilk live "where Art finds no foothold" merits serious attention. The idea is especially provocative because the hatred Browning dramatizes through misanthropes and other mavericks explodes aesthetic and philosophical assumptions about reciprocity and collective harmony. His intellectual interest—and, surely, poetic delight—lies in exposing the flip side of these ideals as rancorous and antiharmonious. Indeed, his antiheroes wreak revenge on society by insisting energetically that all such ideals about social and interpersonal harmony contain the seeds of their destruction.

As we saw in the introduction, many precedents to such misanthropic antiheroism pepper English literature, for instance Milton's Satan and Shakespeare's Iago, who says that Cassio "has a daily beauty in his life, / That makes me ugly."[4] What's distinctive in Browning's villains is a form of excess pushing them beyond normal states of being and motive, conventional reciprocity, and orthodox assumptions about social life. Probing and vital, wild and sly, his malefactors exude an energy that destroys not only interpersonal ties but also relationality as such. *The Ring and the Book*, a series of poetic testimonials about a brutal murder case in Renaissance Italy (1698), dramatizes man's "surplusage of soul," a life force indifferent to moral and physical constraint, and oblivious to personal and collective well-being.[5] Guido alludes to an "overplus of mine," a force "explod[ing]" in murderous violence like the "eruption of the pent-up soul" (11.144, 466, 1494), and the commentator Tertium Quid agrees: "Men, plagued this fashion"—by this force—"get to explode this way, / If left no other" (4.1541–42).

Coupled with Browning's well-known fascination with hatred, these "explosions" accent a set of problems in his poetry that love and redemption can't fully overcome. They mark society's failure to absorb humanity's "surplus" affect, and thwart conventional justice by tarnishing the legal system with malice. Browning comes close to implying that it's irrelevant whether his protagonists are virtuous or corrupt, sociable or misanthropic (see FIGURE 5.1, Hill and Adamson's midcentury photograph of an inscrutable Hugh Miller). Though many scholars rightly maintain that he stopped short of relativism—indeed, retained in his late work an interest in the synthesizing aims of Christian theology—his fascination with excess surpasses the Manichean basis of that theology. Browning amplifies (as would Freud) that we hate more easily than we love, and that extreme experiences corrode the social tie by destroying its central tenets.

FIGURE 5.1 *Hugh Miller* (1843–47). David Octavius Hill and Robert Adamson. *Courtesy Glasgow University Library Special Collections.*

This emphasis on energetic hate and antisocial motive departs from previous approaches to Browning's work, including that he represented virtue as vulnerable while permitting evil to flourish. Certainly, compared with Guido's lupine vigor, Pompilia, his murdered wife, resembles a pallid cipher. Likewise, in "Soliloquy of the Spanish Cloister," Brother Lawrence seems pathetically—annoyingly—naïve beside his rancorous counterpart. My focus, however, is the philosophical and aesthetic ramifications of such excess, which, as Wedgwood's revulsion reminds us, are extraordinary departures from utilitarian and positivist arguments about collective life. Moving from Browning's interest in interpersonal rancor to his near-metaphysical accounts of the way hatred destroys sociality, we'll see how comprehensively he revoked cherished assumptions of the time, including Bentham's maxim that the collective good should override the vagaries of individual will.

In his complex lyric "By the Fire-Side," Browning's speaker—ostensibly the poet *in propria persona*—avows, in a moment that Romantic poetry might have represented by devoted union:

> If two lives join, there is oft a scar,
>> They are one and one, with a shadowy third;
> One near one is too far.[6]

If two people are to connect, to put this in Forsterian terms, then proximity isn't enough, though it keeps us wanting more. In Browning's post-Romantic world, however, the answer to closer intimacy isn't to dislodge this "shadowy third." The paradoxical effect of such attempts is greater estrangement:

> Oh, the little more, and how much it is!
>> And the little less, and what worlds away! (191–92)

The poem ostensibly celebrates Browning's devotion to Elizabeth Barrett, but the desire for union has unforeseen effects, showing that perfect reciprocity doesn't exist, since the lover continually "misses"—surpasses, falters before, and even forgets—his beloved. Though memory and anticipation trick us into believing that the "shadowy third" will disappear, the lyric indicates that we're never fully present with our beloved. The "third" is both an effect of closeness and its precondition.

If this were all that Browning described, it might be enough to say that he revealed, a century before Lacan, the asymmetry of love. But as the poet is also renowned for his "strange interest in morbid psychology" (Leslie Stephen's complaint), we can't call him solipsistic or even contrarian and leave matters there.[7] While the asymmetry he explores is a basis for his villains' motivations, it sounds new and disturbing ethical arrangements, in which his protagonists are answerable less to God and their beloveds than to a form of energy threatening to hurl them—and anyone in their way—into the abyss.

When in "Cleon" the eponymous (and imaginary) Greek poet describes what "joy-hunger" "stings" us into doing, he gauges the volatile consequences, for people and communities, of "life's [being] inadequate to joy" (328–29, 249), an idea comparable to that in "By the Fire-Side":

> We struggle, fain to enlarge
> Our bounded physical recipiency,
> Increase our power, supply fresh oil to life,
> Repair the waste of age and sickness: no,
> It skills not! life's inadequate to joy,
> As the soul sees joy, tempting life to take. (245–50)

Cleon says that "all this joy in natural life" is "exquisitely perfect" (203, 205); humanity alone experiences "failure" because its soul (whether consciousness, mind, or imagination in this pre-Christian context) "craves" more than the human body can absorb or accomplish (241). It is chastening that knowledge points up our sorry limitations, accenting what will always remain elusive happiness:

> There's a world of capability
> For joy, spread round about us, meant for us,
> Inviting us; and still the soul craves all,
> And still the flesh replies, "Take no jot more
> Than ere thou clombst the tower to look abroad!" (239–43)

In standard interpretations of this argument, Cleon invokes the fatigue accompanying aging. We're tempted to live just as "the soul sees joy, tempting life to take" (250), but our frailty makes this impossible: "life," as he says, is woefully "inadequate" to this aim (249). But the phrase "tempting life to take" is also a pun. We can understand it both in apposition to "sees joy"—that is, as the path the soul yearns to pursue—and as alluding to the thoughts of comparison and deficiency surfacing earlier in the poem, contributing to Browning's well-known theory of imperfection.[8] In this second reading, humanity's consciousness perceives the gap between absolute joy and its own paltry ability to feel it. Envying beings (such as animals) that experience this divide less acutely or not at all, consciousness is tempted to appropriate their and others' joy in a bid to top up its own.[9] According to Cleon, the root problem is an "intro-active . . . quality [that] arise[s]" in man's soul; but the impulse to reflect on—and correct—the ensuing malaise is a "force" ruling our behavior (211–13).

Although there's evidence here and in many other poems supporting conventional and counterintuitive interpretations of joy, Browning did not turn these notions of ecstasy, appropriation, and theft into a larger maxim. Indeed, his poetry offers many exceptions to the counterintuitive perspective, celebrating more-orthodox visions of love and harmony. Nevertheless, his vampiric portrayal of hatred often depletes the virtue that eventually, perhaps miraculously, overwhelms it; and hatred and ugliness are frequently zero-sum qualities in his work, their hostile relation to virtue proving corrosive rather than dialectical. Browning often doesn't replace hatred with love or convert the first element into the second, that is, because both can be as dissimilar as proximate lovers hoping to unite. Triumphant virtue acquires extra piquancy after withstanding the onslaught, but the result is anticlimactic, even bizarre, because the vulnerability of goodness *provokes* Browning's villains into attack: They are disgusted by modesty, and violating it gives them exquisite pleasure.

Given the recurrence of Browning's counterintuitive emphasis, meekness acquires almost outrageous strength. Its representatives mustn't in turn appear to enjoy outwitting evil, and in fact survive by disdaining schadenfreude. But whether the reader is as scrupulous in renouncing this glee is more doubtful. As we saw in the introduction, "Soliloquy of the Spanish Cloister" increases our satisfaction by making Brother Lawrence unaware of the hatred he inspires. His ignorance is presented as a factor that invites punishment, as if his naïveté cries out to be harmed. That we hear nothing from him directly compromises us, given the complicity established between speaker and audience "(He-he! There his lily snaps!)," but it doesn't diminish our joy in overhearing the speaker's rant against this harmless monk. Perhaps we laugh after hearing how the former keeps Lawrence's flowers "close-nipped on the sly!" while plotting how to trip him, cursing, and thus "send him flying / Off to hell" (48, 55–56). With such robust imagery, the speaker's mockery, blasphemy, onomatopoeia ("Gr-r-r-"), and feverish exclamations (four in the first stanza alone) make his hatred compelling. As the casuist Bishop Blougram declares elsewhere, in feigned apology, "Our interest's on the dangerous edge of things. . . . We watch while th[o]se in equilibrium keep / The giddy line midway" ("Bishop Blougram's Apology" 395, 399–400). When colorful rhetoric frames this "dangerous edge," it's tempting to dismiss malice as "a splendid fault whereat we wink, / Wishing your cold correctness sparkled so!" (*Ring* 1.196–97). In the face of such entertainment, probity and decorum seem tedious indeed.

This dynamic is a central concern in "The Pied Piper of Hamelin," which begins by describing the fearless rats that feast on everything from fine cheese to "gowns lined with ermine," as if part of their pleasure lies in ruining everyone else's (3.25). Their gorging anticipates the piper's struggle with the mayor's and council's greed, the rats proving also metaphoric. After refusing to pay the agreed sum, the mayor winks, delighted that as the rats can't return, the piper must settle for less reward. The musician takes revenge by "stealing" the villagers' children. Indeed, after he assures them they'll be happy in "a joyous land," they vanish through a "wondrous portal," so reaffirming a link in Browning's poetry between "stolen" pleasure and the abyss (13.240, 227). Such conflicts over joy are structurally inevitable, enhancing the poem's energy and restlessness (anapests, trochees, and amphibrachs syncopate its iambic beats) while helping us believe that correct payment would offset the imbalance between those taking happiness and those forced to relinquish it.

However, this "surplus" energy doesn't merely enhance the dynamism of Browning's poetry; it adds, scandalously, to the works' aesthetic effect by making hatred ebullient. We saw in "Soliloquy of the Spanish Cloister" how the speaker's rant overwhelms any impression that timid Brother Lawrence could make, and the same is true of Pompilia and others in *The Ring and the Book*, book 11, when Guido vents his bilious rage. When admitting, moreover, that he hates Pompilia "for no one cause / Beyond my pleasure so to do," Guido rescinds his claim that he had her killed *honoris causa* after she cuckolded him (11.1432–33). The satisfaction he experiences in voicing his tirade snares him into betraying the more "reasonable" defense. As well, his rage pushes the poem's conception of justice beyond conventional ideas of restraint, confounding legal disinterestedness. Since the murder occurs after a crisis of understanding, reciprocity is a crucial issue here, and it recurs when the poem must identify a punishment equal to his crime. Exulting in "wolfish" cruelty, Guido becomes increasingly contemptuous of others' humanity, while those seeking legal redress, like Giuseppe Caponsacchi, appear as lacking in objectivity as the man they would gladly execute.

This asymmetrical vision of power and pleasure, by no means limited to *The Ring and the Book*, is in Browning's poetry inevitable and oddly gratifying. A mechanism driving his plots, the vision also exposes relational difficulties among his characters. Roy Gridley lists how often Guido, bragging about his vigor, dismisses Pompilia as a heifer, a "Calf-creature," a lamb, a brood-hen, a pullet, a hare, and a horse "fearful of the fire which is Guido" (11.977, 989, 1174, 1321, 1423, 1328, 1395).[10] More important, he repeats Guido's claim that Pompilia is "a nullity in female shape . . . [an] insipid harmless nullity" (11.1111, 1127). Such statements are a key to understanding this remarkable poem: They highlight then check a demand for freedom and release through which Guido tries to rescind all consequences. His pleasure in finding such freedom increases, moreover, from knowing that others will suffer immeasurably from its effects.

While Guido plays up his wife's exasperating meekness, his fantasy of Pompilia and her parents magnifies their power, as if *in their nothingness* they deplete his vitality. Thus he likens Pompilia to a "sheep-like thing" whose meekness temporarily blinds Guido to "the veritable wolf beneath" (11.1174, 1176). He's already called her, in book 5, a hawk with the semblance of a pigeon (5.703, 701), and in book 11 insists she's like "some timid chalky ghost / That turns the church into a charnel" (11.2120–21). One might dismiss these claims as hyperbolic, but that would ignore the strength with which he sustains them as projections. At such moments, *"negativity as such has a positive function,"* since it "enables and structures our positive consistency."[11] By extension, Guido depends on such virtue to justify his acts, briefly allowing Pompilia to embody goodness, as this increases the pleasure of violation.[12]

Hence her declaring, on her deathbed,

> And as my presence was importunate,—
> My earthly good, temptation and a snare,—
> *Nothing about me* but drew somehow down
> His hate upon me,—somewhat so excused
> Therefore, since hate was thus the truth of him.
> (7.1723–27; my emphasis)

Similarly, when Guido calls the Comparini "two abominable nonde-scripts," "taenia[e] that had sucked [him] dry of juice" (11.1114, 1604), what matters is the strength he attributes to Pompilia's parents, the en-joyment they seem to experience in their betrayal.

Let's approach this issue and its ethical problems by engaging simpler poems where hatred seems to be only an interpersonal affair. "Porphyr-ia's Lover" is partly an outrageous rationalization of murder, stemming from the lover's attempt to destroy Porphyria's status and sexual power. Yet the poem's most revealing lines describe how the speaker "warily oped her lids" to check whether Porphyria was still alive, only to find that "again / Laughed the blue eyes without a stain" (44–45). In one sense, this phrase conveys the lover's psychotic belief that Porphyria, though dead, has achieved "her darling one wish" (57). The laughing eyes seem to mock him, extending her joy, which infuriates him at the start of the poem when Porphyria "glide[s]" into the cottage without apologizing for her delay (6). The inverted active voice marking the phrase "again / Laughed the blue eyes" emphasizes the lover's inability to control Porphyria's happiness, one of the factors that enrages him, culminating in "a kind of revenge for all her decision-making."[13] Lying beyond his control and reach is a form of happiness to which he fears he's entirely incidental.

"My Last Duchess," also published in *Dramatic Lyrics*, describes a similar scenario. What intrigues then repels the Duke is his wife's "spot of joy" (twice mentioned), for such happiness surpasses him, pointing to other "cause[s]" that apparently are "enough / For calling up" her pleasure (20–21). He tells the Count's emissary that he lacked the rhetorical wherewithal to accuse his now deceased wife, in a sentence nonetheless accompanied by his quotation marks,

> "Just this
> Or that in you disgusts me; here you miss,
> Or there exceed the mark." (37–39)

Yet even without these quotation marks we would doubt his claim, for the Duke is articulate and quick to speak his mind, and Browning's dramatic monologues shrewdly expose his speakers' self-delusions, especially when attributing faults to others. The Duke's haughty contempt—projected onto his wife because, by his lights, she wanders indiscriminately among other people and things—indicates that he has contemplated many times this "weakness," despite claims to the contrary. And her "spot of joy"—arising, maddeningly, whether or not he's present—betrays his apparent irrelevance to her:

> She had
> A heart—how shall I say?—too soon made glad,
> Too easily impressed; she liked whate'er
> She looked on, and her looks went everywhere. (21–24)

Finally, his nonspecific objections ("Just this / Or that"), combined with the language of default and overreach ("here you miss / Or there exceed the mark"), mirror Browning's account of energy and contempt in *The Ring and the Book*—as, for instance, when "Half-Rome" speaks about "the natural over-energy" lulling Guido into "Vault[ing] too loftily over what barred him late" (2.1534, 1532). What goads these speakers, we might say, is both the ineffable quality of joy and the intangible quality of this "over-energy"—the fact that one can't possess, or reproduce unfailingly, the enigmatic factor that sparks another's fancy. Consequently, hatred extends beyond interpersonal relations, raising larger questions about these characters' relation to the world, and to the nothingness beyond it.

The Duke, Guido, and Porphyria's lover aren't simply obsessed with their lovers' experience of joy—a claim that simplifies their psychological turmoil. Among other factors, they fear that other people—especially lovers—will experience happiness at their expense, and that strangers will glean this secret and mock them accordingly.[14] (Consider Lippi's mischievous glee in "play[ing] hot cockles, all the doors being shut, /

Till, wholly unexpected, in there pops / The hothead husband!" [381–83].) What these "hotheads" covet, but of course can't access, is less the key to their lover's or spouse's happiness than possession of the peculiar "something" *beyond* them, of which neither party has full control or understanding.[15] As Earl G. Ingersoll explains of the Duchess, the Duke "murders desire in her."[16] Although this result outwardly is the same as taking her life, the motive for murder acquires different meaning in this light: It makes her person subordinate to what her desire represents to him, a shocking but fascinating outcome. Minimizing the power of this transference neutralizes the strength of Browning's insights, the complexity of his ethical arrangements, and how the ensuing conflicts implicate us as readers. In detailing a lover's apparently limitless contempt for his beloved's joie de vivre, Browning's poems do scandalous justice to a series of fantasies that most lovers would deny had ever crossed their minds.

Killing the Thing One Loves

"If we are to be judged by our unconscious wishful impulses," says Freud in the second half of "Thoughts for the Times on War and Death" (1915), "we ourselves are, like primaeval man, a gang of murderers."[17] Although clearly inadvertent on Freud's part (Browning making no appearance in his written work),[18] he could almost be alluding to Guido's thugs in *The Ring and the Book*. Freud's provocative assertion, intended as a rebuke to those "pious souls . . . who would like to believe that our nature is remote from any contact with what is evil and base," surfaces after his discussion of our "denial of death" and its relation to the biblical proscription of murder ("Thoughts" 295). "The first and most important prohibition made by the awakening conscience was," he claims,

> "Thou shalt not kill." It was acquired in relation to dead people who were loved, as a reaction against the satisfaction of the hatred hidden behind the grief for them; and it was gradually extended to strangers who were not loved, and finally even to enemies. This final extension of the commandment is no longer experienced by civilized man. (295)

Because of the erosion of this proscription's symbolic power, we no longer love our neighbors—or, perhaps the same thing, our enemies—quite as we ought. Advancing this thesis after the outbreak of World War I, Freud views hostility among nations as intrinsic to civilizations, asking near the end of his essay whether humanity shouldn't begin viewing peace as an exception rather than the rule.

But despite its varied historical and symbolic significance, the injunction against murder can't eradicate "the satisfaction of the hatred" underpinning not only interpersonal relations but also modern civilization as such. This satisfaction is, Freud says, a legacy of evolutionary struggle, a pitiable consequence of our alienation in language, and an effect of the hostility we feel toward even loved ones. These are, in his words, "on the one hand an inner possession, components of our own ego; but on the other hand they are partly strangers, even enemies. With the exception of only a very few situations, there adheres to the tenderest and most intimate of our love-relations a small portion of hostility which can excite an unconscious death-wish" (298). As no one is exempt from this hatred, the question becomes whether we bestow hostility freely or temper it by apparent affection. As Freud put it, in a claim so devoid of romanticism that it sounds almost scandalous: "It might be said that we owe the fairest flowerings of our love to the reaction against the hostile impulse which we sense within us" (299).

One consequence of this assertion, to which most poems discussed in this chapter also point, is that we try covertly to rid ourselves of attachments. In the unconscious, at least, we are all partly misanthropic. As Tim Dean paraphrases Freud's argument above: "We not only wish for the deaths . . . of our enemies, but often desire the speedy elimination of our nearest and dearest too, as a consequence of the ambivalence that infects all love."[19] In chapter 2, we saw this dynamic recur in Dickens's *Martin Chuzzlewit*. The erosion of guards against such hatred widens the gap between hostility and its sanctioned release, leaving us fewer ways of processing it. Hence, according to Hazlitt, the role of literature and the arts in representing aggression or, today, the proliferation of true-to-life video programs, sadistic game shows, and "reality" TV, whose popularity flourishes the more observers decry the malice involved.[20]

As I explained in the introduction, Bentham also anticipated this discussion, hoping the principle of utility would regulate "the pleasures of the malevolent or dissocial affections" to "prevent [their] doing mischief."[21] Still, Hazlitt countered that part of the "pleasure of hating" consists in "throw[ing] aside the trammels of civilisation, the flimsy veil of humanity" when we read.[22] "The wild beast resumes its sway within us" as we do, "we feel like hunting-animals, and as the hound starts in his sleep and rushes on the chase in fancy, the heart rouses itself in its native lair, and utters a wild cry of joy, at being restored once more to freedom and lawless, unrestrained impulses" (12:129).

Browning often replayed this last conflict in his work. When Guido pretends in 1698 to voice the equivalent of Benthamite concerns, he piously announces:

> Who breaks law, breaks pact, therefore, helps himself
> To pleasure and profit over and above the due,
> And must pay forfeit,—pain beyond his share:
> For pleasure is the sole good in the world,
> Anyone's pleasure turns to someone's pain. (11.526–30)

Though this last claim is probably irrefutable, Guido's statement is completely insincere.[23] Indeed, because his speech in book 11 would challenge the foundations of Benthamite thought, given his fundamental indifference to others' satisfaction *and* pain, the resulting philosophical vacuum makes us ask whether Victorian and contemporary readers remain loyal to Bentham or succumb, with Guido, to the lure of Hazlittian and Browningesque schadenfreude. As Daniel Karlin shows in *Browning's Hatreds*, the poet certainly capitalized on that energy, representing hatred as emblematic of struggle in the broadest sense, and schadenfreude as a force transporting readers in excitement, helping them "Yoke Hatred, Crime, Remorse," before they "break . . . through the tumult" in search of radiancy (*The Two Poets of Croisic* 159.1269, 1271).[24]

But if Browning's understanding of hatred (ostensibly resembling Freud's) is coeval with love, is enlightenment in his poetry contingent on his characters' renouncing enmity? The poetry I've interpreted suggests not; it shatters our assumption that desire serves life and collective harmony. Browning implies, scandalously, that we achieve enlightenment through hatred as well as its renunciation, a proposition that I'll defend against some of his scholars. Indeed, as the poet understands hatred independently of love and conventional desire, even Freud's argument that we unconsciously desire the elimination of loved ones can't take us far enough when interpreting this poetry. Such assertions don't turn Browning into a moral relativist. Nor do they dispute his poetry's gesturing, in Clyde de L. Ryals's words, "to the infinite and the Absolute."[25] We may still view Browningesque negativity psychoanalytically, in other words, but we can't reduce it to Freudianism, at least in its 1950s American idiom. We are more likely to grasp the cause of hatred in Browning's poetry if we associate it with "life envy," a principle that Lacan outlined in his 1959–60 seminar on the ethics of psychoanalysis.

"Isn't it strange, very odd," asks Lacan, "that a being admits to being jealous of something in the other to the point of hatred and the need to destroy, jealous of something that he is incapable of apprehending in any way, by any intuitive path? . . . I don't think one has to be an analyst to see such disturbing undulations passing through subjects' behaviors."[26] This rhetorical question surpasses Freud's argument by associating "the need to destroy [*besoin de détruire*]" not with "ordinary" loathing or repressed desire but with jealousy of "something in the other"—something, as we saw earlier in Browning's poetry, that needn't exist in any material sense to have profound transferential power.[27] As this something is always mediated, we're incapable of apprehending it directly—a lesson that *Silas Marner* taught us. We gauge our happiness, that is, by assessing—enviously or not, as the case may be—other people's contentment. Lacan adopted the German term *Lebensneid* ("life envy") to highlight the "strange malaise" resulting from such hostile comparisons. Life envy "is not an ordinary jealousy," he insists; "it is the jealousy born in a subject in his relation to an other, insofar as this other is held to enjoy a certain form of *jouissance* or superabundant vitality [*surabondance vitale*], that the subject perceives as something that he cannot apprehend by means of even the most elementary of affective movements" (237; 278). That such vitality and malign joy elude us doesn't diminish their imaginary power, then, but intensifies it. We might even experience the ensuing comparisons as a form of theft, resulting in murderous rage. As Dean puts it, extrapolating Lacan's argument, "*He whom I suppose to know how to enjoy, I hate*."[28] Those with apparently limitless joy are perceived—irrationally, of course—as robbing others of the opportunity to feel the same bliss.

By implication, gratuitous cruelty in Browning's poems needs no primal basis in love. So, despite earlier allusions to the "eruption of the pent-up soul" (*Ring* 11.1494), the repressive hypothesis cannot help us here. And though Freud's model sometimes ties conflict to repressed desire, keeping hatred in the realm of love, Browning's and Lacan's arguments free hatred from conventional ontology and affect. This idea converges with Browning's "malleolable" understanding of character and speech (1.702). Both factors point up a performative dimension of identity, as well as an understanding of identification that repeatedly fails, since speech and character face an impasse beyond which they no longer mean anything. We might expect joy to support meaning, to carry significance, but in Browning's poetry the opposite is generally true, and since the results are so devastating and violent it's important to consider why. Forming a basis for life envy, joy points more often to a void, or what Lacan called "'holes' in . . . meaning."[29]

In *The Ring and the Book*, Guido alludes to "the honest instinct, pent and crossed through life, / Let surge by death into a visible flow / Of rapture" (11.2062–64). The instinct is "honest" here, not because it accords with consciousness but, on the contrary, because it exposes an ecstatic hankering for death-in-life. Not surprisingly, Browning's characters and speakers often view death as both a blissful end to suffering and a final epiphany, as if, to invoke *Easter-Day*, annihilation would help them "at last awake / From life, that insane dream we take / For waking now" (14.479–81).[30] Yet despite enabling this discovery, the "honest instinct" is indifferent to the damage it causes. Put differently, if the death drive cuts through swaths of social and psychic dishonesty, it is *jouissance*, the malign joy and "superabundant vitality" lying beyond the pleasure principle, that bounces us into the void.

Despite Guido's infectious enthusiasm for "rapture," then, what goads him is, he says, a "hunger I may feed but never sate, / Tormented on to perpetuity" (5.1966–67). Here, as elsewhere, Browning blends insatiable "hunger" with nonredemptive "honesty," making Guido's expectation of lasting happiness result in greater suffering and joylessness. But though we witness, in book 11, Guido's realization that he'll be "tormented on to perpetuity," the realization comes too late to cancel earlier manifestations of enmity, leaving these to reverberate at the poem's end as gnashing rage and distress.

Consequently, scholars have disputed Robert Langbaum's much-discussed assertion that Guido is saved soon after book 11 ends. Because Guido cries out, "Pompilia, will you let them murder me?" (11.2425) and shuns the hypocrisy he earlier voiced in his apparent defense, Langbaum comments: "Far from making Guido the devil incarnate, this self-portrayal is a station on his way to self-understanding and therefore salvation."[31] Like other critics, I dispute especially the final transition in this argument ("and therefore salvation"), believing that the poem frustrates Langbaum's expectation. Biographical details can't settle literary debates, especially given Browning's fondness for impersonation, but we should at least acknowledge the evidence. When, in the letter cited earlier, Wedgwood urged him: "Oh, be merciful to us in Guido's last display!,"[32] Browning responded with exasperation that the story is factual rather than imaginary, adding: "Guido 'hope?'—do you bid me turn him into that sort of thing? No, indeed! Come, I won't send you more, if you will but lift your finger!"[33]

This well-known reply is, Langbaum concedes, "the strongest argument against me, and I must do what I can to try to diminish its force." He tries to do so by arguing that the "letter was written in pique" (292). One could as easily claim that Langbaum shares with Wedgwood the same recalcitrant belief in happy endings that Browning wanted to dislodge—the same regret that "so large a part of your canvas is spent in delineating what is merely hateful."[34] "Given Browning's often stated views of the afterlife," Langbaum explains, "there should be no doubt of Guido's eventual salvation" (291–92). But especially in Browning's case, there's always some doubt about poetic intention; and other concerns also press this reading: Why should we assume, as Langbaum puts it, that redemption is the necessary conclusion to draw once Guido attains self-understanding?[35]

Because Guido's pride in consistency impedes any suggestion of evil's use-value—its being bent toward virtue—he betrays Victorian expectations about reform that Wedgwood also exemplifies. Since Guido's near-final words are "All that was, is; . . . / Nor is it in me to unhate my hates" (11.2397–98), his impulse clearly is not to forgo revenge, but to embrace the seeds of rancor nourishing it, thereby "go[ing] inside my soul / And shut[ting] its door behind me" (11.2289–90):

> Let me turn wolf, be whole, and sate, for once,—
> Wallow in what is now a wolfishness
> Coerced too much by the humanity
> That's half of me as well! Grow out of man,
> Glut the wolf-nature,—what remains but grow
> Into man again, be man indeed
> And all man? (11.2054–60)

As we saw earlier, the "honest instinct" that Guido believes will help him "glut the wolf-nature" thwarts his ideas of wholeness and satiation. The energy he boasts about defies containment and conventional limits. That "growing out of" manhood will, paradoxically, help him "grow [back i]nto" it is fallacious for other reasons, too; one can't augment part of an already split identity and expect to restore balance. What Guido's fantasy exposes is the violent division and crisis of understanding between Pompilia and him that provoked the murder in the first place.[36] That he wants to substitute wolfishness for his existing identity ideally would free the result—"all man"—from any residual loyalty to humanity. "Away with man!" he exclaims, before asking mockingly, "What shall I say to God?" (*Ring* 11.934). Similar accounts of Guido's misanthropy recur throughout the poem, as when "Half-Rome" insists: "'Twas in his very brow / Always to knit itself against the world" (2.283–84).

Guido is in this respect not only ill-suited to sociability, but also poised to shatter its central tenets, in ways resembling his earlier Renaissance counterparts, like Vindice in Tourneur's *Revenger's Tragedy* and Edmund in *King Lear* ("Wherefore should I / Stand in the plague of custom ...?" [1.2.2–3]). More than an attribute associated with Guido's villainy, this misanthropy bears out Browning's notion of evil as arelational and antiharmonious. Denying the most elemental reciprocity, Guido's rebellion against the world culminates in his near-perfect estrangement from "civilized life" (11.1660), compounding the conflicts that beset most relations in the poem. His hatred exposes the emptiness—the relational inadequacies—that we encountered before in Browning's poetry. So, after his rejection of society, Guido's near-metaphysical strife is inevitable, for he has no one left to argue with.

If we followed Langbaum here, our perspective on Guido's condition would "depend on whether we see [him] as human and therefore capable of development, or whether we see him as belonging to another order of existence, as an Iago or devil figure" (290). But the lines are too starkly drawn here and, as Freud and Lacan have shown, the summation of psychological possibilities too limited. A commitment to evil is, after all, still a form of development. Critics—especially those influenced by theology—often recoil from Guido's contempt for virtue, saying it disqualifies him from membership in humanity. As Wedgwood urged Browning, he should write as "one who has been taught supremely to believe in goodness by the close neighbourhood of a beautiful soul."[37] But this cant dissociates evil from humanity, ignoring all that we've learned from anticommunitarian philosophy, including Freud's indictment of human cruelty: "Homo homini lupus," man is a wolf to man. "Who," asks Freud, "in the face of all his experience of life and of history, will have the courage to dispute this assertion?"[38] Since Guido brags (*pace* Ovid) that the cruel Lycaon lived forever when he became a wolf, Browning—had he lived to hear Freud's rhetorical question—would surely have agreed with it (11.2050–51).

While Guido clearly perceives what redemption entails, then, he voices an ethics of detachment, not of moral improvement. Coupled with his commitment to destruction, this perspective indicates what aspects of community life are to him intolerable. Granted, his understanding occurs after Pompilia is murdered, a crime we can't ignore. But his refusal to cede to religious, legal, and community demands has important ethical ramifications of its own, stemming partly from his failure to sacrifice radically antisocial forms of enjoyment. And though we would call abhorrent the consequences of this violence when it's unleashed on Pompilia, the unflinching honesty with which Guido directs violence at himself, before confronting his own abyss of being, remains striking. As Žižek explains, such honesty is focused on those limit-experiences in which the subject finds himself confronted with the death drive at its purest, prior to its reversal into sublimation. . . . What "Death" stands for at its most radical is not merely the passing of earthly life, but the "night of the world," the self-withdrawal, the absolute contraction of subjectivity, the severing of its links with "reality."[39]

Partly for this reason, Guido's brief amplification of "Benthamite" thought clashes with his disingenuous attempt at appeasing Cardinal Acciaiuoli and Abate Panciatichi. Instead, Guido raises profound doubts about what constitutes the good and why we would even dream of renouncing our enjoyment and vitality for collective gain. The significance of his misanthropy lies in his refusing to sacrifice this bliss for a community in which he's ceased to believe and about which he no longer cares.

Guido isn't alone in enduring this problem or in feeling "hate / Of all things in, under, and above earth." Consequently, it's worth examining why glee in general obstructs justice in *The Ring and the Book* and related works. In book 6, Caponsacchi, the man with whom Pompilia eloped to Rome, voices what Karlin calls a "lurid, violent, and nauseating daydream," though one that's also, in Karlin's view, "the most powerful expression of hatred in the poem."[40] Caponsacchi's joyous rumination on Guido's imminent suffering is at least three dozen lines long, but one of its recurring motifs, influenced by Dante's *Inferno*, is a wish that Guido "slide out of life,"

> Pushed by the general horror and common hate
> Low, lower,—left o' the very ledge of things,
> I seem to see him catch convulsively
> One by one at all honest forms of life,
> . . . .
> And still they disengage them from his clutch. (6.1911–18)

One pictures Guido in a kind of moral free fall, suffering from the very "disengage[ment]" that his bid for freedom first led him to pursue. Karlin observes valuably that Caponsacchi's is "a quintessentially Victorian, and post-Darwinian, vision, one of devolution, of regression from the high to the low."[41]

Further, Caponsacchi hopes Guido will suffer the consequences of his misanthropy by having the community sever all ties to him, as if returning hatred to its apparent source could neutralize Caponsacchi's own bile.

As his fantasies transport Caponsacchi, however, this last expectation is denied him. Browning thereby mocks those who believe that their vicious judgments of others are disinterested, unfettered by rage. Caponsacchi's investment in Guido's suffering defeats his hope of relinquishing ties to Guido, betraying any notion that hatred is self-contained and reducible to misanthropes. His conception of justice is almost as punitive and sadistic as his enemy's.

The Lure of Self-Extinction

But nowhere in Browning's work does this coupling of revenge and hatred recur more powerfully than in "'Childe Roland to the Dark Tower Came,'" a popular, allusive 1855 poem whose speaker pursues a form of exploration that flirts with personal harm, even self-extinction. In ways similar to Guido's resistance to salvation, the wandering speaker of "Childe Roland" is goaded, revolted, and excited by a quest into which he's partly trapped into consenting and over which he apparently has little control. Both the poem's setting and its speaker's identity are disturbingly vague, the former resembling a horrific dreamscape (fostering a host of allegorical and quasi-psychoanalytic readings) that replaces the merciless "eye" Guido imagines drives him relentlessly toward annihilation (11.924). And we can't finally say whether the narrator is Roland—legendary knight of Charlemagne—one of his peers, or someone wanting to eulogize him. At the start of the poem, Browning directs us to Edgar's song in *King Lear*, which gives the work its title, but the Norman poet Turold was probably the first to herald Charlemagne's knight in the French epic *La chanson de Roland* (c. 1100).

What, however, could one celebrate in Browning's poem? In it, the giddy sense of freedom accompanying the speaker's missing self-concern collides with a set of metaphysical forces rendering his courage humiliatingly small. The poem anticipates why Hardy's protagonists—themselves recording a debt to Browning[42]—battle stubbornly against a faceless "Immanent Will." Also uniting "Childe Roland's" speaker with

Guido is a "daemonic energy" and a belief that integrity consists in turning away from the collective good, rather than sacrificing themselves for it.[43] (The isolation and medievalism of "Childe Roland" underscore this even more powerfully than does the Renaissance setting of *The Ring and the Book*.) Put differently, both poems substitute brutal confrontations between the subject and nothingness for courtship and kinship, highlighting how the individual might withstand the impersonal forces that would obliterate it. As Karlin observes, "Childe Roland" is not "about relationship, and indeed . . . might . . . be thought to achieve [its aim] by the sacrifice of relationship."[44] This far-reaching insight returns us to "By the Fire-Side" and the implications of Browning's swerving away from reciprocity even when invoking it, by advocating a more elemental, precarious understanding of being. Departing from conventional Victorian morality, he often considers it irrelevant whether his protagonists are pure or corrupt, altruistic or misanthropic—one reason critics often (and inaccurately) call him a relativist.[45]

Like "Porphyria's Lover," with its opening references to the "sullen wind" tearing down treetops "for spite" (2, 3), "Childe Roland" frequently uses the pathetic fallacy to capture this widespread hostility. The speaker crosses a vast plain that initially seems "grey . . . all round: / Nothing but plain to the horizon's bound" (52–53), but on closer examination it is pockmarked with holes, extrusions leaking "substances like boils" (153), and grass that "gr[ows] as scant as hair / In leprosy" (73–74), as if the speaker were stumbling across a massive head. Since the river confronting him is "petty yet so spiteful!" and nature as a whole is "starved [and] ignoble" (115, 56), the landscape is not only hostile to humanity, but also anthropomorphized as one of its enemies. In this sense it is more alive than the speaker, whose character, as John Willoughby astutely notes, is so thinly drawn as to appear "not quite there." He "seems unreal or more than real, a patent fiction or a symbol for something more than himself."[46] Thus does the speaker anticipate Guido's self-surpassing aims. Devoid of conventional being, he is closer to resembling pure drive.

For the duration of this poem, then, we inhabit a Browningesque terrain familiar only to the extent that it describes a fierce zero-sum game, in which the landscape, the "hoary cripple," and presumably the secret inhabitant of the Dark Tower seek every possible opportunity to rob the speaker of life. If this is a pre-Freudian allegory about the unconscious, as many have claimed, it's also one in which destructive forces of nature and the speaker's own reckless quest prove indistinguishable. "Freudian" readings of the poem forestall this conclusion, arguing that we awake from such nightmares and so put them in their proper place.[47] But Browning's poem inverts this fantasy, making clear that our "awakening" as such is to an alienated state that guards against our ongoing attraction to death. It is society, we might say, that intercedes between the tower and us, though no community can really dupe us into forgetting the powerful lure of self-extinction.

According to this stronger psychoanalytic reading, for which Freud's thoughts on hatred and Lacan's on life envy have prepared us, the speaker accepts—even perversely embraces—his likely extinction. As this proposition is counterintuitive (most critics viewing triumph as the experience of "cheating" death, rather than of surrendering to it),[48] they've long been baffled by the poem's opening lines:

> My first thought was, he lied in every word,
>   That hoary cripple, with malicious eye
>   Askance to watch the working of his lie
> On mine. (1–4)

The speaker suspects this "cripple," and intuits that following his bad advice will give the old man such malign joy that his mouth will be "scarce able to afford / Suppression of the glee" (4–5), a dynamic we've witnessed before in Browning's poetry. But why does the speaker accept his directions when any sensible hero would run the other way? Raising still greater complications, the cripple doesn't lie—his advice, resulting in extraordinary hardship, is correct. And, though he perceives this accuracy, the speaker curiously implies that he would follow the directions anyway:

>   I guessed what skull-like laugh
> Would break, what crutch 'gin write my epitaph
>   For pastime in the dusty thoroughfare,
>
> If at his counsel I should turn aside
>   Into that ominous tract which, all agree,
>   Hides the Dark Tower. (10–15)

As we soon learn, the speaker is prepared to ignore his own cautionary "if" clause here (line 13) and proceed regardless, with

> neither pride
> Nor hope rekindling at the end descried,
> So much as gladness that some end might be. (16–18)

Following the cripple's directions ends the speaker's equivocation, then, along with any firm conviction that he'll prevail. Such rationalizations may be paradoxical, but they turn, finally, on this third stanza's last line, the overall conclusion to the poem's introductory material: knowledge that "some end might be" results in "gladness," not fear or anxiety. The speaker isn't suicidal, we stress, but his inability to rule out death makes him oddly pleased.

Although the poem elaborates this disturbing idea in thirty more stanzas, the speaker explains in the fourth what's at stake in rationalizing this outcome. He concedes that failure has accompanied him for so long now that his hope has

> Dwindled into a ghost not fit to cope
> With that obstreperous joy success would bring. (21–22)

The admission reverses Guido's boast that, concerning life and, of course, virility, he could "spill this overplus of mine" among those who would "make . . . hay of juicy me," and still "brighten hell and streak its smoke with flame!" (11.144, 148, 150). "Childe Roland's" speaker experiences the joy accompanying success as so "obstreperous"—so clamorous and troublesome—that he can't bring himself to "rebuke the spring / My heart made, finding failure in its scope" (23–24). If we viewed desire only as serving life, survival, and the good, as I've strongly discouraged in this chapter, then the speaker's elation that he needn't do so would puzzle us. The lines acquire piquancy, in Browningesque terms, by supporting the disturbing, counterintuitive idea that defeat and self-extinction are the stronger aim of life, surpassing community, redemption, and even affection for other people.

This second emphasis puts in doubtful light the speaker's ostensibly triumphant blowing of his "slug-horn" (203). Like many critics, I view this final act as paradoxical rather than relief-filled and optimistic, though I stress once more that Browning's fascination with hatred's antisocial effects didn't muzzle his love poetry and doesn't expose as disingenuous the adoration he expressed for his wife, son, and friends. Although I have identified places in his poetry where Browning challenges, even confounds, the idea of perfect reciprocity, the poems rarely spiral off into solipsism. More commonly, they show that love and hatred aren't coeval in his poetry, and that the expectations we've inherited from much Victorian fiction, in which misanthropy either "expires" or passes into love, are not merely facile and naïve but also conceptually impoverished descriptions of humanity's *attachment* to enmity.

I have argued in this chapter—and throughout this book—that this attachment highlights at least one ethical principle, since it underscores what forms of community life induce anguish, rather than pleasure. During this book, we've seen Victorians portray self-righteous neighbors as invasive, even grotesque, but few could match Browning for the horror and repulsion his characters voice when contemplating endless, involuntary life among strangers or rivals. It would be easy to pronounce him merely curmudgeonly in this regard, as if we could take comfort in tracing his characters' inspired rancor back to him. Certainly, there are ample records of him fulminating at critics, unscrupulous editors ("their paws in my very bowels"), and deriders of his wife's poetry ("to spit there glorifies your face," concludes "To Edward Fitzgerald," the vituperative sonnet that caused an uproar when Browning rashly published it in the *Athenæum*).[49] His work also shows artists working in a rage—among them, *Paracelsus*, *Sordello*, and of course "Of Pacchiarotto, and How He Worked in Distemper."

But as Browning was also immensely sociable, a devoted husband and father, and the author of some of the most famous love poetry in the language, the psychobiographical path cannot help us here, and it's fitting that it cannot. We must struggle instead with the impasse arising when conventional wisdom and platitudes fall away. Moreover, this resistance to conventional explanation is emancipatory, since it frees his works from simple motivation and allows them to pursue, with Browningesque detachment, a more profound inquiry into what Conrad—our final study, and a writer arguably indebted to Browning's dramatic monologues—called the "sombre" elements that "lead into the heart of an immense darkness."[50] Granted, this phrase is now a cliché, inviting us to parse the virtuous from the damned in ways that neither Conrad nor Browning surely intended. For Conrad retitled his best-known work, first published in *Blackwood's* as "The Heart of Darkness,"[51] deleting the definite article and reprinting the novella as simply *Heart of Darkness*. The phrase floats ominously, somewhat detached from identifiable cultures and landscapes, peoples and causes. Its effect is disorienting, paring clichés that used to comfort. We're forced to acknowledge, with him and Browning, that the symbolism we've inherited about the heart no longer protects us from all that humanity desires.

Joseph Conrad and the Illusion of Solidarity

> Betray. A great word. What is betrayal? They talk of a man betraying his country, his friends, his sweetheart. There must be a moral bond first.
> —Razumov in *Under Western Eyes*

> I am independent—and therefore perdition is my lot.
> —Razumov in *Under Western Eyes*

IN THE OPENING CHAPTER OF THIS BOOK, I examined a short story by Bulwer that inspired Edgar Allan Poe and, arguably, Joseph Conrad. Bulwer's "Monos and Daimonos" portrays a violent tension between desired solitude and unwanted company, which Conrad's characters experience at sea, though the latter's debt is conceptual and not merely inspirational. Conrad aggravates and recasts the dualistic conflict facing Bulwer's allegorical figures, describing whole communities as hostile and woefully inadequate to their protagonists' needs.[1]

Bulwer's short story emphasizes the allure of solitude. Severed from society, his Monos is left at the mercy of a tormenting "Daimonos," the opposite of what Socrates called a ministering spirit. But whereas Bulwer's Monos can't tell whether the Daimonos ends up inside him, Conrad made that uncertainty integral to his fiction. In all senses remote, his disenchanted protagonists wander from communities that are rife with suspicion and hatred. Though they find society intolerable, their hostile impulses are more harrowing. Hating society yet impelled to stay on its periphery, they discover that they can't just leave.

Perhaps surprisingly, then, Conrad's motley cast of villains and mavericks includes few misanthropes. Despite giving his protagonists every imaginable reason to leave society, he generally resolves that they must put up and make do. Yet although this compromise seems conservative, even typically Victorian, it represents a sea change in eighteenth- and nineteenth-century arguments about sociability, with Conrad jeopardizing group loyalty and self-sovereignty. He also pushes some of his antiheroes into a register where conventional psychology has little relevance. As the fake mystic Madame de S— explains in *Under Western Eyes*, "a belief in a supernatural source of evil is not necessary; men alone are quite capable of every wickedness" (108). Armed with this secular wisdom, Conrad confirmed and sometimes extended his predecessors' narrative conventions (Bulwer's among them), putting misanthropy to fresh uses.

First titled "The Other Self," Conrad's novella *The Secret Sharer* develops Bulwer's interest in the vexed, uncertain boundaries of selfhood.[2] Blurring the line where illusions begin and end, Conrad weakens ties among his characters, many of whom become "isolatoes."[3] The captain-narrator appears to rescue Leggatt naked from the sea after the latter murdered a crew member of the *Sephora*, a nearby ship, but he can't easily distinguish truth from fiction, and himself from Leggatt. He admits privately that the pressure of concealing Leggatt from his crew "distracted me almost to the point of insanity" (99–100). As all truth claims in this first-person narrative depend on a mind possibly hallucinating from madness or exhaustion, Conrad accents the frenzy of an ego defending its reality from an adverse community that's also incapable of understanding it. The bewildered captain is, as Conrad remarked of a similar context, unable to forget "the inseparable being always at [its] side—master and slave, victim and tormentor—who suffers and causes suffering."[4]

Conrad, here, did more than quiz nineteenth-century communitarianism. He dove further into the past, turning Gothic fiction's uncanny scenarios and obsession with space into widespread emblems of psychosocial hostility. *The Secret Sharer* is but one example flaunting an air of unreliability, because it allows narrators to lie to us, to other characters, and to themselves. And as in novels that praise solidarity among shipmates, including *The Nigger of the "Narcissus,"* social bonds often cede to destructive forces. Conrad may aspire to show "the latent feeling of fellowship . . . , the subtle but invincible, conviction of solidarity that knits together the loneliness of innumerable hearts,"[5] but even his rhapsodic narrator can't help noticing how quickly this feeling dissipates when the sailors reach London. That's a city, he says, "where men, in fur caps, with brutal faces and in shirt sleeves, dispense out of varnished barrels the illusions of strength, mirth, happiness" (127). Granted, some fellowship prevails beforehand on the *Narcissus*, but the elements inciting mutiny—almost destroying the community—are dangerously volatile. When the sailors aren't blaming one another "with a deadly hate" or spitting with disgust at the apparent "malinger[er]" James Wait, they react to his illness with a "latent egoism of tenderness to suffering . . . in the developing anxiety not to see him die" (68, 53, 102–3).

As we saw in the introduction, many eighteenth- and some nineteenth-century novelists and philosophers applauded "tenderness to suffering," viewing empathy a sign of self-sacrifice, but Conrad tainted this sentiment with self-regard and drew attention to its "latent egoism." He limited altruism to those, like Singleton, whose "unsentimental concern for work and duty sustains solidarity and helps to preserve the ship and her voyagers,"[6] thereby modifying, without rescinding, what philosophers such as Adam Smith and the third Earl of Shaftesbury had argued just over a century earlier.[7]

Because later works by Conrad, including *Nostromo*, *Under Western Eyes*, and *Victory*, denude his protagonists after highlighting their "latent egoism," let's consider how they strip away illusions, leaving little in their place. These works sling characters between the world and nothingness—a miserable fate, since they call the former "a bad dog. It will bite [us] if [we] give it a chance," and the latter "swallow[s us] up in the immense indifference of things."[8] To add insult to injury, malice in these works is irreducible to fate and other people. Related, indeterminate forms of aggression harry his protagonists internally, making them anxious and exhausted. As Almayer, Willems, Jim, Decoud, Razumov, and a host of others discover, the "worst that can happen to us in the temperamental depths of our being" is experiencing an attack of self-directed fury—the kind that guides these characters swiftly to their annihilation.[9] The dramatic particulars may be unique, but the crisis afflicts them all.

Hoping to escape such insoluble dilemmas and thus to mollify the Schopenhauerian belief that "he who forms a tie is lost," protagonists like Axel Heyst resolve to "drift" (*Victory* 215, 129). Events and other people nonetheless puncture their isolation. As Davidson observes, Heyst's "detachment from the world was not complete. And incompleteness of any sort leads to trouble" (79).[10] Certainly, Heyst Sr. predicts the emotional turmoil of his son, whose troubles with Schomberg and Jones explode after he elopes with Lena to Samburan, but Heyst himself experiences intense emotional and sexual longing—a pressure similar to the captain's in *The Secret Sharer*. Despite craving isolation, these characters can't or won't give up on at least the idea of other people.

Critics can therefore marshal a host of quotations from Conrad's letters and novels wavering between bleak pessimism and guarded optimism. Leaning toward the latter, he once insisted that "to be hopeful in an artistic sense it is not necessary to think that the world is good. It is enough to believe that there is no impossibility of its being made so."[11] And despite the allusion in *Chance* to "hate of invisible powers interpreted, made sensible and injurious by the actions of men," Conrad stipulated: "One becomes useful only on recognizing the extent of the individual's utter insignificance within the arrangement of the universe."[12] Though the last statement is bleak, even solipsistic, when coupled with what is "useful" it implies a remedy for hubris; as Conrad added, "By oneself, one is nothing," sounding the ambiguity that intrigues me.[13] Draining the individual of conceit is precisely the modest value he accords to the collective. Nevertheless, there's no shortage of Conradian aphorisms conveying greater despondency. While writing *Nostromo*, Conrad feared he was "growing into a sort of . . . mental and moral outcast. I hear of nothing—I think of nothing—I reflect upon nothing—I cut myself off."[14] Two years later, despite hoping for "the advent of Concord and Justice," he couldn't resist adding that "the efforts of mankind to work its own salvation present a sight of alarming comicality."[15]

Notwithstanding his formal innovations in narrative, point of view, and characterization, Conrad was also conventionally Victorian in his willingness to punish those who resisted the rule of law. His antiheroes may be profoundly disruptive—Jones says he's "the world itself, come to pay [Heyst] a visit . . . an outcast—almost an outlaw" (*Victory* 35)— but they perish at the work's end. As in novels by Eliot and Dickens, Conrad's fictional mavericks can't tilt his fictional communities entirely toward unfettered hatred. For every Kurtz we find a baffled Marlow; for every corrupt de Barral in *Chance*, a Captain Anthony who's "a hermit withdrawn from a wicked world."[16] What's typically Conradian is the ensuing tension between individual disbelief in collective life—including despair at what humanity is capable of doing—and narrative insistence that society is, at bottom, all we have.[17]

Conrad downplays neither this somber conclusion nor its psychological price. Instead, as Paul Armstrong observes of *Nostromo*, he "alternates between endorsing and demystifying the ideal of community—between advocating social oneness and demonstrating its impossibility."[18] Characters like Martin Decoud and Dr. Monygham spotlight this quandary, as does Heyst. But whereas the latter suffers unremittingly after heeding the "barbed hook" of "action" and forming tentative ties (*Victory* 193), Decoud, the reformed dilettante who for much of the novel wisely abstains from joining suspect political ventures, exasperates the narrator into calling his "enormous vanity" the "finest form of egoism" (*Nostromo* 261). Indeed, Decoud's suicide from dejection and solitude apparently renders him a "victim of the disillusioned weariness which is the retribution meted out to intellectual audacity" (416)!

Invoking such lines, many critics have accused Conrad of attaching his despair to Decoud and using the latter's death to purge himself of suicidal tendencies. Martin Ray suggests more usefully that Decoud became "a means by which Conrad [could] test some of his own aesthetic practices, especially the acknowledged source of his writing in a confrontation with the forces of darkness and annihilation."[19] Seen in this light, Decoud appears to curb—even to eliminate—the novel's interest in eschatology, his death forming a hiatus or break in meaning that allows the narrator to reconstitute the fragile community around his traumatic absence.

Decoud's suicide also helps reform Dr. Monygham, the novel's cynic, whose misanthropy eventually burgeons into love. But unlike in a host of nineteenth-century novels, including *A Philanthropic Misanthrope*, *Paul Clifford*, and *Shirley*, discussed earlier, this process is neither straightforward nor devoid of irony. Monygham deceives Sotillo (and so saves Mrs. Gould) by believing *too* strongly in his own treachery. The ardor he offers Emily Gould—a rare example of altruism—stems from self-serving disgust: Monygham falls in love with "the utter absorption of a man to whom love comes late, not as the most splendid of illusions, but like an enlightening and priceless misfortune" (424). With absurd gravity, he quells a desire to "kiss . . . the hem of [Mrs. Gould's] robe" by increasing his "grimness of speech" (424). That carefree love could evaporate Monygham's misanthropy is as illusion-coated, we might say, as the "love" altering his outlook on society.

Transforming Victorian accounts of misanthropy, then, Conrad implies that those least disposed to trust others are—owing to compromised self-regard—the only ones capable of even nominal self-sacrifice. He recasts assumptions, dating from at least the eighteenth century, that misanthropes hate only for want of love. While giving Monygham some of the idealism characterizing erstwhile people-haters (the kind Bulwer hoped to resurrect in "The Modern Misanthrope"), Conrad partly offsets that hatred by underscoring the corruption plaguing life in Costaguana.

The "bitter, eccentric" Monygham is thus right to express through his "short, hopeless laugh . . . an immense mistrust of mankind" (69). As he says ironically, "Really, it is most unreasonable to demand that a man should think of other people so much better than he is able to think of himself" (69). Given Monygham's profound self-disgust, the statement conveys less egoism than an unrepentant Decoud would have attached to it. Despite forming "an ideal conception of his disgrace" and falsifying his past to exacerbate his misery (319), Monygham corroborates Freud's doubts, in *Civilization and Its Discontents* and "Mourning and Melancholia," that we should turn the other cheek or—which is similar—treat our neighbor as ourselves. Indeed, in the latter article Freud cites a passage from *Hamlet* suggesting that to treat other people as we do ourselves is brutally unkind: "Use every man after his desert, and who shall scape whipping?"[20] Sociability, by Freudian and Conradian standards, prevails as a viable illusion only if it can surpass these violent psychic dynamics, yet individuals—and society itself—undercut that possibility.

While Monygham self-flagellates, for example, his "outward aspect of an outcast" incurs the wrath of Europeans in Sulaco, who circulate then profess to disbelieve rumors that he "had betrayed some of his best friends" after Guzman Bento had imprisoned him years earlier (270, 271). Though the narrator finds it impossible to confirm or discredit these reports, ironically the Europeans view Monygham's self-contempt as corroborating them. The narrator isn't so sure: "So much defiant eccentricity and such an outspoken scorn for mankind seemed to point to mere recklessness of judgement, the bravado of guilt" (270). Echoing the Europeans' scorn, the narrator suggests archly that their contempt for Monygham successfully displaces their own self-criticism. Maybe they should treat themselves with a fraction of the contempt they blithely direct at him.

That one can reform misanthropy is a delicate, but finally pivotal idea in *Nostromo*. Thereafter, Conrad (like Dickens) aligned societal contempt more schematically with his antiheroes and self-directed violence with his isolates. Monygham's "aimless wandering" (270) anticipates Heyst's decision to "drift" (*Victory* 129); he evokes in observers the same horror that characters in *Victory* experience when Mr. Jones stares at them. After speaking with Monygham, Sotillo can't "bear [his] expressionless and motionless stare, which seemed to have a sort of impenetrable emptiness like the black depth of an abyss" (*Nostromo* 300). Like Conrad's villain in *Victory*, too, the misanthropic doctor exposes social and interpersonal duplicity, joining Browning's Guido and Eliot's Latimer in eliminating swaths of falsehood.

Monygham's transformation and Mrs. Gould's eventual detachment from her husband's mine indicate glimmerings of hope, but by the time Conrad completed *The Secret Agent*, just over two years later, his optimism had dimmed considerably. Conrad was even more harried by financial concerns and by his wife's and his own ill health ("sick with worry and overwork" is a common refrain in his letters). Rendering more extreme the psychopolitical tensions besetting his earlier works, *The Secret Agent* offers few practical solutions to the ensuing suffering and despair. Based on an actual attempt by Victorian anarchists to blow up London's Greenwich Observatory, this 1907 novel amplifies *Nostromo*'s concerns about treachery and social ties without "saving" any of its characters.

When in February 1894 Martial Bourdin caused the "Greenwich Bomb Outrage," Britain's imperial power was at its zenith. Located near the heart of London, Greenwich is "at the very centre," Conrad's narrator reminds us, "of the Empire on which the sun never sets" (198); it also lies at the meridian, the imaginary line indicating zero-degree longitude and standardizing "universal time." Destroying the observatory regulating world time and space would have had profound symbolic ramifications, making it seem, to paraphrase *Macbeth*, that the frame of things had become disjoint. Bourdin succeeded only in killing himself during his attack on time, just as Stevie, in Conrad's novel, dies undertaking a comparable terrorist plot. Foiling Conrad's anarchists is ineptitude and treachery, then, but also—the Conradian twist—contempt for their "mediocr[ity]."[21] Indeed, Conrad can't resist using the 1894 plot to amplify bleaker concerns about human motives and ostensibly inhuman satisfactions. Whereas Ossipon is so appalled by his betrayal of Winnie that he finally calls himself "seriously ill," the deranged Professor remains serenely indifferent about others and himself. Insisting that "mankind . . . does not know what it wants," he believes the solution is to blow himself up in a crowded street (265).

Clutching at all times a detonator that can kill him and many others, the Professor exhibits a readiness for terrorism that clearly serves more than political ends. Conrad conveys the extraordinary intensity of this character, always mindful of death and prepared for self-extinction. Before making what's presumably his last foray into the crowd, this character toasts "the destruction of what is" and echoes Kurtz's directive, "Exterminate all the brutes!"[22] It's with "perfect sincerity," Conrad later told R. B. Cunninghame Graham, that the Professor informs Ossipon: "The weak" are "the source of all evil on this earth!"—"our sinister masters"—and thus must be "taken in hand for utter extermination. . . . First the blind, then the deaf and the dumb, then the halt and the lame—and so on. Every taint, every vice, every prejudice, every convention must meet its doom" (*Secret* 263).[23] Thus does the idea of anarchic disruption devolve in this novel into proto-fascism and monomaniacal self-justification. Indeed, when Ossipon inquires, "And what remains?" the Professor replies: "I remain—if I am strong enough" (263).

After denouncing Ossipon for his humanity, the Professor shuffles off menacingly into the crowd, his once political animus flourishing as generalized hatred of humanity:

> And the incorruptible Professor walked, too, averting his eyes from the odious multitude of mankind. He had no future. He disdained it. He was a force. His thoughts caressed the images of ruin and destruction. He walked frail, insignificant, shabby, miserable—and terrible in the simplicity of his idea calling madness and despair to the regeneration of the world. Nobody looked at him. He passed on unsuspected and deadly, like a pest in the street full of men. (269)

These are the novel's final words. The Professor isn't just parasitic; he's also an entity so devoid of doubt—and so hostile to society—that the narrator, depersonalizing him, can call him a "force." Releasing misanthropy from realist understandings of character, Conrad's novel points to a form of affect beyond socialization and political remedy. And though it's difficult to consider this a gain, I'll conclude by indicating what's most pressing and sobering about this representation.

Throughout this book, we've seen comparable descriptions—of Guido in *The Ring and the Book*, Raffles in *Middlemarch*, and even Codlin and Quilp in *The Old Curiosity Shop*—that confirm one of my central claims: Victorian literature increasingly portrayed antiheroes (conventionally distinct from misanthropes) as lacking in psychology. Once flattened into pure motive, they appear incapable of reflection. Conrad's narrator doesn't faithfully reproduce this tradition; he blurs what are anyway porous distinctions, establishing in his first description of the Professor a set of motives by which we're meant to account for his hatred. He's "treated with revolting injustice" at a laboratory and technical institute, and thereafter "his struggles, his privations, his hard work to raise himself in the social scale, had filled him with such an exalted conviction of his merits that it was extremely difficult for the world to treat him with justice" (98).

But since the Professor later scorns humility, venting a rage that no one could appease or reform, he's radically different from misanthropes like Monygham. The above psychological sketch given by Conrad's narrator is thus, at bottom, irrelevant. Similar to Browning's Guido and Childe Roland, a "force" driving him on toward annihilation overwhelms this terrorist. The misanthropy Conrad depicts unusually makes obsolete all conventional psychological accounts of it. Sundering the idea that human motivation is rational and self-evident, Conrad takes us beyond psychology, into the realm of eschatology. Once more, however, he backs away from this vision, rendering his terrorist so deranged that he appears finally absurd. Asks an indignant Ossipon:

"But what do you want from us? . . . What is it that you are after?"
"A perfect detonator," was the peremptory answer. (93)

Though he's intriguing and ethically disturbing, the Professor becomes little more than a caricature. The crowning moment of Conradian misanthropy appears not in *The Secret Agent*, but in *Under Western Eyes*, four years later, when Razumov imagines himself confessing to Natalia Haldin. She's the person Razumov deceives for most of the novel, causing immeasurable suffering after betraying her brother to despotic authorities. Like Dr. Monygham, Razumov is compromised by love. Yet unlike in *Nostromo*, his confession ruins any chances of securing Natalia's forgiveness, and it destroys her memory of her brother (a lawless assassin) as morally courageous. "I was given up to evil," Razumov writes in his diary, as if forming the very words the Professor swallows:

I had to confirm myself in my contempt and hate for what I betrayed. I have suffered from as many vipers in my heart as any social democrat of them all—vanity, ambitions, jealousies, shameful desires, evil passions of envy and revenge. I had my security stolen from me, years of good work, my best hopes. . . . Victor Haldin had stolen the truth of my life from me, who had nothing else in the world.[24]

Named after the Russian *razhum*, meaning "reason," "intelligence," or "mind," the orphaned Razumov is repeatedly drawn into conspiracies in which he wants no part. One couldn't ask for a better metaphor for the misanthrope's necessary implication in society. Despite yearning to be left alone to pursue his studies, he's condemned to participate in activities in which he has neither faith nor illusion. Among these is love itself, which Razumov admits pursuing as a form of revenge: he imagines retaliating against Haldin by "steal[ing] his sister's soul from her" (252). Once Haldin is hanged, Razumov is reduced to acts of gratuitous cruelty against his innocent sister. His fantasy of ruining Natalia's life replicates the Professor's asymmetrical retribution, which Guido and Caponsacchi promoted in Browning's *Ring and the Book*. "Stealing" Razumov's joy and freedom, Haldin launches another zero-sum game that Conrad's hapless narrator, a "mute witness," claims incorrectly "unroll[s] . . . their Eastern logic under my Western eyes" (267). Because readers witness and eavesdrop on this revenge scenario, the statement is disingenuous: our "Western eyes" are greedy participants in schadenfreude.

As Razumov's complicity is itself a response to harrowing psychological needs, the novel turns much of his misanthropy into spectacular self-betrayal. The scenario resembles Dostoyevsky's ambivalent involvement in the anticzarist Petrashevsky circle, whose revolutionary aims he sometimes maligned. Yet for Conrad and Dostoyevsky, this self-betrayal is neither exceptional nor entirely perverse. As we saw in chapter 2 when engaging Dostoyevsky's work, self-interest is an inadequate guide to human behavior, motivation, and satisfaction. Parodying Bentham and other nineteenth-century philosophers who forged "systems . . . for the happiness of mankind," Dostoyevsky's antihero in *Notes from Underground* laments that such thinkers omit from consideration a "prompting of something inside [ourselves] that is stronger than all [our] self-interest."[25] "It is indeed possible, and sometimes *positively imperative* (in my view)," he insists, in sentences I am requoting, "to act directly contrary to one's own best interests. One's own free and unfettered volition, one's own caprice, however wild, one's own fancy, inflamed sometimes to the point of madness—that is the one best and greatest good, which is never taken into consideration" (33–34; original emphasis).

Conrad's Razumov experiences this "prompting," but associates it intriguingly with panic and guilt, not "free and unfettered volition." The "wild . . . fancy" of acting against one's self-interest is in *Under Western Eyes* neither enjoyable nor felt in isolation; horrifically, it destroys the lives of other people or at least radically curbs their freedom. Unlike in *Notes from Underground*, too, Razumov isn't self-satisfied, but utterly alone:

> He was as lonely in the world as a man swimming in the deep sea. The word Razumov was the mere label of a solitary individuality. There were no Razumovs belonging to him anywhere. His closest parentage was defined in the statement that he was a Russian. Whatever good he expected from life would be given to or withheld from his hopes by that connection alone. This immense parentage suffered from the throes of internal dissensions, and he shrank mentally from the fray as a good-natured man may shrink from taking sides in a violent family quarrel. (10)

Nothing orients Razumov, in other words, except the abstract and fraught signifier "Russia." Lacking such common intermediaries as parents, family, and friends, Razumov is from the beginning largely beyond the social tie and thus especially vulnerable to political and predatory forces, including "free and unfettered volition" (*Notes* 33). "I want to guide my conduct by reasonable convictions," he soliloquizes, "but what security have I against something—some destructive horror—walking upon me as I sit here?" (*Under Western* 57).

As Conrad's narrator points out, it's both fitting and ironic that Razumov's saddest musings on loneliness occur in spy-haunted Geneva, home to "the author of the *Social Contract*" (206). Skidding away from Rousseauesque sensibility, Razumov is compelled to humiliate and destroy himself in a way "a happy lover would have [given] the name of ecstasy" (246). Metaphorically speaking, Razumov "stab[s] himself" in front of others "as though he were turning the knife in the wound and watching the effect" (246). Adam Gillon calls this "spiritual masochis[m]," but Razumov's extreme distress far surpasses this term.[26]

Instead, "his moral supports falling away from him one by one," Razumov reels from the "giddiness" of near-perfect moral freedom, including the terrible ecstasy of knowing he can destroy himself *and* the "bond of common faith, of common conviction" that barely connects him to other people (56, 29).

The Professor and Razumov hate with almost irrational fury. These antiheroes enter a new realm, where conventional psychology has little heuristic value. Conventional emphasis on their professional grievances, orphanhood, and anger at unwanted complicity fails to explain their hostility to the world (consider, for instance, the repellent "surplus" violence with which Razumov batters the drunken Ziemianitch in chapter 2). Like Browning, his predecessor, Conrad binds such characters to a "force" overturning rational accounts of "the good"—a force thus conceptually at odds with the central tenets of nineteenth-century philosophy and psychology. He shows why a character would be drawn to forms of satisfaction, like violent self-annihilation, that are psychically appealing and liberating, even as they result is awful bodily and social harm.

Conrad's paradoxical achievement, then, is to explain in *Under Western Eyes* why individuals turning away from society seek perverse, counterintuitive solace in their own destruction. Only this emphasis can explain, at bottom, why the Professor would constantly clutch his detonator. Yet as my analysis of his earlier novels indicates, Conrad couldn't leave matters there, and certainly wasn't prepared to indict all of society. Despite Stein's well-known directive in *Lord Jim*—"submit . . . to the destructive element"—and Conrad's belief that "man must drag the ball and chain of his individuality to the very end," his isolatoes rarely achieve or enjoy lasting solitude (one of "only two things," including death, that apparently "make life bearable!").[27] As the narrator avows, "The most miserable outcast hugs some memory or some illusion. . . . No human being could bear a steady view of moral solitude without going mad" (30). Though we might credibly call him insane, the Professor is similarly described "caress[ing] . . . images of ruin and destruction" (*Secret* 269).

Conrad's misanthropes and antiheroes alike perceive that sociability can't ward off the agony of moral solitude. Nor does fellowship stop them from examining the shortcomings of emotional ties. Unlike for many of his predecessors, society is in Conrad's fiction an insoluble problem. It's a sign of this paradox that society gives his protagonists enough wisdom to declare: "We live, as we dream—alone" (*Heart* 79; see FIGURE 6.1).

FIGURE 6.1 *Der Augenturm* (*The Eye Tower*; 1977).
Copyright Dieter Appelt. Gelatin silver print.
Courtesy Kicken Berlin and the Pace/MacGill Gallery, New York.

Acknowledgments

1. Robert Lewis Taylor, *W. C. Fields: His Follies and Fortunes* (New York: Doubleday, 1949), 3–4.

Prologue

1. Megan Mullally, *The More You Know* series, airing June 9, 2001, and on many other days in 2001: http://nbctv.nbci.com/tmyk/pgv_psa_prejudice.html. NBC has since removed this and other short infomercials from its Web site.

2. *New Hope for People with Social Anxiety Disorder* (paroxetine HCI; SmithKline Beecham Pharmaceuticals, September 1999).

3. Eric Lewin Altschuler, Ansar Haroun, Bing Ho, and Amy Weimer, "Did Samson Have Antisocial Personality Disorder?" [Letters to the Editor], *Archives of General Psychiatry* 58.2 (2001), 202–3. The *DSM-IV*'s seven criteria for this disorder are:

> (1) failure to conform to social norms with respect to lawful behaviors as indicated by repeatedly performing acts that are grounds for arrest; (2) deceitfulness, as indicated by repeated lying, use of aliases, or conning others for personal profit or pleasure; (3) impulsivity or failure to plan ahead; (4) irritability and aggressiveness, as indicated by repeated physical fights or assaults; (5) reckless disregard for safety of self or others; (6) consistent irresponsibility, as indicated by repeated failure to sustain consistent work behavior or honor financial obligations; (7) lack of remorse, as indicated by being indifferent to or rationalizing having hurt, mistreated, or stolen from another.

American Psychiatric Association, *Diagnostic and Statistical Manual of Mental Disorders*, 4th ed. (Washington, D.C.: American Psychiatric Association, 1994), 649–50.

4. Murray B. Stein, John R. Walker, and David R. Forde, "Setting Diagnostic Thresholds for Social Phobia: Considerations from a Community Survey of Social Anxiety," *American Journal of Psychiatry* 151.3 (1994), 412, 408.

5. Robert D. Putnam, *Bowling Alone: The Collapse and Revival of American Community* (New York: Simon and Schuster, 2000), 47.

6. Michael Elliott, "Rude Britannia," *Prospect* 63 (May 2001), 22. Despite his being interrupted by hearty applause, Benjamin Disraeli apparently was wrong to declare in 1872 that "increased means and increased leisure are the two civilizers of man." Disraeli, April 3, 1872, qtd. in "Mr. Disraeli at Manchester," the *Times* (April 4, 1872), 5.

7. Elliott, "Rude Britannia," 25, 23.

8. *Random House Webster's Unabridged Dictionary*, 2d ed. (New York: Random House, 1998), 1321, 1201.

9. Kathryn Hughes, "The Way of All Flesh: Kathryn Hughes Finds That the Victorians Differed Little from Us in Their Response to Nudity," *New Statesman* (November 19, 2001), 41, 40.

10. Matthew Sweet, *Inventing the Victorians* (New York: St. Martin's, 2001).

11. Roger Kimball, "Undressing the Victorians," *New Criterion* 21.2 (October 2002), 13, 17.

12. Ibid., 16–17. Indeed, Andrew Lambirth, the London *Spectator*'s reviewer, was so disturbed that the exhibition might revise these conceptions that he found himself more interested in the "single men of a certain age in raincoats" deriving pleasure from the paintings and sculpture than in the art itself. Lambirth, "Coquetry and Abandon," *Spectator* (November 17, 2001), 61. Karen Wilkin was more restrained than either Lambirth or Kimball in her review, "Victorian Art: We Are Amused, That's ALL," *Wall Street Journal* (October 16, 2002), D8, column 2.

13. Walter E. Houghton, *The Victorian Frame of Mind, 1830–1870* (1957; New Haven: Yale UP, 1985), 394–95.

14. Robert Louis Stevenson, *Strange Case of Dr Jekyll and Mr Hyde* (1886; Harmondsworth: Penguin, 2002), 60, 68. Subsequent references give pagination in main text.

15. Oscar Wilde, *An Ideal Husband*, ed. Russell Jackson (1895; 1899; New York: Norton, 1993), III, lines 14–17, 87.

16. Thomas Hardy, *The Woodlanders* (1887; Harmondsworth: Penguin, 1998), 197.

17. See, for instance, Florence King, *With Charity Toward None: A Fond Look at Misanthropy* (New York: St. Martin's, 1992); Nicolaus Mills, *The Triumph of Meanness: America's War Against Its Better Self* (Boston: Houghton Mifflin, 1997); Alexander Evans, "Misanthropy," *Salisbury Review* 15.4 (1997), 34–36; and, most recently, Garret Keizer, "How the Devil Falls in Love: Misanthropy, Prejudice, and Other Follies," *Harper's Magazine* (August 2002), 43–51.

18. In a celebrated article, and from a very different perspective, T. M. Scanlon addresses this question in "Contractualism and Utilitarianism," *Utilitarianism and Beyond*, ed. Amartya Sen and Bernard Williams (New York: Cambridge UP, 1992), 103–28, now expanded into Scanlon's full-length study *What We Owe to Each Other* (Cambridge: Harvard UP, 1998).

19. Lord Byron, *Don Juan* (1819–24), *The Complete Poetical Works*, ed. Jerome J. McGann (Oxford: Clarendon P, 1986), 7 vols., 5:13.6.47–48.

20. William Morris, *A Dream of John Ball* (1888), *The Collected Works of William Morris*, introduced by May Morris (1910–15; London: Routledge/Thoemmes P, 1992), 24 vols., 16:230. Although many other Victorians (including Ruskin and James Thomson) shared Morris's thoughts on urban strife, the latter is best known as a poet who idealized medieval conduct.

21. Morris, "How I Became a Socialist," first published in *Justice* (June 16, 1894), *Collected Works* 23:279.

22. Morris, "Apology," *The Earthly Paradise: A Poem* (1868–70), *Collected Works* 3:1 (line 22); *News from Nowhere* (1890; 1891), *Collected Works* 16:3.

23. Fyodor Dostoyevsky, *The Brothers Karamazov*, trans. David McDuff (1880; Harmondsworth: Penguin, 1993), 61. Subsequent references give pagination in main text.

24. *The Oxford English Dictionary*, 2d ed., prepared by J. A. Simpson and E. S. C. Weiner (Oxford: Clarendon P, 1989), 20 vols., 9:846. The references are to James Harris, *Philological Inquiries* (London: C. Nourse, 1781), and William Rounseville Alger, *The Solitudes of Nature and of Man; or, The Loneliness of Human Life* (Boston: Roberts Brothers, 1867), 123.

25. Thomas Carlyle, "Characteristics," *Edinburgh Review* 54.108 (December 1831), 359.

26. Ibid., 366.

27. Hardy, *Far from the Madding Crowd* (1874; Harmondsworth: Penguin, 1978), a title culled from Thomas Gray's "Elegy Written in a Country Churchyard" (1751), which alludes to what is "Far from the madding crowd's ignoble strife" (l. 73); and Hardy, *Jude the Obscure* (1894; 1895; Harmondsworth: Penguin, 1998), 29.

28. Hardy, "In a Wood" (1887; 1896), *The Variorum Edition of the Complete Poems of Thomas Hardy*, ed. James Gibson (New York: Macmillan, 1979), 64.

29. Hardy, *Jude the Obscure*, 336.

30. See Arnold's "A Summer Night" (1852; 1855; 1869), whose speaker says that "most men [live] in a brazen prison" and that even closed windows are as "repellent as the world." *The Poetical Works of Matthew Arnold*, ed. C. B. Tinker and H. F. Lowry (London: Oxford UP, 1950), 242, ll. 37 and 5.

31. Excellent books on this subject include Peter France, *Hermits: The Insights of Solitude* (London: Chatto and Windus, 1996), and Isabel Colegate, *A Pelican in the Wilderness: Hermits, Solitaries, and Recluses* (Washington, D.C.: Counterpoint, 2002).

32. George Eliot, *Romola* (1862–63; Harmondsworth: Penguin, 1996), 269.

33. Still, Lyndall Gordon's recent biography notes Brontë's concern about her misanthropic tendencies. See Gordon, *Charlotte Brontë: A Passionate Life* (New York: Norton, 1995), esp. 239. Eliot's letters, discussed briefly in chapter 4, periodically betray similar fears.

34. Eliot, *Impressions of Theophrastus Such*, ed. Nancy Henry (1879; Iowa City: U of Iowa P, 1994), 32.

35. Charles Dickens, *Hard Times for These Times* (1854; Harmondsworth: Penguin, 1995), 9.

36. Robert Browning, "A Bean-Stripe," *Ferishtah's Fancies* (1884), *Robert Browning: The Poems*, ed. John Pettigrew with Thomas J. Collins (New Haven: Yale UP, 1981), 2 vols., 2:756 (ll. 287–88), and "A Pillar at Sebzevah," *Ferishtah's Fancies* (l. 124).

37. Peter Gay, *Savage Reprisals: Bleak House, Madame Bovery, Buddenbrooks* (New York: Norton, 2002), 26.

38. Ibid., 68–69.

39. Thomas R. Preston, *Not in Timon's Manner: Feeling, Misanthropy, and Satire in Eighteenth-Century England* (University: U of Alabama P, 1975).

40. Peter Gay, *The Cultivation of Hatred*, vol. 3 of *The Bourgeois Experience: Victoria to Freud* (New York: Norton, 1993), and Gay, *Savage Reprisals*; Daniel Karlin, *Browning's Hatreds* (Oxford: Clarendon P, 1993); Victor Brombert, *In Praise of Antiheroes: Figures and Themes in Modern European Literature, 1830–1980* (Chicago: U of Chicago P, 1999).

41. Adam Gillon, *The Eternal Solitary: A Study of Joseph Conrad* (New York: Bookman Associates, 1960); John Portmann, *When Bad Things Happen to Other People* (New York: Routledge, 2000), esp. xi–xxi and 3–44.

42. Barbara Ehrenreich, *The Snarling Citizen: Essays* (New York: Farrar, Straus, and Giroux, 1995); Wisława Szymborska, "Hatred," *The End and the Beginning* (1993), rept. in *Poems New and Collected 1957–1997*, trans. Stanislaw Baranczak and Clare Cavanagh (New York: Harcourt Brace Jovanovich, 1998), 231, 230.

43. Giorgio Agamben, *Language and Death: The Place of Negativity*, trans. Karen E. Pinkus with Michael Hardt (1982; Minneapolis: U of Minnesota P, 1991); Alain Badiou, *Ethics: An Essay on the Understanding of Evil*, trans. Peter Hallward (1998; New York: Verso, 2001); Joan Copjec, ed., *Radical Evil* (New York: Verso, 1996); Renata Salecl, *(Per)Versions of Love and Hate* (New York: Verso, 1998); and Slavoj Žižek, *Tarrying with the Negative: Kant, Hegel, and the Critique of Ideology* (Durham: Duke UP, 1993).

44. Florence King, *With Charity Toward None: A Fond Look at Misanthropy*.

Introduction: Victorian Hatred, a Social Evil and a Social Good

1. Joseph Somebody, *A Philanthropic Misanthrope: A Story* (London: Remington and Co., 1880), 35. Subsequent references give pagination in main text.

2. Thomas Babington, Lord Macaulay, *The History of England from the Accession of James the Second* (1849–61), *The Complete Works of Lord Macaulay* (London: Longmans, Green, and Co., 1898), 12 vols., 1:443, 445. I am grateful to Peter Gay's *Cul-*

tivation of Hatred, vol. 3 of *The Bourgeois Experience: Victoria to Freud* (New York: Norton, 1993), for this and several other references in this introduction.

3. Edmund Burke, *Reflections on the Revolution in France* (1790), *The Writings and Speeches of Edmund Burke*, ed. L. G. Mitchell (Oxford: Clarendon P, 1989), 9 vols., 8:97–98.

4. G. H. E., "Evil Often a Stimulant to Good," *Universalist Quarterly and General Review* 19 (Boston; July 1862), 312; W. S., "Moral Evil Not Incompatible with Divine Goodness," *Universalist Quarterly and General Review* 18 (April 1861), 184.

5. "Hate as a Motive Force," *Spectator* 64 (February 8, 1890), 197.

6. Ibid.

7. George Moore, *Confessions of a Young Man*, ed. Susan Dick (1887; 1888; Montréal: McGill-Queen's UP, 1972), 165. Subsequent references to Moore's autobiographical novel give pagination in main text.

8. Gertrude Himmelfarb, *The De-Moralization of Society: From Victorian Virtues to Modern Values* (1994; New York: Knopf, 1995), esp. 3–20, and *Marriage and Morals Among the Victorians and Other Essays* (Chicago: Ivan R. Dee, 2001). Margaret Thatcher first praised Victorian values in an interview on *Weekend World*, January 16, 1983.

9. Influential works by Foucauldian Victorianists include D. A. Miller, *The Novel and the Police* (Berkeley: U of California P, 1988), and Mary Poovey, *Making a Social Body: British Cultural Formation, 1830–1864* (Chicago: U of Chicago P, 1995). Both adapt Foucault's claim that Bentham's Panopticon epitomizes social and individual surveillance, in *Discipline and Punish: The Birth of the Prison*, trans. Alan Sheridan (1975; Harmondsworth, Middlesex: Peregrine, 1979), as well as his claims about madness, society, and sexuality in *Madness and Civilization: A History of Insanity in the Age of Reason*, trans. Richard Howard (1961; London: Tavistock, 1967), and *The History of Sexuality*, vol. 1: *An Introduction*, trans. Robert Hurley (1976; New York: Pantheon, 1978).

10. "The Decline of Hatred," *Scribner's* 29.2 (February 1901), 250.

11. Ibid., 249.

12. Ibid.

13. *The Oxford English Dictionary*, 2d ed., prepared by J. A. Simpson and E. S. C. Weiner (Oxford: Clarendon P, 1989), 20 vols., 9:846.

14. In *A Picture of Society; or, The Misanthropist*, the character Augustus declares: "The [misanthrope] expects too much from the world: never satisfied with his fellow-creatures as they are, nor watchful to be himself what he ought, he raises an ideal model of perfection, and then quarrels with mankind because they are what nature made them." *A Picture of Society; or, The Misanthropist* (London: Printed for T. Hookham, Jr., and E. T. Hookham, 1813), 88–89.

15. David Konstan, "A Dramatic History of Misanthropes," *Comparative Drama* 17.2 (1983), 97. Subsequent references give pagination in main text. See also Gary Saul Morson, "Misanthropology," *New Literary History* 27.1 (1996), esp. 59.

16. The noun *misanthrope* is gender-neutral. Hence William Makepeace Thackeray's narrator calls Becky Sharp a "young misanthropist" in the opening pages of *Vanity Fair* (1847–48; Harmondsworth: Penguin, 1985), 47. See also Alexandre Duval, *La femme misanthrope, ou Le depit d'amour, comedie en trois actes et en vers, Œuvres* complètes (Paris: J. N. Barba, 1823), 7:183–278; and Justin McCarthy, *Miss Misanthrope, A Novel* (New York: Sheldon and Co., 1877). In Dickens's work alone, Miss Wade, Miss Havisham, and Rosa Dartle are strongly misanthropic.

17. Auguste Comte, *System of Positive Polity, or Treatise on Sociology, Instituting the Religion of Humanity*, trans. John Henry Bridges (1851; London: Longmans, Green, and Co., 1875–77), 4 vols., 1:7. Subsequent references give pagination in main text.

18. William Rounseville Alger, *The Solitudes of Nature and of Man; or, The Loneliness of Human Life* (Boston: Roberts Brothers, 1867), 122. Subsequent references give pagination in main text.

19. Max Nordau, *Degeneration* (1892; Lincoln: U of Nebraska P, 1993), 313.

20. Barnabe Googe, *Eglogs, Epytaphes, and Sonettes* (London: Thomas Colwell, 1563). According to the *OED* (9:846), the noun *misanthropy*—meaning the condition of people-hating rather than the type of individual disposed to do so—first appeared in English in Thomas Blount's *Glossographia: Or a Dictionary, Interpreting All Such Hard Words . . . With Etymologies, Definitions, and Historical Observations on the Same* (London: Thomas Newcomb, 1656). *Philanthropy* first appeared as a published English noun in Sir Francis Bacon's *Essaies. Religious Meditations* (London: William Jaggard, 1606).

21. Sir Thomas North translated Plutarch's *Lives* into English in 1579, and although *Timon of Athens* was published in 1623, it was probably composed in 1607–8. For elaboration, see W. H. Clemons, "The Sources of *Timon of Athens*," *Princeton University Bulletin* 15 (1903–4), 208–23. Imaginative reconstructions of Timonian rage highlight these variations and clarify how the Victorians reached their own symbolic understanding of them. Published just over a century after *Timon of Athens*, John Kelly's *Timon in Love: or, The Innocent Theft. A Comedy* (London: J. Watts, 1733) begins after Timon has given away his money; and unlike in Shakespeare's play his anger is considered "peevish" and antisocial rather than hubristic (Introduction, scene 2, p. 2). Instead of railing about humanity to Apemantus, Kelly's Timon begins in dialogue with Mercury, who decides to reconcile him to the world by teaching Eucharis how to win his heart. Thus does Kelly betray Augustan sentiment. Eucharis seduces Timon by pretending to rail against the world. The two forge sympathy from their real and feigned disappointment, Timon quickly telling himself that that "very Hatred, which thou hast thank'd the Gods for, is the fatal Knot that confirms thy Slavery" (2.3, p. 31). The play ends with Eucharis and him thanking the gods "for their Favours" and "swear[ing] an everlasting Constancy" (3.7, p. 55). Yet the most provocative line is in the Introduction, when Pierot declares: "A Man becomes a Savage who flies from Society, and wilfully neglects the Pleasures in his Power" (o.3, p. 8). At the outset, then, Kelly's choric figure indi-

cates that our stake in the play rests on Timon's willingness to forgo misanthropy. For related examples, see Thomas Shadwell, *The Sullen Lovers, or, The Impertinents: A Comedy* (London: Printed for Henry Herringman, 1668); Justus van Effen, *Le misanthrope* (1726), ed. James L. Schorr, *Studies on Voltaire and the Eighteenth Century*, vol. 248 (Oxford: Voltaire Foundation at the Taylor Institution, 1986); William Wycherley, *The Plain Dealer: A Comedy* (London: Printed for W. Griffin, 1766); John Charles Villiers, Third Earl of Clarendon, *Chaubert, or, The Misanthrope: A Tragic Drama* (London: Printed by H. Goldney for T. Cadell, 1789). *Fraser's Magazine* published a translation of Lucian's *Timon; or, The Misanthrope* in January, February, and April 1839 (19.109, 110, and 112, pp. 89–95, 215–21, and 470–76).

22. *The Dialogues of Plato*, trans. Benjamin Jowett (New York: Random House, 1892, 1920), 2 vols., 1:474. Subsequent references give pagination in main text.

23. Menander, *The Bad-Tempered Man; or, The Misanthrope: A Play in Five Scenes* (316 B.C.), trans. Philip Vellacott (London: Oxford UP, 1960). The play is also translated as *The Curmudgeon*.

24. Horace, *Odes* 3.1, 1 and 3.6, 17, *The Complete Odes and Epodes*, trans. David West (Oxford: Oxford UP, 1997), 76 and 85. See also *Epodes* 5.89–102 and *Odes* 1.1, 7–8, 2.16, 37–40.

25. Percival Stockdale, *An Essay on Misanthropy* (London: B. Law, 1783), 10. Subsequent references give pagination in main text. See also David Hume, "Of the Dignity or Meanness of Human Nature" (1741), *Essays Moral, Political, and Literary*, ed. T. H. Green and T. H. Grose (London: Longmans, Green, and Co., 1875), 2 vols., 1:151; and "Of Misanthropy," *Library: or, Moral and Critical Magazine* 1 (October 1761), 364.

26. David Bromwich, *Hazlitt: The Mind of a Critic* (1983; New Haven: Yale UP, 1999), 85; my emphasis.

27. William Hazlitt, "On the Pleasure of Hating" (1823), *The Complete Works of William Hazlitt*, ed. P. P. Howe (London: Dent, 1931–34), 21 vols., 12:127; original emphasis. Subsequent references give pagination in main text.

28. Robert Owen, *A New View of Society, or, Essays on the Principle of the Formation of the Human Character, and the Application of the Principle to Practice* (1813–16), *A New View of Society and Other Writings*, ed. Gregory Claeys (Harmondsworth: Penguin, 1991), 1–92; Jeremy Bentham, *An Introduction to the Principles of Morals and Legislation*, ed. J. H. Burns and H. L. A. Hart (1780; 1789; 1823; London: Athlone P, 1970), 44.

29. See "The Natural History of Hatred" (reprinted from the *Examiner*), *Littell's Living Age*, series 4:111, no. 1427 (October 14, 1871), 116.

30. Edward Lytton Bulwer, "The Modern Misanthrope," *Blackwood's Magazine* 93.21 (April 1863), 477. Subsequent references give pagination in main text.

31. *Merriam-Webster's Collegiate Dictionary*, 10th ed. (Springfield, Mass.: Merriam-Webster, Inc., 1997), 1343. The German Romanticist Jean Paul (pseudonym of

Johann Paul Friedrich Richter) coined this term in a 1827 novel, but *weltschmerz* wasn't adopted into English until 1875.

32. John Reed, *Victorian Will* (Athens: Ohio UP, 1989), 9, 16.

33. "The Natural History of Hatred," 115.

34. "Hate as a Motive Force," 197–98.

35. "Japanese Hatred of Christianity" (reprinted from *Fraser's Magazine*), *Littell's Living Age*, series 3:77, no. 984 (April 11, 1863), 61; "Irish Hatred of England" (reprinted from the *Examiner*), *Littell's Living Age*, series 3:88, no. 1138 (March 24, 1866), 859–61; also "Irish Hatred for England," *Spectator* 55 (May 20, 1882), 651–52; "Race-Hatred in India," *Spectator* 57 (October 11, 1884), 1335–36; and Wilfrid Scawen Blunt, "Ideas about India, II: Race Hatred," *Fortnightly Review* 42.214 (n.s. 36; October 1, 1884), 445–59; Goldwin Smith, "The Hatred of England," *North American Review* 150.402 (May 1890), 547–62; "The Growth of National Hatred," *Literary Digest* 11.26 (October 26, 1895), 22; "The Hatred of Authority," *Saturday Review of Politics, Literature, Science and Art* 79 (March 23, 1895), 377–78; E. L. Godkin, "American Hatred of England," *Nation* 62.1, 594 (New York; 1896), 46–47; also A. Cleveland Coxe, "Do We Hate England?" *Forum* 11 (1891), 19–28; "The Hatred of the Poor for the Rich," *Spectator* 76 (June 6, 1896), 801–2; "Hatred of Jews ['The New Hep! Hep!']" *Spectator* 79 (December 11, 1897), 851–52; Rev. C. C. Starbuck, "Hatred of Foreigners ['General Missionary Intelligence']," *The Missionary Review of the World* 20.2 (n.s. 10.2; February 1897), 144–45; John W. Diggle, "Holy Hatred," *Expositor* (London, 5th series) 9 (1899), 434–42; editorial, "International Hatred," *Century Illustrated Monthly Magazine* 60 (May–October, 1900), 955; Charles Winslow Hall, "Racial Hatred," *Colored American Magazine* 1.4 (September 1900), 246–52.

36. See Sir Francis Galton, *Hereditary Genius: An Inquiry into Its Laws and Consequences* (1869; 2d ed. New York: Macmillan, 1892); *Inquiries into Human Faculty and Its Development* (New York: Macmillan, 1883), in which he coined the term *eugenics*; and *Natural Inheritance* (New York: Macmillan, 1889).

37. "On the Coincidence between the Natural Talents and Dispositions of Nations, and the Development of Their Brains," *Phrenological Journal* 2.5 (1824–25), 16; original emphasis. Jenny Bourne Taylor and Sally Shuttleworth reprint this and other notable articles in their excellent collection, *Embodied Selves: An Anthology of Psychological Texts, 1830–1890* (New York: Oxford UP, 1998).

38. Not for all, though. In his 1861 essay "Uncivilised Man,' George Henry Lewes drew more-liberal conclusions: "Many of the things noticeable as characteristic of the savage," he declared, "are found lingering amongst ourselves, either in remote provinces, in uncultivated classes, or in children." Lewes, "Uncivilised Man," *Blackwood's Magazine* 89 (January 1861), 39. See also Herbert Spencer's attacks on British imperialism in "Re-Barbarization" and "Imperialism and Slavery," both from 1902, in *Selected Works of Herbert Spencer: Westminster Edition* (New York: D. Appleton and Co., 1902), 18 vols., 15:172–88 and 157–71.

39. Robert Knox, *The Races of Men: A Fragment* (Philadelphia: Lea and Blanchard, 1850), 162. Subsequent references give pagination in main text. For analyses of Knox's claims, see Robert J. C. Young, *Colonial Desire: Hybridity in Theory, Culture, and Race* (New York: Routledge, 1995) esp. 119–22; and Laura Callanan, "Reading Race in Mid-Victorian England" (Ph.D. diss., Emory University, 1999), chapter 1.

40. Karl Pearson, *National Life from the Standpoint of Science. An Address Delivered at Newcastle, November 19, 1900* (London: Adam and Charles Black, 1901), 19. Subsequent references give pagination in main text. For an excellent account of Pearson's lamentable intellectual development, see Christopher Herbert, "Karl Pearson and the Human Form Divine," *Victorian Relativity: Radical Thought and Scientific Discovery* (Chicago: U of Chicago P, 2001), esp. 176–79.

41. Christopher Lane, *The Ruling Passion: British Colonial Allegory and the Paradox of Homosexual Desire* (Durham: Duke UP, 1995), esp. 16–17, 23–26, 57–61, 159–61, 172, 221, and so on, as well as Lane, "The Psychoanalysis of Race: An Introduction" and "'Savage Ecstasy': Colonialism and the Death Drive," *The Psychoanalysis of Race*, ed. Lane (New York: Columbia UP, 1998), esp. 5–13 and 291–301.

42. Gay, *The Cultivation of Hatred*, 5.

43. Ibid., 5–6.

44. Miss M. J. M'intosh, "The Young Misanthrope: An O'er True Tale" (reprinted from *Neal's Saturday Gazette*), *Littell's Living Age* 11.135 (December 12, 1846), 492–96; *Hatred, or the Vindictive Father: A Tale of Sorrow* (London: Minerva P for Lane and Newman, 1802); Miss [Catharina] Smith, *The Misanthrope Father; or, The Guarded Secret: A Novel in Three Volumes* (London: Printed for Appleyards, 1807).

45. Charles Dickens, *Our Mutual Friend* (1864–65; Harmondsworth: Penguin, 1997), 297. Another example would be "The Misanthropes," *Too Late; and Other Interesting and Amusing Stories by Eminent Authors, Nimmo's Popular Tales* (Edinburgh: William P. Nimmo, 1866), 9:146–47.

46. Dickens, "The Bloomsbury Christening" (April 1834), *Sketches by Boz, Illustrative of Every-Day Life and Every-Day People*, ed. Dennis Walder (1833–39; Harmondsworth: Penguin, 1995), 552. See also a piece that Dickens may well have authored: "The Misanthropic Society," in "Our Eye-Witness in Low Spirits," *All the Year Round* (February 25, 1860), 425.

47. James Beresford, *The Miseries of Human Life; or the Groans of Samuel Sensitive and Timothy Testy, with a Few Supplementary Sighs from Mrs. Testy: In Twelve Dialogues*, 3d ed. (London: Printed for William Miller, 1806), 129; original emphases.

48. "Ishmael," *Our Own Misanthrope* (London: Chapman and Hall, 1876), 10.

49. Thomas R. Preston, *Not in Timon's Manner: Feeling, Misanthropy, and Satire in Eighteenth-Century England* (University: U of Alabama P, 1975), 29.

50. Walter Bagehot, "The Character of Sir Robert Peel" (1856), *The Works of Walter Bagehot*, ed. Forrest Morgan (Hartford, Conn.: Travelers Insurance Co., 1889), 5 vols., 3:4.

51. "The Confession of a Misanthrope," *Atlantic Monthly* 71 (April 1893), 569.

52. Gay, *The Cultivation of Hatred*, 35.

53. Macaulay, *The History of England from the Accession of James II*, 445.

54. Gay, *The Cultivation of Hatred*, 134.

55. Macaulay, "Hallam's History" (1828), *Critical and Historical Essays* (London: J. M. Dent and Co., 1909), 2 vols., 1:40.

56. "Laus Iracundiæ," *New Eclectic Magazine* 5 (Baltimore; November 1869), 529, 528; original emphasis. Subsequent references give pagination in main text.

57. The author of "Laus Iracundiæ" might have taken heart from four sketches, titled "The Gallery of a Misanthrope," in the New York-based *American Monthly Magazine*. Each sketch lovingly records a form of treachery, the better to shake readers' faith in humanity. See "The Gallery of a Misanthrope 1: The Man of Pleasure," *American Monthly Magazine* 5.2 (New York; April 1835), 97–101; "2: Woman's Love," 5.3 (May 1835), 183–87; "3: Filial Affection," 5.4 (June 1835), 257–63; and "4: The Dignity of Human Nature," 5.5 (July 1835), 335–39.

58. Reverend John Keble, "National Apostasy," *Sermons, Academical and Occasional* (1833; Oxford: John Henry Parker, 1847), 6:143–44.

59. Reverend Francis Brothers, *The Hatred of the World: The Test of Our Abiding in Christ, a Sermon Preached at the Parish of All Saints, Cuddesdon, in the Diocese of Oxford* (London: Joseph Masters, 1860), 10; original emphases.

60. James Cowles Prichard, *A Treatise on Insanity and Other Disorders Affecting the Mind* (1835; New York: Arno P, 1973), 17; original emphasis.

61. Herbert, *Culture and Anomie: Ethnographic Imagination in the Nineteenth Century*, (Chicago: U of Chicago P. 1991), 51.

62. C. P. Bronson, *Stammering: Its Effects, Causes and Remedies; Involving Other Nervous Diseases; Such as Hysterics, St. Vitus' Dance, Spasmodic Asthma, Croup, Trembling Palsy, Epileptic Fits, Hypochondria, Misanthropy, Depression of Spirits, Peculiar Weaknesses, &c. &c.* (Boston: Bronson and Beers, 1855), 149. Subsequent references give pagination in main text.

63. John Conolly, *An Inquiry Concerning the Indications of Insanity, with Suggestions for the Better Protection and Care of the Insane* (1830; London: Dawsons, 1964), 227. Subsequent references give pagination in main text.

64. See Reed, *Victorian Will*, esp. 29–37.

65. George Eliot, *Felix Holt, the Radical* (1866; Harmondsworth: Penguin, 1995), 50. Subsequent references give pagination in main text.

66. Eliot, "Birth of Tolerance" in "Leaves from a Note-Book," *Essays of George Eliot*, ed. Thomas Pinney (New York: Columbia UP, 1963), 449.

67. Lewes, *Problems of Life and Mind* (Boston: Houghton, Mifflin, and Co., 1874–79), first series, 5 vols., 1:115.

68. Lewes, *Problems of Life and Mind* (Boston: Houghton, Mifflin, and Co., 1879), third series, 5 vols., 1:164.

69. Robert Browning, *The Ring and the Book*, ed. Richard D. Altick (1868–69; New Haven: Yale UP, 1981), 1.1294.

70. Auguste Widal (aka Daniel Stauben), *Des divers caractères du misanthrope, chez les écrivains anciens et modernes* (Paris: Auguste Durand, 1851), 5 and 3; my trans. Subsequent references give pagination in main text.

71. Spencer, *First Principles* (1862; New York: D. Appleton and Co., 1896), 433.

72. *OED* 1:371. See also Lewes, *Comte's Philosophy of the Sciences: Being an Exposition of the Principles of the Cours de philosophie positive of Auguste Comte* (1853; London: George Bell, 1887), 1:224. For elaboration on what Darwin and Freud inherited intellectually from Comte, see C. R. Badcock, *The Problem of Altruism: Freudian-Darwinian Solutions* (Oxford: Basil Blackwell, 1986).

73. Raymond Williams, *Keywords: A Vocabulary of Culture and Society*, 2d ed., (1976; London: Fontana, 1985), 76.

74. See "Hatred" (reprinted from *The Saturday Review*), *Littell's Living Age*, series 3:79, no. 1011 (October 17, 1863), esp. 104, and "The Natural History of Hatred," 115–17.

75. Arthur Schopenhauer, "On Human Nature" (1851), *Arthur Schopenhauer: Essays from the Parerga and Paralipomena*, trans. T. Bailey Saunders (London: Allen and Unwin, 1951), 17; my emphasis. The pages in this edition are not continuous.

76. John Oxenford, "Iconoclasm in German Philosophy," *Westminster Review* 3.2 (n.s., April 1853), 388–407. For a later nineteenth-century perspective on Schopenhauer's misanthropy, see P. Janet, "Un Philosophe misanthrope," *Académie des sciences morales et politiques, Séances et travaux*, n.s. 9 (Paris; janvier–juin 1878), 369–98.

77. Max Stirner, *The Ego and Its Own* (1844–45), ed. David Leopold, first trans. in 1907 by Steven T. Byington (New York: Cambridge UP, 1995), 47. Subsequent references give pagination in main text. See also Ludwig Feuerbach, *The Essence of Christianity*, trans. George Eliot (1841; New York: HarperTorch, 1957), which distinguishes between "self-interested love" and "the true human love [that] impels the sacrifice of self to another" (53).

78. Fyodor Dostoyevsky, *Notes from Underground and The Double* (1864; first English trans. 1913), trans. Jessie Coulson (Harmondsworth: Penguin, 1986), 15; original ellipsis; trans. modified. Subsequent references give pagination in main text.

79. Sigmund Freud, "Dostoevsky and Parricide" (1928), *The Standard Edition of the Complete Psychological Works of Sigmund Freud*, ed. and trans. James Strachey (London: Hogarth, 1953–74), 24 vols., 21:173–94.

80. Freud, *Civilization and Its Discontents* (1929, rev. 1930), *Standard Edition*, 21:112; original emphasis.

81. Ibid., 109. Joan Copjec extends this argument brilliantly in "Beyond the Good Neighbor Principle," *Read My Desire: Lacan Against the Historicists* (Cambridge:

MIT P, 1994), 88–98; see also Kenneth Reinhard, "Freud, My Neighbor," *American Imago* 52.4 (1997), 165–95.

82. "Prophetic Misanthropy," *Spectator* 55 (April 8, 1882), 462–63. The writer explains, in tortuous prose: "For though [Carlyle's] misanthropy is closely allied with prophetic wrath, though it is not hatred of that which is good in man, but of that which is petty and poor in man, still it is hatred of what is petty and poor even more than of what is evil in man, and it is wholly unaccompanied with vivifying and restoring life" (462).

83. Thackeray, *The History of Henry Esmond, Esq., A Colonel in the Service of Her Majesty Queen Anne, Written by Himself* (1852; Oxford: Oxford UP, 1991), 109.

84. According to G. Barnett Smith, Thackeray was wrongly accused of cynicism; see "The Works of Thackeray," *Edinburgh Review* 137.279 (January 1873), esp. 119–20. Similarly, in *The Way We Live Now*, Trollope indicts the Victorians' obsession with money without countenancing misanthropy. The closest the novel comes to hatred is Roger Carbury's measured contempt for the fraudulent Augustus Melmotte: "I look upon him as dirt in the gutter!" (Anthony Trollope, *The Way We Live Now* [1874–75; Oxford: Oxford UP, 1982, 1999], 138). But Carbury's judgment is so allied with Trollope's here that unless we share this perspective, the novel implies, there's something very wrong with us too. The only acceptable outlets for aggression in the book are commerce and book reviewing: Despite Lady Carbury's cultivated friendship with Ferdinand Alf, pedantic editor of the *Evening Pulpit*, the latter sets one of his "most sharp-nailed subordinates . . . upon her book," the latter "pull[ing] it to pieces with almost rabid malignity. . . . Error after error was laid bare with merciless prolixity" (95–96).

85. Thackeray, *The English Humourists of the Eighteenth Century* (1851; London: Macmillan and Co., 1911), 23, 24.

86. Browning, "Soliloquy of the Spanish Cloister" (1842), *Robert Browning: The Poems*, ed. John Pettigrew with Thomas J. Collins (New Haven: Yale UP, 1981), 2 vols., 1:356 (ll. 1–4).

87. "Moral Evil," a review article in the *London Quarterly Review* 52.104 (1879), 392–93; my emphasis. In her later essay "Fear and Hate," May Kendall also comes close to conceding the power of this argument. See *Longman's Magazine* 15.85 (1889–90), esp. 81.

88. James Fitzjames Stephen, *Liberty, Equality, Fraternity* (1873; Cambridge: Cambridge UP, 1967), 152.

89. Ibid. Stephen advanced a very similar argument in "Of Crimes in General and of Punishments," in *A History of the Criminal Law of England*, 3 vols. (1883; New York: Burt Franklin, 1964), 2:75–85, 91; also 179.

90. Gay, *The Cultivation of Hatred*, 175. Dickens's judgment appears in "A Letter to the Daily News" (February 28, 1846), qtd. in Gay, *The Cultivation of Hatred*, 177. See also chapter 2, n. 17.

91. Joseph Conrad, *Under Western Eyes* (1911; Harmondsworth: Penguin, 1996), 252.

92. Eliot, *Adam Bede* (1859; Harmondsworth: Penguin, 1985), 135. Subsequent references give pagination in main text.

1. Bulwer's Misanthropes and the Limits of Victorian Sympathy

To avoid confusion, I refer throughout this chapter to "Bulwer," but indicate in the notes below when he published as "Bulwer-Lytton," "Bulwer Lytton," and "Lytton Bulwer."

1. Edward Lytton Bulwer, "The Modern Misanthrope," *Blackwood's Magazine* 93.21 (April 1863), 477. Subsequent references give pagination in main text.

2. John Woolford, in Woolford and Daniel Karlin, *Robert Browning* (London: Longman, 1996), 168–69. As Woolford explains, Bulwer's "pamphlet, *Letter to a Late Cabinet Minister on the Present Crisis* (publ. Nov. 1834), was widely credited with having prevented the Tories from winning the General Election which shortly followed, an event that would have threatened reverse to the reforms put in place in the 1833 Reform Act" (169n.18). See also Victor Alexander Lytton, Second Earl of Lytton, *The Life of Edward Bulwer, First Lord Lytton, by his Grandson* (London: Macmillan and Co., 1913), 2 vols., 1:471–90.

3. Bulwer, *The New Timon: A Romance of London* (London: Henry Colburn, 1846), 7.10 and 8.1. Subsequent references give pagination in main text.

4. See, for instance, Giorgio Agamben, *The Coming Community*, trans. Michael Hardt (1990; Minneapolis: U of Minnesota P, 1993); Étienne Balibar, *Politics and the Other Scene*, trans. Christine Jones, James Swenson, and Chris Turner (1997–98; London: Verso, 2002); Jacques Derrida, *Specters of Marx: The State of the Debt, the Work of Mourning, and the New International*, trans. Peggy Kamuf (1993; New York: Routledge, 1994); Ernesto Laclau, *Emancipation(s)* (London: Verso, 1996); Claude Lefort, *The Political Forms of Modern Society: Bureaucracy, Democracy, Totalitarianism*, ed. John B. Thompson (1971–81; Cambridge: MIT P, 1986); Carl Schmitt, *The Concept of the Political*, trans. George Schwab and J. Harvey Lomax (1932; Chicago: U of Chicago P, 1996); and Slavoj Žižek, *Tarrying with the Negative: Kant, Hegel, and the Critique of Ideology* (Durham: Duke UP, 1993).

5. John Sutherland, *The Stanford Companion to Victorian Literature* (Stanford: Stanford UP, 1989), 390. See also G. K. Chesterton's account of Bulwer in *The Victorian Age in Literature* (New York: H. Holt and Co., 1913), 135–37.

6. This assessment is George Darley's, qtd. in Michael Sadleir, *Bulwer: A Panorama: Edward and Rosina, 1803–1836* (London: Constable and Co., 1931), 361.

7. For example, C. P. Bronson, *Stammering: Its Effects, Causes and Remedies; Involving Other Nervous Diseases; Such as Hysterics, St. Vitus' Dance, Spasmodic Asthma, Croup, Trembling Palsy, Epileptic Fits, Hypochondria, Misanthropy, Depression of Spirits, Peculiar Weaknesses, &c. &c.* (Boston: Bronson and Beers, 1855), 151; Auguste Comte, *System of Positive Polity, or Treatise on Sociology, Instituting the Religion of Humanity*, trans. John Henry Bridges (1851; London: Longmans, Green, and Co., 1875–77), 4 vols., 1:11, 18; and John Conolly, *An Inquiry Concerning the Indications of*

Insanity, with Suggestions for the Better Protection and Care of the Insane (1830; London: Dawsons, 1964), 227.

8. See Thomas Carlyle, *Past and Present*, ed. Richard D. Altick (1843; New York: New York UP, 1965), 4 books, 3:148; Auguste Widal (aka Daniel Stauben), *Des divers caractères du misanthrope, chez les écrivains anciens et modernes* (Paris: Auguste Durand, 1851), 5.

9. As Amanda Anderson writes of mid-Victorian precepts, paraphrasing Lorraine Daston, "The rigorous cultivation of objectivity in the natural sciences was linked to individual moral ascesis as well as a larger ideal of sociability." Anderson, *The Powers of Distance: Cosmopolitanism and the Cultivation of Detachment* (Princeton: Princeton UP, 2001), 12.

10. William Godwin, *Enquiry Concerning Political Justice and Its Influence on Morals and Happiness*, ed. F. E. L. Priestley (1793; Toronto: U of Toronto P, 1946), 2 vols., 1:xxiv. Subsequent references give pagination in main text. To improve readability I have altered Godwin's spelling, turning his "f"s into "s"s.

11. Thomas Reid outlined a similar argument in "Of the Nature and Obligation of a Contract," *Essays on the Active Powers of the Human Mind* (1788), *The Works of Thomas Reid* (New York: N. Bangs and T. Mason, 1822), 3 vols., esp. 3:288.

12. Godwin to Bulwer (May 13 and September 10, 1830), qtd. in Victor Alexander Lytton, Second Earl of Lytton, *The Life of Edward Bulwer, First Lord Lytton, by his Grandson* (London: Macmillan and Co., 1913), 2 vols., 1:364, 401. C. Kegan Paul dates the second letter to September 16, 1830 (see Paul, *William Godwin: His Friends and Contemporaries* [Boston: Robert Brothers, 1876], 2 vols., 2:302–9; original emphasis). Godwin was alluding to Bulwer's flippant statement, voiced in mid-July that year, that he was pursuing "the 'selfish system,' as it is commonly interpreted," in seeking election to Parliament. Evidently nettled that Godwin thought him unprincipled, Bulwer replied defensively on September 17, 1830: "With respect to the utilitarian, not 'self-love,' system of morals, all I can say is, that I am convinced that, if I commit a blunder, it is in words, not things. I understand by the system that benevolence may be made a passion; that it is the rule and square of all morality; that virtue loses not one atom of its value, or one charm from its loveliness" (qtd. in V. A. Lytton, *The Life of Edward Bulwer, First Lord Lytton*, 1:402). For insight into Bulwer's relationship with Godwin, see Keith Hollingsworth, *The Newgate Novel, 1830–1847: Bulwer, Ainsworth, Dickens, and Thackeray* (Detroit: Wayne State UP, 1963), 71–73.

13. See also Michael Lloyd, "Bulwer-Lytton and the Idealising Principle," *English Miscellany* 7 (1956), 25–39; Bulwer, "On Art in Fiction," *Monthly Chronicle: A National Journal of Politics, Literature, Science, and Art* 1 (London; March–June 1838), 42–51; and Harold H. Watts, "Lytton's Theories of Prose Fiction," *PMLA* 50.1 (1935), 274–89.

14. E. G. Bell, *Introductions to the Prose Romances, Plays, and Comedies of Edward Bulwer, Lord Lytton* (Chicago: Walter M. Hill, 1914), 275.

15. Bulwer, "The Sympathetic Temperament," *Blackwood's Magazine* 92 (November 1862), 535–43, rept. in *Caxtoniana: A Series of Essays on Life, Literature, and Manners* (New York: Harper and Brothers, 1863), 173–86. Subsequent references give pagination to the reprinted edition in main text.

16. Adam Smith, *The Theory of Moral Sentiments*, ed. D. D. Raphael and A. L. Macfie (1759; Oxford: Clarendon P, 1976), 9. Subsequent references give pagination in main text.

17. See also Audrey Jaffe, *Scenes of Sympathy: Identity and Representation in Victorian Fiction* (Ithaca: Cornell UP, 2000), 4, 10–11.

18. Bulwer Lytton, *The Disowned* (1828; London: Henry Colburn, 1829), 4 vols., xl, xxxix.

19. Bulwer Lytton, *The Last Days of Pompeii* (London: Richard Bentley, 1834), 3 vols., 2:210. For details about his earlier works, see Edward Robert Bulwer Lytton, Earl of Lytton (Owen Meredith), *The Life, Letters, and Literary Remains of Edward Bulwer, Lord Lytton, by His Son* (New York: Harper and Brothers, 1884), 2 vols., 1:414 (the first volume of this New York edition contains volumes 1 and 2 of the English edition).

20. Jeremy Bentham, *An Introduction to the Principles of Morals and Legislation*, ed. J. H. Burns and H. L. A. Hart (1780; 1789; 1823; London: Athlone P, 1970), 44. Subsequent references give pagination in main text.

21. Lytton Bulwer, *England and the English*, ed. and intro. Standish Meacham (Chicago: U of Chicago P, 1970), 286. Subsequent references give pagination in main text. The first draft of this work, conceived and written in 1824, was titled "History of the British Public."

22. Nor was he alone in this respect. Byron's *Manfred* and *Childe Harold's Pilgrimage* spawned many lesser imitations invariably detailing the plight of a rejected lover who struggles to reconcile nature's beauty with man's treachery and woman's "fickle" heart. Among these works are *Childe Albert, or, the Misanthrope and Other Poems, Imitative and Original* (Edinburgh: William Aitchison, 1819); Joseph Snow, *Misanthropy, and Other Poems* (London: Printed for John Miller, 1819); Thomas Furlong, *The Misanthrope; with Other Poems* (1819; Dublin: W. Underwood, 1821), rept. in Sean Mythen, *Thomas Furlong: The Forgotten Wexford Poet* (Ferns, Co. Wexford, Ireland: Clone Publications, 1998), 53–62; T. Gordon Hake, *Poetic Lucubrations; Containing The Misanthrope and Other Effusions* (London: Hunt and Clarke, 1828); George W. Sands, "The Misanthrope Reclaimed: A Dramatic Poem," *Mazelli, and Other Poems* (Philadelphia: Lindsay and Blakiston, 1849), 57–108; *The Misanthrope of the Mountain: A Poem*, attributed to Joseph W. Bennett (New Haven: A. H. Maltby, 1833); and Charles Henry St. John, "The Misanthrope Melted: A Scene from an Unfinished Drama," *Poems* (Boston: A. Williams and Co., 1859), 121–27.

23. I examine Bulwer's revisions to such "dandiacal" novels as *Pelham; or, The Adventures of a Gentleman* (1828; rev. 1835 and 1840) in *The Burdens of Intimacy:*

Psychoanalysis and Victorian Masculinity (Chicago: U of Chicago P, 1999), 45–54.

24. Bulwer, qtd. in *The Life, Letters, and Literary Remains of Edward Bulwer, Lord Lytton, by His Son*, 1:420.

25. Although the latter's name probably was inspired by Godwin's 1817 novel, *Mandeville. A Tale of the Seventeenth Century in England*, it may also allude to Bernard Mandeville, the eighteenth-century philosopher who mocked Shaftesbury's claims for innate sociability in his dazzling satire, *The Fable of the Bees* (1714; rev. 1724).

26. Edwin M. Eigner, *The Metaphysical Novel in England and America: Dickens, Bulwer, Melville, and Hawthorne* (Berkeley: U of California P, 1978), 69–70.

27. Allan Conrad Christensen, *Edward Bulwer-Lytton: The Fiction of New Regions* (Athens: U of Georgia P, 1976), 5.

28. See Sadleir, *Bulwer: A Panorama*, esp. 362.

29. "Epistles to the Literati: No. 1. to E. L. Bulwer," *Fraser's Magazine for Town and Country* 4.23 (London; December 1831), 521–22, 525–26.

30. William Makepeace Thackeray, qtd. in Ellen Moers, *The Dandy: Brummell to Beerbohm* (New York: Viking, 1960), 213 and 201. See Sadleir, *Bulwer: A Panorama*, 248–51 and 263n., for explanations about William Maginn's personal vendetta against Bulwer.

31. "Liston Bulwer's Song," *Fraser's* 5.25 (February 1832), 125. Rich with in-jokes and scurrilous allusions, this stanza invokes, first, Letitia Elizabeth Landon's article on Bulwer in the *New Monthly Magazine*, so fulsome in praise that *Fraser's* scandalously implied that Bulwer had written it. Bulwer and Landon also engaged in "an apparent philandering" in 1828, and the *appearance* of an affair quickly overruled any likelihood that it occurred (Sadleir 139, but also 250). Ms. Landon was a protégée of William Jerdan, editor of the *Literary Gazette*, invoked here because he praised Bulwer's satirical poem *The Siamese Twins* (1831) and was anyway an enemy of Charles Molloy Westmacott, editor of *The Age* from roughly 1827, a close associate of William Maginn, editor of *Fraser's*. Bulwer took his revenge on Westmacott in "Supplementary Illustrations of Character," *England and the English*, esp. 355.

32. Sibylla Jane Flower, *Bulwer-Lytton: An Illustrated Life of the First Baron Lytton, 1803–1873* (Aylesbury, UK: Shire Publications, 1973), 20. See also Virginia Blain's interesting essay "Rosina Bulwer Lytton and the Rage of the Unheard," *Huntington Library Quarterly* 53.3 (1990), 211–36.

33. Louisa Devey, Executrix to the Dowager Lady Lytton, *Letters of the Late Edward Bulwer, Lord Lytton, to His Wife, with Extracts from Her Mss., "Autobiography," and Other Documents, Published in Vindication of Her Memory* (1884; New York: G. W. Dillingham, 1889), 411. Subsequent references give pagination in main text.

34. These words appear in Benjamin Disraeli's 1833 "Mutilated Diary," qtd. in William Flavelle Monypenny and George Earle Buckle, *The Life of Benjamin*

Disraeli, Earl of Beaconsfield (1910–20; New York: Macmillan, 1929), 2 vols., 1:239.

35. Bulwer, "On the Want of Sympathy" (1835), *Miscellaneous Prose Works* (London: Richard Bentley, 1868), 3 vols., 2:108. Subsequent references give pagination in main text.

36. Bulwer, "On Self-Control," *Caxtoniana: A Series of Essays on Life, Literature, and Manners*, 210. Subsequent references give pagination in main text.

37. Bulwer-Lytton, *Pelham*, ed. and intro. Jerome J. McGann (Lincoln: U of Nebraska P, 1972), 84. Subsequent references give pagination in main text. Bulwer even claimed, two years later, that "Pelham . . . was meant to be . . . a practical satire on the exaggerated, and misanthropical romance of the day—a human being whose real good qualities put to shame the sickly sentimentalism of blue skies and bare throats, sombre coxcombries and interesting villainies." "If he be at all like this," he added, "I am extremely proud to be mistaken for him." Bulwer, "Dedicatory Epistle," *Paul Clifford* (London: Henry Colburn and Richard Bentley, 1830), 3 vols., xixn. Subsequent references give pagination in main text.

38. Bulwer-Lytton, unsigned review of *The Autobiography, Times, Opinions, and Contemporaries of Sir Egerton Brydges, Bart.* (1834), *Edinburgh Review* 59.120 (July 1834), 441–42.

39. See, for instance, Bulwer, "The Faults of Recent Poets: Poems by Alfred Tennyson," *New Monthly Magazine and Literary Journal* 8 (January 1833), 69–74.

40. For details (including the quoted material), see Hollingsworth, *The Newgate Novel, 1830–1847*, 199–200. The insult appears in Michael Angelo [*sic*] Titmarsh (i.e., Thackeray), "A Grumble about the Christmas-Books," *Fraser's* 35.205 (January 1847), 115.

41. See "Alcibiades" (i.e., Tennyson), "The New Timon, and the Poets," *Punch* 10.242 (February 28, 1846), 103. Deeming his statement unworthy of a bard, Tennyson retracted it in "After-thought," *Punch* 10.243 (March 7, 1846), 106, but the damage was done. The passage that irked him appears in Bulwer's *New Timon*, of the same year. Given the weaknesses of Bulwer's own poetry, the following remarks are truly scandalous:

> Not mine, not mine, (O Muse forbid!) the boon
> Of borrowed notes, the mock-bird's modish tune,
> The jingling medley of purloin'd conceits,
> Outbabying Wordsworth, and outglittering Keates [*sic*],
> Where all the airs of patchwork-pastoral chime
> To drowsy ears in Tennysonian rhyme!
> Am I enthrall'd but by the sterile rule,
> The formal pupil of a frigid school,
> . . . . ?
> Let School-Miss Alfred vent her chaste delight
> On "darling little rooms so warm and bright!" (51.1–8, 15–16)

Bulwer then adds, in an extraordinary footnote: "The whole of this *Poem* (!!!) is worth reading, in order to see to what depth of silliness the human intellect can descend" (51n.). After mocking Tennyson's "Mariana" (1830), he continues:

> The most that can be said of Mr. Tennyson is, that he is the favourite of a small circle; to the mass of the Public little more than his name is known— he has moved no thousands—he has created no world of characters—he has laboured out no deathless truths, nor enlarged our knowledge of the human heart by the delineation of various and elevating passions—he has lent a stout shoulder to no sinking but manly cause, dear to the Nation and to Art; yet, if the uncontradicted statement in the journals be true, this Gentleman has been quartered on the public purse; he in the prime of life, belonging to a wealthy family, without, I believe, wife or children; at the very time that Mr. Knowles was lecturing for bread in foreign lands, verging towards old age, unfriended even by the public he has charmed!—such is the justice of our ministers, such the national gratitude to those whom we thank and— starve! (52–53n.)

Bulwer was referring to Tennyson's receiving a pension in 1845, five years before the latter became poet laureate.

42. Carlyle, qtd. in Sadleir, *Bulwer: A Panorama*, 197; Christensen, *Edward Bulwer-Lytton: The Fiction of New Regions*, 10.

43. Bulwer, "Monos and Daimonos: A Legend" (first published in the *New Monthly Magazine* in 1830), *The Student: A Series of Papers* (London: Saunders and Otley, 1835), 2 vols., 1:29. Subsequent references give pagination in main text.

44. On the possible reasons for this aversion, see Sadleir, *Bulwer: A Panorama*, 18.

45. Edgar Allan Poe in April 1835 described "Monos and Daimonos" as an example of "the ludicrous heightened into the grotesque: the fearful coloured into the horrible: the witty exaggerated into the burlesque: the singular wrought out into the strange and mystical. You may say all this is bad taste. I have my doubts about it." Poe, *The Letters of Edgar Allan Poe*, ed. John Ward Ostrom (Cambridge: Harvard UP, 1948), 2 vols., 1:57–58. I'm indebted to Christensen's study, 237n.6, for this reference.

46. See Godwin, *Things as They Are, or The Adventures of Caleb Williams* (1794; Harmondsworth: Penguin, 1988); James Hogg, *The Private Memoirs and Confessions of a Justified Sinner: Written by Himself* (1824; Harmondsworth: Penguin, 1983).

47. Robert Bage, *Hermsprong; or, Man as He Is Not* (1796; New York: Oxford UP, 1985).

48. Mary Shelley, *Frankenstein, or The Modern Prometheus* (1818; Harmondsworth: Penguin, 1992), 96. Subsequent references give pagination in main text.

49. Lord Byron, *Manfred, A Dramatic Poem* (1816), 1.1, 206–7, *The Complete Poetical Works*, ed. Jerome J. McGann (Oxford: Clarendon P, 1986), 7 vols., 4:60; see also 2.2.130 (p. 74: "My solitude is solitude no more, / But peopled with the Furies . . .") and *Cain, A Mystery* (1821), 3.1.545–63, *Complete Poetical Works* 6:294–95.

Both works were of course written while Byron experienced his own exile from England.

50. Bulwer, "Monos and Daimonos: A Legend" (1830), *The Student* (New York: Harper and Brothers, 1836), 2 vols., 2:188; original emphasis.

51. In the extended, London version, the Daimonos adds: "EVIL THOUGHTS ARE COMPANIONS FOR A TIME—EVIL DEEDS ARE COMPANIONS THROUGH ETERNI-TY—THY HATRED MADE ME BREAK UPON THY LONELINESS—THY CRIME DE-STROYS LONELINESS FOR EVER" (1:47–48). The 1835 London edition is in fact the "later" version, too, because Harper and Brothers in New York reprinted from an earlier North American version of the story, ignoring Bulwer's updated revisions to the British edition of *The Student*.

52. Bulwer, 1845 preface to *Night and Morning* (1841; London: Chapman and Hall, 1851), ix. Subsequent references give pagination in main text.

53. Bulwer, *Lucretia; or, The Children of the Night* (London: Saunders and Otley, 1846), 3 vols., 2:280.

54. Bulwer, *Money: A Comedy in Five Acts* (London: Saunders and Otley, 1840), 1.1, p. 29. Subsequent references give pagination in main text.

55. Bulwer to Lord Lytton, his son (June 1871), qtd. in *The Life of Edward Bulwer, First Lord Lytton*, 2:468.

56. Bulwer Lytton, *The Coming Race*, 3d ed. (later subtitled: *or, The New Utopia*) (Edinburgh: William Blackwood and Sons, 1871), 57. Subsequent references give pagination in main text.

57. Bell, *Introductions to the Prose Romances, Plays, and Comedies of Edward Bulwer, Lord Lytton*, 275.

2. Dickensian Malefactors

1. Charles Dickens, *Barnaby Rudge: A Tale of the Riots of 'Eighty* (1841; Harmondsworth: Penguin, 1997), 244. Subsequent references give pagination in main text.

2. Dickens, *Nicholas Nickleby* (1838–39; Harmondsworth: Penguin, 1999), 753.

3. Dickens, *Our Mutual Friend* (1864–65; Harmondsworth: Penguin, 1997), 297. Subsequent references give pagination in main text. Dickens, "The Bloomsbury Christening" (first published in April 1834, in the *Monthly Magazine*), *Sketches by Boz, Illustrative of Every-Day Life and Every-Day People*, ed. Dennis Walder (1833–39; Harmondsworth: Penguin, 1995), 552.

4. See also Dickens, "Thoughts about People," *Sketches by Boz*, 253–54, first appearing in the *Evening Chronicle* on April 23, 1835.

5. Dickens, *The Old Curiosity Shop* (1840–41; Harmondsworth: Penguin, 1985), 192.

6. John Kucich, *Excess and Restraint in the Novels of Charles Dickens* (Athens: U of Georgia P, 1981), 69. Juliet John made similar claims recently in *Dickens's Villains: Melodrama, Character, Popular Culture* (New York: Oxford UP, 2001), esp. chapter 6.

7. As Dickens conceded to John Forster (February 9 [?], 1857), incongruous emotions spoil "The History of a Self Tormentor," an anomalous chapter in *Little Dorrit* purporting to explain Miss Wade's proud contempt, especially for men. See *The Letters of Charles Dickens*, The Pilgrim Edition, ed. Madeline House, Graham Storey, and Kathleen Tillotson (Oxford: Clarendon, 1965–), 11 vols., 8:279–80; and Forster, *The Life of Dickens*, ed. A. J. Hoppé (1872–74; London: Dent, 1966), 2 vols., book 8, chapter 1, 2:184.

8. Victor Brombert, *In Praise of Antiheroes: Figures and Themes in Modern European Literature, 1830–1980* (Chicago: U of Chicago P, 1999), 6, 2.

9. Ibid., 16.

10. In his chapter "Arbitrary and Despotic Characters," John Bowen hints at a similar argument, claiming broadly that Dickens's antiheroes "continue to be radical in quite other [i.e., unconventional] ways," because they "stretch our notions of psychology, aesthetics, and politics alike" (*Other Dickens: Pickwick to Chuzzlewit* [New York: Oxford UP, 2000], 22). Bowen doesn't develop his argument beyond this interesting observation.

11. Ibid., 22. One of many examples of this ferocious desire for retribution would be Abel Magwitch's impulse to drown Compeyson, his enemy and traitor, precisely when Magwitch could board a steamer and escape from the police (Dickens, *Great Expectations* [1860–61; Harmondsworth: Penguin, 1996], 444). More generally, Magwitch uses Pip's advancement to revenge himself against humanity; see 332. Subsequent references give pagination in main text.

12. Dickens, *Dealings with the Firm of Dombey and Son, Wholesale, Retail and for Exportation* (1846–48; Harmondsworth: Penguin, 1985), 875. Subsequent references give pagination in main text.

13. Dickens, qtd. in Peter Ackroyd, *Dickens* (1990; New York: HarperPerennial, 1992), 518.

14. Dickens, *The Life and Adventures of Martin Chuzzlewit* (1843–44; Harmondsworth: Penguin, 1986), 803–4. Subsequent references give pagination in main text.

15. See F. R. and Q. D. Leavis, *Dickens the Novelist* (2d ed.; London: Chatto and Windus, 1970), xv.

16. John Carey, *The Violent Effigy: A Study of Dickens' Imagination* (1973; London: Faber, 1991), 19.

17. During his lifetime, Dickens witnessed several executions and wrote about capital punishment. See "A Visit to Newgate," first published in 1836, but not included in the Penguin edition of *Sketches by Boz and Other Early Papers, 1833–39*, ed. Michael Slater (Columbus: Ohio State UP, 1994), 199–210; Carey, *The Violent Effigy*, 20–22; and the introduction, n. 90 above. Additionally, compare Eliot's account of Bernardo del Nero's and Savonarola's executions in *Romola* (1862–63; Harmondsworth: Penguin, 1996), 496 and 577, discussed more fully in chapter 4.

18. Dickens to Forster (February 24, 1842), *Letters of Charles Dickens*, 3:87.

19. Dickens to Charles Sumner (May 16, 1842), *Letters of Charles Dickens*, 3:239. Although the version in *American Notes* is more tempered, it better captures Dickens's anger and disgust. See Dickens, *American Notes for the General Circulation*, ed. John S. Whitley and Arnold Goldman (1842; Harmondsworth: Penguin, 1985), 244–45.

20. Edwin Chadwick, *Report on the Sanitary Condition of the Labouring Population of Great Britain*, ed. Michael W. Flinn (1842; Edinburgh: Edinburgh UP, 1965).

21. An inspector in 1856, qtd. in Ackroyd, *Dickens*, 382. Most of this paragraph is greatly indebted to Ackroyd's vivid account of urban poverty, esp. 380–84. See also Henry Lorenzo Jephson, *The Sanitary Evolution of London* (New York: Arno, 1978); W. F. Bynum and Roy Porter, eds., *Living and Dying in London* (London: Wellcome Institute for the History of Medicine, 1991); and Andrew Sanders, *Charles Dickens, Resurrectionist* (New York: St. Martin's, 1982), esp. 1–36.

22. A letter with fifty-four signatures appeared in the *Times* on July 5, 1849, complaining: "We are Sur, as it may be, living in a Wilderniss, so far as the rest of London knows anything of us, or as rich and great people care about. We live in muck and filthe. We aint got no privez, no dust bins, no drains, no water splies, and no drain or suer in the whole place," qtd. in Porter, *London: A Social History* (London: Hamish Hamilton, 1994), 259.

23. Dr. Simon, qtd. in Ackroyd, *Dickens*, 382.

24. J. Hillis Miller, *Charles Dickens: The World of His Novels* (1958; Cambridge: Harvard UP, 1965), 104–5.

25. Dickens's original title for the novel was *The Life and Adventures of Martin Chuzzlewit / His Relatives, Friends, and Enemies. / Comprising All His Wills and His Ways: / With an Historical Record of What He Did, and What He Didn't: / Showing, Moreover, Who Inherited the Family Plate, Who Came in for the Silver Spoons, and Who for the Wooden Ladles. / The Whole Forming a Complete Key to the House of Chuzzlewit*. However, he followed Forster's advice in shortening this title before the novel was published in its three-volume format in 1844. For elaboration, see Kathleen Wales, "The Claims of Kinship: The Opening Chapter of *Martin Chuzzlewit*," *Dickensian* 83.3 (1987), 167–79.

26. See Dickens, *The Battle of Life: A Love Story* (London: Bradbury and Evans, 1846).

27. See, for instance, *Our Mutual Friend*, where the narrator—referring to Headstone's mental collapse—declares: "The wild energy of the man, now quite let loose, was absolutely terrible" (389).

28. See Lord James Burnett Monboddo, *Of the Origin and Progress of Language* (Edinburgh: Printed for J. Balfour, Edinburgh, and T. Cadell, 1774–92), 6 vols., which asserts a close biological relation between humans and the orangutan. Although *Chuzzlewit* was published more than a decade before this event, the discovery of what was then called "Neanderthal Man" was made in 1856, in time for Dickens's unorthodox treatment of life and death in *Our Mutual Friend*.

29. Steven Marcus, *Dickens: From Pickwick to Dombey* (London: Chatto and Windus, 1965), 225.

30. Michael H. Futrell, "Dostoyevsky and Dickens," *English Miscellany*, ed. Mario Praz, 7 (1956), 41–89; F. R. and Q. D. Leavis, *Dickens the Novelist*, esp. 35–37; and N. M. Lary, *Dostoevsky and Dickens: A Study of Literary Influence* (London: Routledge and Kegan Paul, 1973), esp. ix–xii.

31. Slow in reaching an English audience—*Crime and Punishment* was translated into English in 1886, but *The Brothers Karamazov* didn't follow until 1912—Dostoyevsky's work influenced only such late-Victorian writers as Stevenson (reading in French), Wilde, and Gissing, as well as Edwardians such as John Middleton Murry, Arnold Bennett (also reading in French), and eventually D. H. Lawrence, after he'd voiced initial antipathy. Friedrich Nietzsche fortuitously read a French translation of *Notes from Underground* in February 1887. For details, see René Wellek, "Introduction: A Sketch of the History of Dostoevsky Criticism," *Dostoevsky: A Collection of Critical Essays*, ed. Wellek (Englewood Cliffs, N.J.: Prentice-Hall, 1962), 1–15; Maurice Beebe and Christopher Newton, "Dostoevsky in English: A Selected Checklist of Criticism and Translations," *Modern Fiction Studies* 4.3 (1958), 271–91; and Helen Muchnic, *Dostoevsky's English Reputation (1881–1936)*, *Smith College Studies in Modern Languages* 20.3–4 (1969).

32. Fyodor Dostoyevsky, *Notes from Underground and The Double*, trans. Jessie Coulson (1864, first trans. 1913; Harmondsworth: Penguin, 1986), 15; original ellipsis; trans. modified. Subsequent references give pagination in main text.

33. For elaboration on this argument, which I am paraphrasing, see Tim Dean, *Beyond Sexuality* (Chicago: U of Chicago P, 2000), esp. 162–67.

34. Brombert, *In Praise of Antiheroes*, 35.

35. See Joseph Frank, "Nihilism and *Notes from Underground*," *Sewanee Review* 69.1 (1961), 1–33. Note, however, that Dostoyevsky's slightly earlier *Winter Notes on Summer Impressions* (1863), based on his 1862 trip to Paris and London, voices *almost* the opposite of anticommunitarianism:

> Understand me: voluntary, fully conscious self-sacrifice utterly free of outside constraint, sacrifice of one's entire self for the benefit of all, is in my opinion a sign of the supreme development of individuality. . . . If we transposed fraternity into rational conscious language, of what then would it consist? It would consist of this: each individual, of his own accord, without any external pressure or thought of profit, would say to society, 'We are strong only when united; take all of me, if you need me; do not think of me when you make your laws; do not worry about me in the least; I cede all my rights to you and beg you to dispose of me as you see fit. My greatest joy is to sacrifice everything to you, without hurting you by so doing. I shall annihilate myself, I shall melt away, if only your brotherhood will last and prosper.'—But the community should answer: 'You

offer us too much. . . . Take everything that is ours, too. (*Winter Notes on Summer Impressions*, trans. Richard Lee Renfield [New York: Criterion Books, 1995], 111, 113.)

Evidently, many problems in Dostoyevsky's fiction stem from the fact that neither side makes this offer—or does so in good faith.

36. Dickens, *A Tale of Two Cities* (1859; Harmondsworth: Penguin, 1985), 115. Subsequent references give pagination in main text.

37. Dickens to Sir Edward Bulwer Lytton (June 5, 1860), *Letters of Charles Dickens*, 9:259.

38. John Keats, "Ode to a Nightingale" (1819), *Selected Poems*, ed. John Barnard (Harmondsworth: Penguin, 1988), 171 (6.2).

39. Dickens, "Going into Society" (1858), *Christmas Stories*, introd. Margaret Lane (New York: Oxford UP, 1985), 229. Subsequent references give pagination in main text.

40. As I mention in the introduction, "Going into Society" should be read beside "The Misanthropic Society," a sketch appearing in *All the Year Round* (February 25, 1860), 425–28.

41. John P. Farrell explains how this emphasis affects the novel's conception of partnership in "The Partners' Tale: Dickens and *Our Mutual Friend*," *ELH* 66.3 (1999), 759–99. Stressing the resilience of partnership, Farrell's conclusion almost reverses mine. Still, as he concedes, "the novel itself seems determined to negate . . . the presence of [this] sociality" (759).

42. Compare this with Sam Weller's amusing belief that "pike-keeper[s]"—that is, turnpike keepers—choose their job because they have "met vith [*sic*] some disappointment in life . . . Consequence of vich, they retires from the world, and shuts themselves up in pikes; partly vith the view of being solitary, and partly to rewenge themselves on mankind by takin' tolls." "If they was gen'lm'n," Weller continues, "you'd call 'em misanthropes, but as it is, they only takes to pike-keepin.'" *The Pickwick Papers* (1836–37; Harmondsworth: Penguin, 1986), 384.

43. Wrayburn's father does finally have Lizzie painted, which Wrayburn infers as understated acceptance of their marriage. In all likelihood, then, Wrayburn would not be cut out of his father's will. But as is clear in the novel's final chapter, in which contempt is voiced for Lizzie and the marriage, social prejudice still thrives. We would be naïve to confuse her and Wrayburn's financial security with even their partial integration into "Society."

3. Charlotte Brontë on the Pleasure of Hating

1. Freud uses this phrase in *Group Psychology and the Analysis of the Ego* (1921), *The Standard Edition of the Complete Psychological Works of Sigmund Freud*, ed. and trans. James Strachey (London: Hogarth, 1953–74), 24 vols., 18:101.

2. The phrase is Caroline Helstone's, voiced internally in Charlotte Brontë, *Shirley: A Tale* (1849; Harmondsworth: Penguin, 1985), 190. Subsequent references give pagination in main text.

3. Sandra M. Gilbert and Susan Gubar, *The Madwoman in the Attic: The Woman Writer and the Nineteenth-Century Literary Imagination* (New Haven: Yale UP, 1979), 314. John Maynard argues persuasively against this approach in *Charlotte Brontë and Sexuality* (New York: Cambridge UP, 1984), ix. While noting that Lyndall Gordon's recent biography alludes to Brontë's fears of her misanthropy (see *Charlotte Brontë: A Passionate Life* [New York: Norton, 1995], esp. 239), I share with Maynard a conviction that psychological factors like fantasy and hatred are irreducible to biographical concerns. In *A Room of One's Own* (1929), by contrast, Virginia Woolf famously (and quite uncharacteristically) claimed otherwise, influencing many later critics when arguing that Brontë wrote "in a rage" when "she should [have] writ[ten] calmly"; that "she [was] at war with her lot"; and that "anger was tampering with the integrity of" her fiction. Woolf, *A Room of One's Own* (New York: Harcourt, 1981), 69, 70, and 73.

4. John Kucich, *Repression in Victorian Fiction: Charlotte Brontë, George Eliot, and Charles Dickens* (Berkeley: U of California P, 1987), 38–39. Subsequent references give pagination in main text.

5. Emily Brontë, *Wuthering Heights* (1847; Harmondsworth: Penguin, 1995), 3. E. Brontë's broadly Romantic conception of misanthropy—resolutely isolationist, stemming from thwarted love and class hatred—helps show why society and the individual, riven by mutual hostility, are incommensurate in her novel.

6. Unsigned review, *Christian Remembrancer* 15 (April 1848), rept. in *The Brontës: The Critical Heritage*, ed. Miriam Allott (London: Routledge and Kegan Paul, 1974), 90.

7. Charlotte Brontë, *Jane Eyre: An Autobiography* (1847; Harmondsworth: Penguin, 1996), 363. Subsequent references give pagination in main text.

8. Nina Auerbach, *Romantic Imprisonment: Women and Other Glorified Outcasts* (New York: Columbia UP, 1985), 203. See also Jerome Beaty, *Misreading "Jane Eyre": A Postformalist Paradigm* (Columbus: Ohio State UP, 1996), esp. 121–22.

9. Brontë, *The Professor* (1846; 1857; Harmondsworth: Penguin, 1989), 40, 41, 42, 44, and 45. Subsequent references give pagination in main text.

10. Heather Glen, Introduction to *The Professor*, 23. See also Janet Gezari's reading of this novel in *Charlotte Brontë and Defensive Conduct: The Author and the Body at Risk* (Philadelphia: U of Pennsylvania P, 1992), 30–58.

11. An excellent, quite different perspective orients John Plotz's chapter "Producing Privacy in Public: Charlotte Brontë's *Shirley*," *The Crowd: British Literature and Public Politics* (Berkeley: U of California P, 2000), 154–93. I am also departing from Arnold Shapiro's suggestion that Brontë's "theme, selfishness, the lack of sympathy between people, connects everything—public or private—in the novel." While agreeing with Shapiro about the ubiquity of selfishness in Brontë's novel, my chapter claims that selfishness conceptually shatters all elements and characters in the novel,

and in this respect is Brontë's means of engaging with anticommunitarian impulses in Victorian society. Shapiro, "Public Themes and Private Lives: Social Criticism in *Shirley*," *Critical Essays on Charlotte Brontë*, ed. Barbara Timm Gates (Boston: G. K. Hall, 1990), 224.

12. Brontë, Preface to *Jane Eyre*, 6–7. In this preface, Brontë also called Thackeray "the first social regenerator of the day" (7). This was before their friendship soured from his revealing publicly her identity as Currer Bell.

13. This passage is partly a rejoinder to Mrs. Pryor's High Toryism, which the narrator reproduces for ironic effect: "Implicit submission to authorities, scrupulous deference to our betters (under which term I, of course, include the higher classes of society), are, in my opinion, indispensable to the wellbeing [*sic*] of every community" (*Shirley*, 365).

14. Lewes, "Currer Bell's *Shirley*," *Edinburgh Review* 91 (January 1850), an unsigned review reprinted in *The Brontës: The Critical Heritage*, 164, 165. Subsequent references give pagination in main text.

15. Brontë to Lewes (January 1850), *The Brontës: Their Lives, Friendships, and Correspondence in Four Volumes*, ed. Thomas James Wise and J. Alexander Symington (Oxford: Blackwell, 1933, 1980), 3:67.

16. See Sally Shuttleworth, *Charlotte Brontë and Victorian Psychology* (New York: Cambridge UP, 1996), 187; also Terry Eagleton, *Myths of Power: A Marxist Study of the Brontës* (London: Macmillan, 1975), 47.

17. Gordon, *Charlotte Brontë*, 180.

18. Brontë to William Smith William, a reader at Smith, Elder (her publishers; January 18, 1849), *The Brontës: Their Lives, Friendships, and Correspondence*, 2:301.

19. Gordon, *Charlotte Brontë*, 190.

20. For elaboration, see Max Stirner's provocative and near-contemporaneous study *The Ego and Its Own* (1844–45), ed. David Leopold, first trans. in 1907 by Steven T. Byington (New York: Cambridge UP, 1995), 40.

21. In "Private and Social Themes in *Shirley*," *Brontë Society Transactions* 13.3 (1958), Asa Briggs calls the axiom "misery generates hate" "as powerful a phrase as any coined by Carlyle, Disraeli or Engels, and it was as relevant to the 1840s as the 1810s" (215).

22. Here he differs radically from Yorke (whom, of course, he earlier resembled). As the narrator observes, "Well did Mr. Yorke like to have power, and to use it: he had now between his hands power over a fellow creature's life: it suited him" (523).

23. "The mercantile classes . . . are too oblivious of every national consideration but that of extending England's (i.e., their own) commerce. . . . A land ruled by them alone would too often make ignominious submission—not at all from the motives Christ teaches, but rather from those Mammon instils" (183).

24. Thomas Carlyle, "Gospel of Mammonism," *Past and Present* (1843; New York: New York UP, 1965), 4 books, 3:148.

25. E. P. Thompson, *The Making of the English Working Class* (1963; Harmondsworth: Pelican, 1984), 613. See also Patrick Brantlinger, "The Case Against

Trade Unions in Early Victorian Fiction," *Victorian Studies* 13.1 (1969), esp. 41–42; and Eagleton, *Myths of Power*: "*Shirley* chooses to ignore contemporary conditions, imaginatively translating them to an earlier phase of the Yorkshire class-struggle, negotiating its feelings in relation to the past rather than the present" (45; see also 46, 49, and 52).

26. Thompson, *The Making of the English Working Class*, 620.

27. My argument and analysis below suggest that this is true even in revolutionary times, as Britain found itself on May 11, 1812, when Prime Minister Spencer Perceval was assassinated in the House of Commons.

28. Anonymous letter (April 19, 1812), qtd. in Thompson, *The Making of the English Working Class*, 620, original emphasis. Matthew Jermyn voices a similar idea in George Eliot's *Felix Holt, the Radical*, when declaring archly to Harold Transome, "You require time to consider whether the pleasure of trying to ruin me—me to whom you are really indebted—is worth the loss of the Transome estates," which Harold is set to inherit (1866; Harmondsworth: Penguin, 1995), 335.

29. Eliot, *Felix Holt*, 319.

30. Eagleton complains: "Even Barraclough's leg is denied authenticity. His counterpart in the novel is William Farren, a model of decency and good manners who is present to provide Shirley and Caroline with an object of patronage; and the novel's attitude to the working class wavers accordingly between panicky contempt and paternalist condescension" (*Myths of Power* 49).

31. Though the following passage in Eliot's *Felix Holt* conveys political overtones, it's worth considering whether, similar to Brontë's narrative concerns in *Shirley*, the judgment of Eliot's narrator and her caution are not partly an effect of her awareness of this surplus content: "As [Felix] was pressed along with the multitude into Treby Park, his very movement seemed to him only an image of the day's fatalities, in which the multitudinous small wickednesses of small selfish ends, really undirected towards any larger result, had issued in widely-shared mischief that might yet be hideous" (320).

32. Thompson, *The Making of the English Working Class*, 603. He argues that Luddism was "a moment of *transitional* conflict. On the one hand, it looked backward to old customs and paternalist legislation which could never be revived; on the other hand, it tried to revive ancient rights in order to establish new precedents" (603). See also Carlyle, "Organic Filaments," *Sartor Resartus: The Life and Opinions of Herr Teufelsdröckh in Three Books* (1833–34; 1836; Berkeley: U of California P, 2000), 3 books, 3:7, 180–86; and Benjamin Disraeli, *Sybil; or, The Two Nations* (1845; London: Frederick Warne and Co., 1868), 131–34.

33. William Shakespeare, *The Tragedy of Coriolanus*, The Arden Shakespeare, ed. Philip Brockbank (1608, 1623; New York: Methuen and Co., 1976), 2.1.252 and 4.7.39. Subsequent references appear in main text.

34. For elaboration on Brontë's interest in *Coriolanus*, see Gezari's chapter on *Shirley* in *Charlotte Brontë and Defensive Conduct*, esp. 108–17; Margaret J. Arnold,

"Coriolanus Transformed: Charlotte Brontë's Use of Shakespeare in *Shirley*," *Women's Re-Visions of Shakespeare: On the Responses of Dickinson, Woolf, Rich, H. D., George Eliot, and Others*, ed. Marianne Novy (Urbana: U of Illinois P, 1990), 76–88; and Uwe Baumann, "'Brotherhood in Error': William Shakespeares *Coriolanus* als Exemplum in Charlotte Brontës *Shirley*," *Exempla: Studien zur Bedeutung und Funktion exemplarischen Erzählens*, ed. Bernd Engler and Kurt Müller (Berlin: Duncker and Humblot, 1995), 315–37.

35. William Hazlitt, *Characters of Shakespear's Plays* [sic], (1817), *The Complete Works of William Hazlitt*, ed. P. P. Howe (London: Dent, 1931–34), 21 vols., 4:216. Subsequent references give pagination in main text. "The love of power in ourselves and the admiration of it in others are both natural to man," explains Hazlitt; "the one makes him a tyrant, the other a slave" (215). My reading of Hazlitt owes much to David Bromwich's superb study *Hazlitt: The Mind of a Critic* (1983; New Haven: Yale UP, 1999), esp. 314–44. See also John L. Mahoney, *The Logic of Passion: The Literary Criticism of William Hazlitt* (New York: Fordham UP, 1981), 107–8.

36. Among the books for which Brontë expressed thanks to Williams on March 19, 1850, was Hazlitt's "Essays." See *The Brontës: Their Lives, Friendships, and Correspondences in Four Volumes*, 3:88 and 174.

37. Wendy Steiner's comments on the book jacket of her *Scandal of Pleasure: Art in an Age of Fundamentalism* (Chicago: U of Chicago P, 1995), and 211. Joan Copjec claims relatedly in *Read My Desire: Lacan Against the Historicists* that psychoanalysis can make us "literate in desire" (Cambridge: MIT P, 1994, 14).

38. Peter Gay, *The Cultivation of Hatred*, vol. 3 of *The Bourgeois Experience: Victoria to Freud* (New York: Norton, 1993), 69n.

39. One of the best accounts of Brontë's partial break with autobiography is Karen Chase's *Eros and Psyche: The Representation of Personality in Charlotte Brontë, Charles Dickens, George Eliot* (New York: Methuen and Co., 1984), 51. For more recent elaborations on this argument, see Angela Hague, "Charlotte Brontë and Intuitive Consciousness," *Texas Studies in Literature and Language* 32.4 (1990), 584–601, and Amanda Anderson, *The Powers of Distance: Cosmopolitanism and the Cultivation of Detachment* (Princeton: Princeton UP, 2001), chapter 1.

40. Hazlitt, "On the Pleasure of Hating" (1823), *Complete Works* 12:136–37n.

41. Ludwig Feuerbach elaborates on "the hatred that belongs to faith" in *The Essence of Christianity*, trans. George Eliot (1841; New York: HarperTorch, 1957), 265.

42. Elizabeth Rigby, *Quarterly Review* 84 (December 1848) (an unsigned review), rept. in *The Brontës: The Critical Heritage*, 109. See also the unsigned review in the *Christian Remembrancer*, rept. in the same volume, esp. 91.

43. John Milton, *Paradise Lost* (1667), in *Milton: Poetical Works*, ed. Douglas Bush (Oxford: Oxford UP, 1966), 1.301–3.

44. For a reading of Brontë's model of heroism differing from both Lewes's and mine in its Carlylean dimensions, see Pam Morris, "Heroes and Hero-Worship in Charlotte Brontë's *Shirley*," *Nineteenth-Century Literature* 54.3 (1999), esp. 299–303.

45. Brontë, *Villette* (1853; Harmondsworth: Penguin, 1979), 445. Subsequent references give pagination in main text. For a related argument, see Karen Lawrence, "The Cypher: Disclosure and Reticence in *Villette*," *Nineteenth-Century Literature* 42.4 (1988), 448–66, and Francesca Kazan, "Heresy, the Image, and Description; or, Picturing the Invisible: Charlotte Brontë's *Villette*," *Texas Studies in Literature and Language* 32.4 (1990), 543–66.

46. The effect of such passages resonates with Max Stirner's argument in *The Ego and Its Own*: "*Are we* that which is in us? As little as we are that which is outside us" (34; original emphasis).

47. Carlyle, *Sartor Resartus* 2.7, 124. Lucy also manifests signs of what Peter Sloterdijk has called "the cynical impulse," though her severity has little in common with Diogenes of Sinope's comic irreverence, indifference to fate, and disengagement from society. See Sloterdijk, *Critique of Cynical Reason*, trans. Michael Eldred, foreword by Andreas Huyssen (1983; Minneapolis: U of Minnesota P, 1987, 1997), esp. 156–74. I am following Sloterdijk in distinguishing conceptually between Diogenes's "kynical impulse" and the cynicism—ironic, but not irreverent—that Lucy often exhibits. Sloterdijk's thesis hinges on the distinction between classical "kynicism" and modern "cynicism."

4. George Eliot and Enmity

1. George Eliot, *The Lifted Veil and Brother Jacob* (Harmondsworth: Penguin, 2001), 14. Subsequent references give pagination in main text. The novella was first published in *Blackwood's* in July 1859 and together with *Brother Jacob* in 1878.

2. Although critics mentioning the story generally discuss its themes and melodramatic ending, when a maid is brought back to life by a blood transfusion, I am focusing on Latimer's misanthropy, because it stems from his noxious mental propinquity to others, especially Bertha. For different perspectives, see Kate Flint, "Blood, Bodies, and *The Lifted Veil*," *Nineteenth-Century Literature* 51.4 (1997), 455–73; Graham Handley, "'The Lifted Veil' and Its Relation to George Eliot's Fiction," *George Eliot Fellowship Review* 15 (1984), 64–69; Charles Swann, "Déjà Vu: Déjà Lu: 'The Lifted Veil' as an Experiment in Art," *Literature and History* 5.1 (1979), 40–57 and 86; Terry Eagleton, "Power and Knowledge in 'The Lifted Veil,'" *Literature and History* 9.1 (1983), 52–61; and Ellen Argyros, "Sympathy and Judgment, Knowledge and Mystery: The Limits of Human Understanding in *The Mill on the Floss* and *The Lifted Veil*," *"Without Any Check of Proud Reserve": Sympathy and Its Limits in George Eliot's Novels* (New York: Peter Lang, 1999), 97–135.

3. The terms *sympathy* and *fellow-feeling* recur frequently in Eliot's writing and, as my introduction showed, derive largely from eighteenth-century philosophy and culture. The phrase I reproduce here appears in chapter 17 of *Adam Bede* (1859; Harmondsworth: Penguin, 1985), 180. Subsequent references give pagination in main text.

4. Eliot in April 1880, qtd. in Georgiana Burne-Jones, *Memorials of Edward Burne-Jones* (London: Macmillan, 1904), 2 vols., 2:104.

5. Benjamin Jowett, qtd. in Evelyn Abbott and Lewis Campbell, *The Life and Letters of Benjamin Jowett, M.A.* (3d ed., New York: Dutton, 1897), 2 vols., 2:108.

6. Thomas A. Noble, *George Eliot's "Scenes of Clerical Life"* (New Haven: Yale UP, 1965), 55–56; Bernard J. Paris, "George Eliot's Religion of Humanity," *George Eliot: A Collection of Critical Essays*, ed. George R. Creeger (Englewood Cliffs, N.J.: Prentice-Hall, 1970), esp. 13.

7. John Blackwood to Eliot (June 8, 1857), *The George Eliot Letters*, ed. Gordon S. Haight (New Haven: Yale UP, 1954–78), 9 vols., 2:344; Eliot to John Blackwood (June 11, 1857), *Letters* 2:348; original emphasis.

8. Neil Hertz, "George Eliot's Pulse," *differences* 6.1 (1994), 35.

9. Eliot, *Romola* (1862–63; Harmondsworth: Penguin, 1996), 308; original emphasis. Subsequent references give pagination in main text.

10. See Carol Christ, "Aggression and Providential Death in George Eliot's Fiction," *Novel* 9.2 (1976), 130–40, as well as David Parker, *Ethics, Theory, and the Novel* (New York: Cambridge UP, 1994), 77–106, and, most recently, Argyros, *"Without Any Check of Proud Reserve": Sympathy and Its Limits in George Eliot's Novels*, esp. 1–12.

11. Will Ladislaw so accuses Dorothea in Eliot's *Middlemarch* (1871–72; Harmondsworth: Penguin, 1994), 219; my emphasis. Subsequent references give pagination in main text.

12. In Eliot's last work, *Impressions of Theophrastus Such*, ed. Nancy Henry (1879; Iowa City: U of Iowa P, 1994), this maxim is subtly reworked as "Do as you are done by," a much more ambiguous imperative (11).

13. Freud would make similar claims in *Civilization and Its Discontents* (1929, rev. 1930), *The Standard Edition of the Complete Psychological Works of Sigmund Freud*, ed. and trans. James Strachey (London: Hogarth, 1953–74), 24 vols., 21:109–11. For elaboration on Eliot's perspectives on society, see Suzanne Graver, *George Eliot and Community: A Study in Social Theory and Fictional Form* (Berkeley: U of California P, 1984), esp. 181–82; *Perspectives on Self and Community in George Eliot: Dorothea's Window*, ed. Patricia Gately, Dennis Leavens, and D. Cole Woodcox (Lewiston, N.Y.: Edwin Mellen, 1997); Daniel Cottom, *Social Figures: George Eliot, Social History, and Literary Representation* (Minneapolis: U of Minnesota P, 1987); and John Preston, "The Community of the Novel: *Silas Marner*," *Comparative Criticism: A Yearbook* 2 (1980), 113–14.

14. Eliot, *Daniel Deronda* (1876; Harmondsworth: Penguin, 1995), 673. Subsequent references give pagination in main text.

15. Eliot, *The Mill on the Floss* (1860; Harmondsworth: Penguin, 1985), 356. Subsequent references give pagination in main text.

16. E. S. Dallas, unsigned review, the *Times* (May 19, 1860), 10.

17. Unsigned review in the *Guardian* (April 25, 1860), qtd. in David Carroll, *George Eliot: The Critical Heritage* (London: Routledge and Kegan Paul, 1971), 130–31. See also the unsigned review in the *Spectator* (April 7, 1860), esp. 331. The Dante reference is to *The Inferno* 3.51.

18. Eliot to Major William Blackwood (May 27, 1860), *Letters* 3:299.

19. Eliot, "The Natural History of German Life," *Westminster Review* 66 (July 1856), 51–79, in *Essays of George Eliot*, ed. Thomas Pinney (New York: Columbia UP, 1963), 271.

20. Ibid., 272. As I noted in the introduction, the *OED* records Lewes's use of the term but fails to mention Eliot's, three years later (1:371).

21. Ludwig Feuerbach, *The Essence of Christianity* (1841), trans. George Eliot (New York: HarperTorch, 1957), 53. Subsequent references give pagination in main text.

22. In 1866, for example, she explained to Frederic Harrison, in an oft-cited remark, that she hoped "to get breathing, individual forms" in *Felix Holt*. She meant to group these forms "in the needful relations, so that the presentation will lay hold on the emotions as human experience—will, as you say, 'flash' conviction on the world by means of aroused sympathy." Eliot to Frederic Harrison (August 15, 1866), *Letters* 4:301. See also *The Journals of George Eliot*, ed. Margaret Harris and Judith Johnston (New York: Cambridge UP, 1998), esp. 122, 131, 137, for further illustrations of this sentiment and self-directed pressure.

23. I disagree here with Parker, who asserts in *Ethics, Theory, and the Novel*, "It is clear that George Eliot herself could not (or would not) grasp the whole significance of what she was imagining. There is not the slightest indication that she understands the ways in which Dorothea unconsciously bullies herself into submission—quite the contrary, her admiring tone gives every indication that she does not" (92).

24. For example, Ruby V. Redinger's *George Eliot: The Emergent Self* (New York: Knopf, 1975), points up correspondences among the letters, essays, poems, and novels, generally viewing them as readily comparable; see also Peggy Fitzhugh Johnstone, *The Transformation of Rage: Mourning and Creativity in George Eliot's Fiction* (New York: New York UP, 1994). In *The Real Life of Mary Ann Evans: George Eliot, Her Letters and Fiction* (Ithaca: Cornell UP, 1994), by contrast, Rosemarie Bodenheimer joins many other Eliot scholars in challenging Eliot's reputation for advancing only religious humanism.

25. For elaboration on Carlylean misanthropy, see "Prophetic Misanthropy," *Spectator* 55 (April 8, 1882), 462–63.

26. Eliot to Charles and Cara Bray and Charles and Rufa Hennell (June 8, 1848), *Letters* 1:267.

27. Eliot, review of Robert William Mackay's *Progress of the Intellect, as Exemplified in the Religious Development of the Greeks and Hebrews* (London: John Chapman, 1850), *Westminster Review* 54 (January 1851), 353–68, in *Essays of George Eliot*, 28.

28. Eliot to John Sibree, Jr. (February 1848), *Letters* 1:251; Eliot to Sibree (May 14 [?], 1848), *Letters* 1:261; and Eliot to Mr. and Mrs. Charles Bray (May 31, 1848), *Letters* 1:263.

29. Haight, *George Eliot: A Biography* (1968; Harmondsworth: Penguin, 1985), 337–40; Eliot, *Journal* (August 28, 1860), qtd. in Haight, ibid., 339; and Eliot to Mrs. Peter Alfred Taylor (April 6, 1861), *Letters* 3:398. While traveling in Germany, their spirits lighter, Lewes told John Blackwood: "We live like Hermits here. . . . It is amazing how well one can do without 'society'!" (August 16, 1858), *Letters* 2:474.

30. See the Weekly Gossip Column, the *Athenæum* (July 2, 1859), 20, qtd. in Haight, *George Eliot*, 290–91.

31. Eliot to Madame Eugène Bodichon (Barbara Leigh Smith; December 26, 1860), *Letters* 3:366–67.

32. Alain Barrat, "George Eliot's Mixed Vision of Human Progress in *Silas Marner*: A Pessimistic Reading of the Novel," *Cahiers victoriens et edouardiens* 35 (1992), 198.

33. See also Eliot's interesting comment in "Life and Opinions of Milton" (August 4, 1855): "We should distrust a man who set up shop purely for the good of the community" (*Essays of George Eliot*, 156).

34. Eliot, "Birth of Tolerance" in "Leaves from a Note-Book," *Essays of George Eliot*, 449.

35. The narrator also remarks on the "strange . . . inversion of the paternal and filial relations" in Squire Cass's Red House (70), an idea *Felix Holt* develops when revealing that Harold Transome is the son of Matthew Jermyn, a man he vehemently hates and physically attacks.

36. I elaborate on this quandary in chapter 5 when interpreting Browning's *The Ring and the Book*. *Romola*'s narrator also meditates briefly on the vagaries of psychic drives when discussing Tito's alternating passions and allegiances: "He was at one of those lawless moments which come to us all if we have no guide but desire, and if the pathway where desire leads us seems suddenly closed; he was ready to follow any beckoning that offered him an immediate purpose" (136).

37. This is one reason Marner's neighbors "argu[e] at their ease" about the "withering desolation of that bereavement" affecting Marner alone (76).

38. Lacan, "The Freudian Thing, or the Meaning of the Return to Freud in Psychoanalysis" (1955), *Écrits: A Selection*, ed. Jacques-Alain Miller, trans. Alan Sheridan (1966; New York: Norton, 1977), 127.

39. Lacan, "The Agency of the Letter in the Unconscious or Reason Since Freud" (1957), *Écrits*, 148.

40. This is true of *Middlemarch*, too, where such conceit is represented sardonically: "A kind Providence furnishes the limpest personality with a little gum or starch in the form of tradition" (21).

41. See Fred C. Thomson, "The Theme of Alienation in *Silas Marner*," *Nineteenth-Century Fiction* 20.1 (1965), 73.

42. Jerome Thale, *The Novels of George Eliot* (New York: Columbia UP, 1959), 61.

43. For related discussion of this problem, see Susan R. Cohen, "'A History and a Metamorphosis': Continuity and Discontinuity in *Silas Marner*," *Texas Studies in Literature and Language* 25.3 (1983), esp. 419–20; Joseph Wiesenfarth, "Demythologizing *Silas Marner*," *ELH* 37.2 (1970), esp. 240–43; David R. Carroll, "*Silas Marner*: Reversing the Oracles of Religion," *Literary Monographs*, vol. 1, ed. Eric Rothstein and Thomas K. Dunseath (Madison: U of Wisconsin P, 1967), 165–200; Brian Swann, "'Silas Marner' and the New Mythus," *Criticism* 18 (1976), 102–5; and, most recently, Kate E. Brown, "Loss, Revelry, and the Temporal Measures of *Silas Marner*," *Novel* 32.2 (1999), 222–49.

44. Eliot to John Sibree, Jr. (February 1848), *Letters* 1:251.

45. *OED*, 2d ed., 10:589.

46. "Hate as a Motive Force," *Spectator* 64 (February 8, 1890), 197.

47. For engaging assessments of group dynamics in *Middlemarch*, see D. A. Miller, *Narrative and Its Discontents: Problems of Closure in the Traditional Novel* (1981; Princeton: Princeton UP, 1989), 110–29, and Philip Fisher, *Making Up Society: The Novels of George Eliot* (Pittsburgh: U of Pittsburgh P, 1981), 196–202.

48. John Bunyan, *The Pilgrim's Progress from This World to That Which Is to Come* (1678), introd. Charles Whibley (London: Constable and Co., 1926), 102–3, also qtd. in *Middlemarch*, 823.

49. Ibid., 103. Eliot's narrator neither quotes nor refers to this passage.

50. The reference is to Johann Wolfgang von Goethe, "Elemente," *West-östlicher Divan* (1819; Tübingen: Max Niemeyer Verlag, 1965), 1:7.17–20.

5. Life Envy in Robert Browning's Poetry

1. Robert Browning to Julia Wedgwood (November 19, 1868), *Robert Browning and Julia Wedgwood: A Broken Friendship as Revealed in Their Letters*, ed. Richard Curle (London: John Murray and Jonathan Cape, 1937), 158.

2. Wedgwood to Browning (December 3, 1868), *Robert Browning and Julia Wedgwood*, 162.

3. Ibid.

4. William Shakespeare, *Othello* (1604), in *The Arden Shakespeare*, ed. M. R. Ridley (New York: Methuen and Co., 1984), 5.1.19–20. I am grateful to Danny Karlin for suggesting this comparison.

5. Browning, *The Ring and the Book*, ed. Richard D. Altick (1868–69; New Haven: Yale UP, 1981), 1.723. All subsequent references to this and other Browning poems give book and line numbers in main text. See also Adam Potkay, "The Problem of Identity and the Grounds for Judgment in *The Ring and the Book*," *Victorian Poetry* 25.2 (1987), 143–57; Michael G. Yetman, "'Count Guido Franceschini': The Villain as Artist in *The Ring and the Book*," *PMLA* 87.5 (1972), 1093–1102; and Roy Gridley, "Browning's Two Guidos," *University of Toronto Quarterly* 37.1 (1967), 51–68.

6. Browning, "By the Fire-Side" (1855), *Robert Browning: The Poems*, ed. John Pettigrew with Thomas J. Collins (New Haven: Yale UP, 1981), 2 vols., 1:560, ll. 228–30.

7. Sir Leslie Stephen, "Browning's Casuistry," *National Review* 40.238 (London; December 1902), 542.

8. See, for instance, Clyde de L. Ryals's excellent reading of this poem in *The Life of Robert Browning: A Critical Biography* (Oxford: Blackwell, 1993, 1996), 123–25 and 241.

9. See also Antony H. Harrison's rather different account of the poem's interest in joy, in "'Cleon' and Its Contexts," *Critical Essays on Robert Browning*, ed. Mary Ellis Gordon (New York: G. K. Hall and Co., 1992), esp. 146–47, as well as W. David Shaw, *The Dialectical Temper: The Rhetorical Art of Robert Browning* (Ithaca: Cornell UP, 1968), 183–84; Roma A. King, Jr., *The Focusing Artifice: The Poetry of Robert Browning* (Athens: Ohio UP, 1968), esp. 107; and Joseph Bristow, *Robert Browning* (New York: St Martin's P, 1991), esp. 114.

10. Gridley, "Browning's Two Guidos," 64.

11. Slavoj Žižek, *The Sublime Object of Ideology* (New York: Verso, 1989), 176. For fascinating elaborations, see also Giorgio Agamben, *Language and Death: The Place of Negativity*, trans. Karen E. Pinkus with Michael Hardt (1982; Minneapolis: U of Minnesota P, 1991), esp. 1–5, and Eric L. Santner, *On the Psychotheology of Everyday Life: Reflections on Freud and Rosenzweig* (Chicago: U of Chicago P, 2001), esp. 80–85.

12. As I'll soon show, this perspective differs considerably from Wedgwood's more liberal idea that "we need the atmosphere of meanness and cruelty to exhibit fully the luminous soul that centres the picture." Wedgwood to Browning (November 15, 1868), *Robert Browning and Julia Wedgwood*, 154. Her tolerance for this atmosphere clearly was less developed than Browning's. As she later wrote: "Did you not . . . contract this debt to us to . . . make us feel that love is the principal thing in this world and the world beyond[?] Oh, do not leave *scorn* in that prominent rivalry with it!" (156; original emphasis). Wedgwood seems to have learned little from this exchange, for despite her calling Stevenson's *Strange Case of Dr Jekyll and Mr Hyde* "remarkable," when she reviewed it twenty years after corresponding with Browning, she extrapolated from Stevenson's work the most conservative lesson possible, arguing, "It is one of those rare fictions which make one understand the value of temperance in art." Wedgwood, "Contemporary Records: I—Fiction," *The Contemporary Review* 49 (April 1886), 594, 595.

13. Barbara Melchiori, "Some Victorian Assumptions behind 'Porphyria's Lover,'" *Browning Society Notes* 5.1 (1975), 6. See also David Eggenschwiler, "Psychological Complexity in 'Porphyria's Lover,'" *Victorian Poetry* 8.1 (1970), 39–48.

14. Ollie Cox captures—but doesn't fully explain—this conflict when asserting, "Although the Duke never says it outright, the principal cause of his irritation is that he wants this joy, *a seemingly unobtainable something for him*, to be shared only between the Duchess and himself. This is why his irritation with the late Duchess

mounts as he recalls the *occasions wherein others shared the joy as much or seemingly more than he*." Cox, "The 'Spot of Joy' in 'My Last Duchess,'" *CLA Journal* 12.1 (1968), 73, my emphases. Although R. B. Jenkins's argument is outrageous when he asserts, "If the Duke really did do away with her (whatever his method and however inexcusable), he was actually driven to the deed by this young woman herself who is praised throughout the literary world as virtuous, kind, generous, loving, humane, and the embodiment of the cardinal virtues," he nonetheless highlights the Duke's apparent helplessness before his hatred. Still, Jenkins downplays Browning's interest in the ethical complexity of describing such hatred. Jenkins, "The Devil's Advocate: A Different Approach to 'My Last Duchess,'" *Journal of English Teaching Techniques* 10.2 (1980), 23.

15. In *The Four Fundamental Concepts of Psycho-Analysis*, Jacques Lacan paradoxically calls this "beyond" what is "in you more than you"—that is, apparently immanent to the lover, but in fact foreign to them, because it is transferential in character. As he explains generically: "*I love you, but, because inexplicably I love in you something more than you . . . I mutilate you.*" Lacan, *The Four Fundamental Concepts of Psycho-Analysis*, ed. Jacques-Alain Miller, trans. Alan Sheridan (1973; New York: Norton, 1978), 268; original emphasis.

16. Earl G. Ingersoll, "Lacan, Browning, and the Murderous Voyeur: 'Porphyria's Lover' and 'My Last Duchess,'" *Victorian Poetry* 28.2 (1990), 156.

17. Sigmund Freud, "Thoughts for the Times on War and Death," Part 2: "Our Attitude Towards Death" (1915), *The Standard Edition of the Complete Psychological Works of Sigmund Freud*, ed. and trans. James Strachey (London: Hogarth, 1953–74), 24 vols., 14:297. Subsequent references give pagination in main text.

18. Ernest Jones does, however, record an amusing episode, in which he "tried to give [Freud] pleasure by showing him some poems in which Browning expressed his transcendent love for Italy. . . . But he waved them aside with a smile, saying: 'I have no need of that; we have our own enthusiasts.'" "No doubt," Jones comments, "Goethe and Heine were foremost in his mind." Jones, *The Life and Work of Sigmund Freud* (New York: Basic Books, 1953–57), 3 vols., 1:331.

19. Tim Dean, *Beyond Sexuality* (Chicago: U of Chicago P, 2000), 124.

20. For different perspectives on this phenomenon, see Salman Rushdie, "Reality TV: A Dearth of Talent and the Death of Morality," the *Guardian* (Manchester; June 9, 2001), 12, who laments the reinvention of "the gladiatorial combat," with its associated "perils of voyeurism" and "tawdry narcissism," and asks: "If we are willing to watch people stab one another in the back, might we not also be willing to actually watch them die?" The question follows Rushdie's discussion of Timothy McVeigh's televised execution. By contrast, argues Julia Kristeva, *Loft Story*, the French equivalent of *Big Brother*, which "hypnotized millions of French viewers this spring," "offered a solution. . . . It was a televised and manipulated representation of what people cannot express, but it responded to people's needs. Parents wondered, 'Why do my kids need this?' It's because at homes [*sic*] they cannot express

what they feel about life, about sex, about their friends. There is no conversation to absorb the psychic malaise." Qtd. in Alan Riding, "Correcting Her Idea of Politically Correct," *New York Times* (July 14, 2001), A19.

21. Jeremy Bentham, *An Introduction to the Principles of Morals and Legislation* (1780; 1789; 1823), ed. J. H. Burns and H. L. A. Hart (London: Athlone P, 1970), 44, 33.

22. William Hazlitt, "On the Pleasure of Hating" (1823), *The Plain Speaker: Opinions on Books, Men, and Things, The Complete Works of William Hazlitt*, ed. P. P. Howe (London and Toronto: Dent, 1931–34), 21 vols., 12:129. Subsequent references give pagination in main text.

23. For elaboration on this insincerity and its philosophical permutations, see Dalton H. Gross, "Browning's Positivist Count in Search of a Miracle: A Grim Parody in *The Ring and the Book*," *Victorian Poetry* 12.2 (1974), 178–80.

24. Daniel Karlin, *Browning's Hatreds* (New York: Oxford UP, 1993), 19–21.

25. Ryals, *The Life of Robert Browning*, 245.

26. Lacan, *The Seminar of Jacques Lacan*, book 7: *The Ethics of Psychoanalysis, 1959–69*, ed. Jacques-Alain Miller, trans. Dennis Porter (New York: Norton, 1992), 237. Subsequent references give pagination in main text.

27. Lacan, *Le Séminaire, livre VII: L'éthique de la psychanalyse, 1959–60*, texte établi par Jacques-Alain Miller (Paris: Seuil, 1986), 278. Subsequent references give pagination in main text.

28. Dean, *Beyond Sexuality*, 127.

29. Lacan, "The Subversion of the Subject and the Dialectic of Desire in the Freudian Unconscious" (1960), *Écrits: A Selection*, ed. Jacques-Alain Miller, trans. Alan Sheridan (New York: Norton, 1977), 299.

30. See also Browning's *La Saisiaz* (1878), whose prologue famously declares:

> Good, to forgive;
> Best, to forget!
> Living, we fret;
> Dying, we live. (1–4)

31. Robert Langbaum, "Is Guido Saved? The Meaning of Browning's Conclusion to *The Ring and the Book*," *Victorian Poetry* 10.4 (1972), 299. Subsequent references give pagination in main text. See also Margaret Doane, "Guido Is Saved: Interior and Exterior Monologues in Book XI of *The Ring and the Book*," *Studies in Browning and His Circle* 5.2 (1977), esp. 61: "Guido thus foresees that in dealing fully with what he is, he can eventually be saved."

32. Wedgwood to Browning (December 3, 1868), *Robert Browning and Julia Wedgwood*, 163.

33. Browning to Wedgwood (January 21, 1869), ibid., 167.

34. Wedgwood to Browning (February 21, 1869), ibid., 184.

35. Doane claims relatedly, "The human heart is never beyond redemption for Browning" ("Guido Is Saved," 64); and both she and Langbaum take "A Bean-Stripe,"

in the later poem *Ferishtah's Fancies*, as representative of Browning's philosophy of evil:

> Of absolute and irretrievable
> And all-subduing black,—black's soul of black
> Beyond white's power to disintensify,—
> Of that I saw no sample. (200–3)

But given this poem's immense complexity and the unreliability of deducing Browning's beliefs from the (frequently self-deluded) statements of his speakers, it is risky to say that such words sum up or even partly represent his philosophy. For starters, neither Langbaum nor Doane cites the words immediately following this statement, which appear after a colon, signaling the repercussions of the speaker's apparent failure to see a "sample" of absolute evil:

> such may wreck
> My life and ruin my philosophy
> Tomorrow, doubtless: hence the constant shade
> Cast on life's shine,—the tremor that intrudes
> When firmest *seems* my faith in white. (203–7; my emphasis)

Besides, near the beginning of this poem we're told: "Forsooth / Black's shade on White is White too! What's the worst / Of Evil but that, past, it overshades / The else-exempted present?" (20–23). Such lines and rhetorical questions come close to calling all later pronouncements on goodness dubious, because stemming from wish fulfillment.

36. For different elaborations, see Shoshana Felman, "Forms of Judicial Blindness, or the Evidence of What Cannot Be Seen: Traumatic Narratives and Legal Repetitions in the O. J. Simpson Case and in Tolstoy's *The Kreutzer Sonata*," *Critical Inquiry* 23.4 (1997), 738–88, and Jane B. Malmo, "The Jouissance of Justice," *Umbr(a): A Journal of the Unconscious* 1 (1997), 153–58.

37. Wedgwood to Browning (December 3, 1868), *Robert Browning and Julia Wedgwood*, 164.

38. Freud, *Civilization and Its Discontents* (1929; revised 1930), *Standard Edition*, 21:111.

39. Žižek, *The Ticklish Subject: The Absent Centre of Political Ontology* (New York: Verso, 1999), 160, 154. See also Alain Badiou, *Ethics: An Essay on the Understanding of Evil*, trans. Peter Hallward (1998; New York: Verso, 2001), and Joan Copjec, "Introduction: Evil in the Time of the Finite World," *Radical Evil*, ed. Copjec (New York: Verso, 1996), vii–xxviii.

40. Karlin, *Browning's Hatreds*, 222, 220.

41. Ibid., 222.

42. See for instance Sue Bridehead's cogent allusion to Browning's "Too Late" (1864), in Hardy's *Jude the Obscure* (1894; 1895; Harmondsworth: Penguin, 1998), 149.

43. Karlin, *Browning's Hatreds*, 244.

44. Ibid., 256. For a differently provocative reading of "Childe Roland," see Loy D. Martin, *Browning's Dramatic Monologues and the Post-Romantic Subject* (Baltimore: John Hopkins UP, 1985), chapters 6 and 7.

45. The best elaboration on, and rejoinder to, this debate is in Ryals, *The Life of Robert Browning*, 241–47.

46. John W. Willoughby, "Browning's 'Childe Roland to the Dark Tower Came,'" *Victorian Poetry* 1.4 (1963), 291.

47. For instance, Joyce S. Meyers, "'Childe Roland to the Dark Tower Came': A Nightmare Confrontation with Death," *Victorian Poetry* 8.4 (1970), 339.

48. See Eugene R. Kintgen, "Childe Roland and the Perversity of the Mind," *Victorian Poetry* 4.4 (1966), esp. 258.

49. Browning to Isabella Blagden (January 19, 1863), *Dearest Isa: Robert Browning's Letters to Isabella Blagden*, ed. Edward C. McAleer (Austin: U of Texas P, 1951), 149; Browning, "To Edward Fitzgerald" (1889), *Robert Browning: The Poems*, 2:972, l. 11.

50. Joseph Conrad, *Heart of Darkness* (1899; 1902), *Youth / Heart of Darkness / The End of the Tether* (Harmondsworth: Penguin, 1995), 148. Cedric Watts alludes to Conrad's likely debt to the Browningesque and Tennysonian dramatic monologue in his chapter "Heart of Darkness," *The Cambridge Companion to Joseph Conrad*, ed. J. H. Stape (New York: Cambridge UP, 1996), 47.

51. John Lyon, "A Note on the Text," *Youth / Heart of Darkness / The End of the Tether*, xlvii.

Epilogue: Joseph Conrad and the Illusion of Solidarity

1. In saying this, I am not ignoring Joseph Conrad's narrator's disparaging remarks about Bulwer. As is well known, the narrator of *The Nigger of the "Narcissus"* (1897; Harmondsworth: Penguin, 1989) refers to Bulwer's "elegant verbiage" and "polished and so curiously insincere sentences" (3). Subsequent references give pagination in main text.

2. Conrad, *The Secret Sharer: An Episode from the Coast* (1910), *'Twixt Land and Sea: Three Tales* (1912; Harmondsworth: Penguin, 1990), 205n.9. Subsequent references give pagination in main text.

3. Adam Gillon, *The Eternal Solitary: A Study of Joseph Conrad* (New York: Bookman Associates, 1960), 56.

4. Conrad to Marguerite Poradowska (July 20 [?], 1894), *The Collected Letters of Joseph Conrad*, ed. Frederick R. Karl and Laurence Davies (New York: Cambridge UP, 1983), 5 vols., 1:162.

5. Conrad, Preface to *The Nigger of the "Narcissus,"* xlviii. This sentiment recurs throughout Conrad's oeuvre, finding an echo in *Lord Jim*, for example, when Marlow extols being "a member of an obscure body of men held together by a community of inglorious toil and by fidelity to a certain standard of conduct" (1899–1900; Harmondsworth: Penguin, 1989), 80.

6. Cedric Watts, Introduction to *The Nigger of the "Narcissus,"* xvii.

7. Adam Smith, *The Theory of Moral Sentiments*, ed. D. D. Raphael and A. L. Macfie (1759; Oxford: Clarendon P, 1976); Anthony A. Cooper, Third Earl of Shaftesbury, *Sensus Communis: An Essay on the Freedom of Wit and Humour*, in *Characteristics of Men, Manners, Opinions, Times*, ed. John M. Robertson (1711; New York: Bobbs-Merrill Co., 1964), 2 vols., 3.2, 1:74. "If eating and drinking be natural," Shaftesbury argued, then "herding is so too. If any appetite or sense be natural, the sense of fellowship is the same" (1:74).

8. Conrad, *Victory: An Island Tale* (1915; Harmondsworth: Penguin, 1989), 101; *Nostromo: A Tale of the Seaboard* (1904; Harmondsworth: Penguin, 1990), 416. Subsequent references to both novels give pagination in main text.

9. Conrad, Author's Note, *The Mirror of the Sea* (1906; New York: Oxford UP, 1988), xxxiv. Conrad similarly described his own self-antagonism and horror of depression: "I face it, I face it but the fright is growing on me. My fortitude is shaken by the view of the monster. It does not move; its eyes are baleful; it is as still as death itself—and it will devour me. Its stare has eaten into my soul already deep, deep. I am alone with it in a chasm with perpendicular sides of black basalt." Conrad to Edward Garnett (March 31 [Good Friday], 1899), *The Collected Letters of Joseph Conrad*, 2:177.

10. I amplify this difficulty in *The Ruling Passion: British Colonial Allegory and the Paradox of Homosexual Desire* (Durham: Duke UP, 1995), chapter 4.

11. Conrad, "Books" (1905), *Notes on Life and Letters* (Garden City, N.Y.: Doubleday, Page, and Co., 1923), 9. Earlier in this article, he insists: "It must not be supposed that I claim for the artist in fiction the freedom of moral Nihilism. I would require from him many acts of faith of which the first would be the cherishing of an undying hope" (8).

12. Conrad, *Chance: A Tale in Two Parts* (1913; Harmondsworth: Penguin, 1974), 260; Conrad to Poradowska (September 4, 1892), *The Collected Letters of Joseph Conrad*, 1:113.

13. Ibid.

14. Conrad to John Galsworthy (August 22, 1903), *The Collected Letters of Joseph Conrad*, 3:54.

15. Conrad, "Autocracy and War" (1905), *Notes on Life and Letters*, 97, 108.

16. Conrad, *Chance*, 187.

17. For elaboration on this tension, see Ursula Lord, *Solitude Versus Solidarity in the Novels of Joseph Conrad: Political and Epistemological Implications of Narrative Innovation* (Montréal: McGill-Queen's UP, 1998) and Robert Hampson, *Joseph Conrad: Betrayal and Identity* (New York: St. Martin's, 1992).

18. Paul B. Armstrong, "Conrad's Contradictory Politics: The Ontology of Society in *Nostromo*," *Twentieth Century Literature* 31.1 (1985), 10.

19. Martin Ray, "Conrad and Decoud," *The Polish Review* 29.3 (1984), 58. Ray's article sums up much of the debate about Conrad's alleged autobiographical portray-

al of Decoud. Mario Curreli cites many relevant letters by Conrad in "Fictional Suicide and Personal Rescue: The Case-History of *Nostromo*," *Studi dell'Istituto lin-
guistico* 4 (Florence; 1981), 97–121.

20. *Hamlet* (2.2.524–25), qtd. in Freud, "Mourning and Melancholia" (1917 [1915]),
The Standard Edition of the Complete Psychological Works of Sigmund Freud, ed. and
trans. James Strachey (London: Hogarth, 1953–74), 24 vols., 14:246n.

21. Conrad, *The Secret Agent: A Simple Tale* (1907; Harmondsworth: Penguin,
1990), 268. Subsequent references give pagination in main text.

22. Conrad, *Youth / Heart of Darkness / The End of the Tether* (Harmondsworth:
Penguin, 1995), 110. Subsequent references give pagination in main text.

23. Conrad to R. B. Cunninghame Graham (October 7, 1907), *The Collected Letters
of Joseph Conrad*, 3:491.

24. Conrad, *Under Western Eyes* (1911; Harmondsworth: Penguin, 1996), 252. Subsequent references give pagination in main text.

25. Fyodor Dostoyevsky, *Notes from Underground and The Double*, trans. Jessie
Coulson (1864, first trans. 1913; Harmondsworth: Penguin, 1986), 31, 30. Subsequent references give pagination in main text.

26. Gillon, *The Eternal Solitary*, 127.

27. Conrad, *Lord Jim*, 200; Conrad to Poradowska (July 20 [?] 1894), *The Collected
Letters of Joseph Conrad*, 1:162.

INDEX